CROCHET
With Bits & Pieces™

Edited by Carol Alexander

HOUSE of
WHITE
BIRCHES

PUBLISHERS
SINCE 1947

Crochet With Bits & Pieces™

Editor: Carol Alexander
Art Director: Brad Snow
Publishing Services Manager: Brenda Gallmeyer

Associate Editor: Brenda Stratton
Assistant Art Director: Nick Pierce
Copy Supervisor: Michelle Beck
Copy Editors: Nicki Lehman, Beverly Richardson, Mary O'Donnell
Technical Editor: Agnes Russell

Graphic Arts Supervisor: Ronda Bechinski
Book Design: Edith Teegarden
Graphic Artist: Erin Augsburger, Joanne Gonzalez
Production Assistants: Cheryl Kempf, Marj Morgan

Photography: Tammy Cromer-Campbell
Photo Stylist: Martha Coquat

Chief Executive Officer: John Robinson
Publishing Director: David McKee
Marketing Director: Dan Fink
Printed in China
First Printing: 2005

Library of Congress Control Number: 2005922872
Hardcover ISBN: 1-59217-084-6
Softcover ISBN: 1-59217-085-4

Every effort has been made to ensure the accuracy and completeness of the instructions in this book. However, we cannot be responsible for human error or for the results when using materials other than those specified in the instructions, or for variations in individual work.

1 2 3 4 5 6 7 8 9

A Note From the Editor

One common thread (so to speak) that we crocheters share is that we love yarn! When we see a new yarn, we want to touch it and think about the perfect project to make with it. Of course, not having a specific project in mind usually doesn't stop true-blue, die-hard crocheters from taking advantage of any opportunity to buy new yarn!

As a result, we often have yarn left over from many of our projects. While there are some crocheters who never purchase more yarn than they need, many of us take the "better safe than sorry" route and buy more than is needed for a particular project. Thus, we have a continually growing stash of yarn that usually doesn't contain a lot of any one kind, but small amounts of lots and lots of different yarns.

In *Crochet With Bits & Pieces*, we have included an appealing collection of more than 80 colorful, creative projects specially designed for using up a wide variety of scrap odds and ends of yarn. And we haven't forgotten thread crochet lovers, either! You'll find a pleasing array of thread designs throughout the book, including an entire chapter devoted to the fun of working with color in thread. With all of the great ideas in *Crochet With Bits & Pieces*, you'll not only save money with these projects, but you'll also free up lots of space to fill with new yarn and thread supplies!

From projects designed to give your home a variety of decorator looks without the decorator price to fun, trendy fashions and accessories that are big on style but small in cost, you'll appreciate the creative opportunities within these pages to make some crochet magic with just a little bit of this and that from your stash of colorful scraps!

I'm sure your reasons and uses for the delightful ornaments in this vibrant and fun collection will be equally clever and wonderful!

With warm regards,

Carol Alexander

3

Contents

Little Bits for the Family

Retro Revisited

One of a Kind

Fun With Color in Thread

Every Day's a Holiday

From Scraps to Sensational

Little Bits for the Family

What crocheter doesn't love to turn all those odds and ends of yarn and thread that accumulate from other projects into fabulous new crochet creations? With the enticing variety of patterns featured in this chapter, you can turn your stash of scraps into creative crochet works of art your family will love!

Design by Kim Harmon

The Blues Belt

Stitch a trendy beaded belt in alternating sections of blue and navy to add a fun, carefree look to a favorite skirt, jeans or shorts.

EASY

Finished Size

Instructions given fit
   medium to large; for
   extra-large, add one
   motif; for extra-small,
   delete one motif
Each motif of belt
   measures 1⅛ x 6½ inches

Materials

- Lily Sugar 'N Cream
  medium (worsted)
  weight cotton yarn (2.5
  oz/120 yds/70.9g per ball):
  1 ball each #83
     cornflower blue and
     #09 bright navy blue
- Sizes G/6/4mm and
  H/8/5mm crochet hooks
  or size needed to
  obtain gauge
- Yarn needle
- Sewing needle
- Silver sewing thread
- 5mm silver beads: 12
- Pony beads:
  64 (6 x 9mm) silver
  39 (6 x 9mm) light blue
  2 (6 x 9mm) navy

Gauge

Size H hook: 9 sc = 2½ inches
Check gauge to save time.

Pattern Notes

Weave in loose ends as work progresses.
Join rounds with a slip stitch unless otherwise stated.
Belt can be adjusted to any size simply by adding or decreasing the number of motifs. For large sizes remember to purchase sufficient yarn and beads.

Motif

Make 3 each cornflower blue and bright navy blue.
Rnd 1 (RS): With size H hook, ch 23, 3 sc in 2nd ch from hook, sc in each of next 20 chs, 3 sc in last ch, working on opposite side of foundation ch, sc in next 20 chs, join in beg sc, turn. *(46 sc)*
Rnd 2 (WS): Ch 1, [sc in each of next 20 sc, 2 sc in each of next 3 sc] twice, join in beg sc, fasten off. *(52 sc)*

Joining Motifs

Alternating Motif colors and using bright navy blue to join

Motifs, cut 5 lengths of bright navy blue each 12 inches long.
For each joining, thread yarn needle with bright navy blue and 1 each a silver pony bead, light blue pony bead and silver pony bead.
Working on RS, thread beaded 12-inch piece of bright navy blue through center sc at each end of 1 cornflower blue and bright navy blue Motifs. Working on WS, thread 1 end of 12-inch piece of bright navy blue through next sc above center on 1 Motif end to next sc above center on other Motif end, rep once more to double this connec-

Continued on page 26

8

Design by Belinda "Bendy" Carter

Rainbow Purse

Add a kick of color to any casual outfit with this stylish bag crocheted in bright rainbow stripes of medium weight plastic canvas yarn.

Gauge

10 sc = 3 inches; 12 rnds = 3 inches
Check gauge to save time.

Pattern Notes

Weave in loose ends as work progresses. Join rounds with a slip stitch unless otherwise stated.

Do not join rnds unless otherwise stated, mark rnds with a stitch marker.

Purse Bottom

Rnd 1 (RS): With A, ch 17, sc in 2nd ch from hook, sc in each of next 14 chs, 3 sc in next ch, working on opposite side of foundation ch, sc in each of next 14 chs, 2 sc in same ch as beg sc. *(34 sc)*

Rnd 2: 2 sc in next sc, sc in each of next 14 sc, 2 sc in each of next 3 sc, sc in each of next 14 sc, 2 sc in each of next 2 sc. *(40 sc)*

Rnd 3: [2 sc in each of next 2 sc, sc in each of next 14 sc, 2 sc in each of next 2 sc, sc in each of next 2 sc] twice. *(48 sc)*

Rnd 4: Sc in next sc, *2 sc in each of next 2 sc, sc in each of next 16 sc, 2 sc in each of next 2 sc**, sc in each of next 4 sc, rep from * around, ending last rep at **, sc in each of next 3 sc. *(56 sc)*

Rnd 5: Sc in each of next 2 sc, *2 sc in each of next 2 sc, sc in each of next 18 sc, 2 sc in each of next 2 sc**, sc in each of next 6 sc, rep from * around,

Continued on page 29

BEGINNER

Finished Size
Purse bottom is
  2½ x 7 inches and,
  excluding handles,
  7 inches tall

Materials
- Uniek Needloft
  plastic canvas
  nylon 2-ply medium
  (worsted) weight
  yarn (10 yds
  per skein):
  2 skeins each brown
    (A) and Holly *(E)*
  3 skeins each
    Christmas red *(B)*,
    bright orange *(C)*,
    yellow *(D)*, royal
    (F) and bright
    purple *(G)*
- Size H/8/5mm
  crochet hook or
  size needed to
  obtain gauge
- 1 sheet 7-count stiff
  plastic canvas
- Uniek 5-inch craft
  moon: 2
- 22mm red
  shank button
- Sheet red felt
- Tacky glue
- Stitch marker

Designs by Vashti Braha

Mini Tech Totes

Take your CD player, cell phone and other small electronics with you in ultracool style wherever you go in these fun and colorful high-tech totes.

Finished Size
Inside measurements:
2½ x 1½ x 5 inches

Materials
- Patons Grace fine (sport) weight yarn (1.75 oz/136 yds/50g per skein):
  1 skein #60104 azure
- DMC Embroidery Floss (8.7 yds/8m per skein):
  4 skeins cotton #336 dark blue
  6 skeins #5287 metallic dark silver
- Sizes F/5/3.75mm and H/8/5mm crochet hooks or size needed to obtain gauge
- 8 stitch markers
- 4 machine screw hex nuts size ¼-20 stainless steel

Cell Phone Holder

Gauge
Size F hook: 9 hdc = 2 inches; 3 puff st rows and 3 hdc rows = 2 inches
Check gauge to save time.

Pattern Notes
Weave in loose ends as work progresses.
Join rounds with a slip stitch unless otherwise stated.
When working puff stitch, skip 2 top loops of half double crochet and insert hook in the next lower loop facing.

Special Stitches
Puff stitch (puff st): Yo, sk 2 top lps of hdc, insert hook in lp facing below 2 top lps, yo, draw up a lp level the height of turning ch, [yo, insert hook in same st, yo, draw up a lp level with previous lp] twice, yo, draw through all 7 lps on hook.

Front post puff st (fp puff st): Yo, insert hook front to back to front again around the vertical post of next hdc, yo, draw up a lp, [yo, insert hook around same hdc post from front to back to front again, yo, draw up a lp] twice, yo, draw through all 7 lps on hook.

Holder
Row 1 (RS): Beg with bottom of holder, with size F hook and azure, ch 14, hdc in 3rd ch from hook, hdc in each rem ch across, turn. *(12 hdc)*

Row 2: Ch 2 *(does not count as a st throughout bottom of holder)*, **puff st** *(see Special Stitches)* in first st, puff st in each of next 11 sts, turn. *(12 puff sts)*

Row 3: Ch 2, working in 2 top lps of each puff st, hdc in each of next 12 puff sts, turn. *(12 hdc)*

Row 4: Rep row 2.

Row 5: Rep row 3.

Rnd 6: Now working in rnds and beg sides of holder, with RS facing, ch 2 *(counts as first hdc throughout sides of holder)*, work

7 hdc across side edge of rows, 12 hdc across opposite side of foundation ch, 8 hdc across next side edge of rows, 12 hdc across row 5, join in first hdc, turn. *(40 hdc)*

Rnd 7: Ch 2, [work **fp puff st** *(see Special Stitches)* around next hdc] 39 times, join in top of beg ch-2, turn. *(40 sts)*

Rnd 8: Working with 1 strand of azure and 1 strand *(6 plies)* metallic dark silver embroidery floss, ch 2, hdc in each puff st around, join in beg ch-2, drop metallic dark silver, turn.

Rnd 9: Working with 1 strand azure, ch 2, work puff st into bottom 3rd lp of join and in bottom 3rd lp of each hdc around, join in beg ch-2, pick up dropped strand of metal-lic dark silver, turn. *(39 puff sts)*

Rnd 10: Ch 2, hdc in each puff st around, join in beg ch-2, drop metallic dark silver, turn.

Rnds 11–20: Rep rnds 9 and 10.

Rnd 21: Ch 2, work a puff st into bottom 3rd lp of joining and in bottom 3rd lp of each hdc around, pick up dropped strand of me-tallic dark silver, join in beg ch-2, turn.

Rnd 22: Sl st in front lp of each puff st around, fasten off.

Corded Edging

***Note:** Place a st marker in each corner of holder at each bottom corner and each top edge corner.*

With size H hook and 1 strand (6 plies) each of dark blue embroidery floss and metallic dark silver embroidery floss held tog, attach to any bottom corner of Holder with a sl st, ch 1, work 2 sc in the bottom row, then progress up the side in a straight vertical line to the corresponding st marker at the top edge of Holder, placing 1 sc in each hdc row and 2 sc in each puff st row, ending with 1 sc in sl st row, to create side handle for Strap, loosely ch 12, at the next closest corner attach handle with sc and continue down side in a vertical path toward corresponding st marker at the bottom corner working in the same manner as the first corded edge of 2 sc in the puff st rows and 1 sc in the hdc rows, at the bottom do not turn, reverse sc into the top 2 lps of each sc just made and in each ch of handle and in each sc back to the first corner. Now do a row of sc into the top 2 lps of each hdc of row 6 to edge the perimeter of the bottom, sl st to join into the top of the first sc of the first corner. Rep this process to edge the other 2 corner sides and create the other handle for strap with a row of sc and then a row of **reverse sc** (see illustration). Complete the Corded Edging by doing a row of reverse sc around the bottom edge of sc, fasten off.

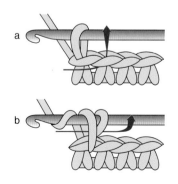

Reverse Single Crochet

Strap
With size H hook and 2 full strands (6 plies each strand) of dark blue embroidery floss, ch 112 to desired length. Pass through the 2 side handles of bag then string the 4 hex nuts onto handle, using care not to twist ch, join end of ch to beg with a sl st, drop 1 strand of dark blue embroidery floss, attach a full strand of metallic dark silver embroidery floss and change to size F hook, ch 1, [sl st into top 2 lps of next ch, ch 1] across strap, fasten off.

CD/Walkman Case

Gauge
Size H hook and 1 strand each chenille and crochet cotton held tog: 12 sc = 4 inches
Check gauge to save time.

Pattern Notes
Weave in loose ends as work progresses. Join rnds with a slip stitch unless otherwise stated.
Case is worked with 1 strand each chenille (garnet) and crochet cotton size 10 (victory red) held together unless otherwise stated. Take care to catch both strands as work progresses as the crochet cotton reinforces the chenille yarn.

Special Stitch
Picot: Ch 3, sl st in top front lp of last st made.

Case Back
Rnd 1 (RS): With size H hook and 1 strand each garnet and victory red, ch 5, sl st to join in beg ch to form a ring, ch 3 (counts as first dc throughout), 11 dc in ring, join in top of beg ch-3. (12 dc)
Rnd 2: Ch 3, **fptr** (see Stitch Guide) around ch-3 of rnd 1, [dc in next dc, fptr around

■■■□
INTERMEDIATE

Finished Size

6 inches in diameter x
2 inches deep

Materials

- Lion Brand Chenille
  medium (worsted)
  weight yarn (3 oz/174
  yds/85g per skein):
  2 skeins #113 garnet
- J. & P. Coats Aunt
  Lydia's Classic Crochet
  size 10 crochet cotton
  (350 yds per ball):
  1 skein #494 victory
  red
- Bulky (chunky) weight
  fur-like yarn (1.75
  oz/70 yds/50g per
  skein):
  1 skein tangerine
- DMC Embroidery
  Floss (8.7 yds
  per skein):
  1 skein each rayon
  #30744 or #30307
  yellow, #5270
  metallic dark red,
  #815 dark red
- Sizes E/4/3.5mm and
  H/8/5mm crochet
  hooks or size needed
  to obtain gauge
- Large-eyed
  yarn needle
- 16 inches
  round elastic
- Stitch marker

post of same dc] 11 times, join in top of beg ch-3. *(24 sts)*

Rnd 3: Ch 3, *dc in next fptr, fptr around same fptr as last st was worked**, dc in next dc, rep from * around, ending last rep at **, join in top of beg ch-3. *(36 sts)*

Rnd 4: Ch 2 *(counts as first hdc throughout)*, hdc in next dc, hdc in next fptr, **fpdc** *(see Stitch Guide)* around same fptr as last st was worked, [hdc in each of next 3 sts, fpdc around same st as last hdc was worked] around, join in top of beg ch-2. *(48 sts)*

Rnd 5: Ch 2, hdc in each of next 3 sts, fpdc around same st as last hdc was worked, [hdc in each of next 4 sts, fpdc around same st as last hdc was worked] around, join in top of beg ch-2. *(60 sts)*

Rnd 6: Ch 2, hdc in each of next 3 sts, 2 hdc in next st, [hdc in each of next 4 sts, 2 hdc in next st] around, join in top of ch-2, fasten off. *(72 sts)*

Case Front

Rnd 1 (RS): With size H hook and 1 strand each garnet and victory red, ch 6, sl st to join in beg ch to form a ring, ch 6 *(counts as first dc, ch 3)*, [dc in ring, ch 3] 5 times, join in 3rd ch of beg ch-6. *(6 ch-3 sps)*

Rnd 2 (RS): Ch 1, *in next ch sp work 1 sc, ch 1, 7 tr, ch 2, turn, dc in first st, **bptr** *(see Stitch Guide)* around each tr, hdc in sc, ch 1, turn, fpdc around first tr, **picot** *(see Special Stitch)*, [sk next st, fpdc around next st] 3 times, picot ch 1, sl st in top of turning ch, ch 1, sl st in base of same turning ch, ch 2, sc in same ch sp, rep from * around, join in beg sc, turn. *(6 petals)*

Rnd 3 (WS): Sl st into bottom 2 lps of first tr at base of petal, sc in bottom 2 lps of next tr, ch 3, sk next 3 tr, sc in base of next tr, [ch 3, sc in base of 2nd tr of next petal, sk next 3 tr, sc in next tr] around, ch 3, sl st in first sc to join, turn. *(12 ch-3 lps)*

Rnd 4 (RS): Ch 1, *in next ch sp work sc, ch 1, sl st into strand midway up side of nearest right-hand petal made in rnd 2, 7 tr in same ch sp as beg sc, ch 2, turn, dc in first st, bptr around each tr, hdc in end st, ch 1, turn, fpdc around first tr, [sk next st, fpdc around next st] 3 times, ch 1, sl st in top of end turning ch, ch 1, sl st in base of same turning ch and adjacent side strand of nearest left-hand petal from rnd 2, fold this petal forward to work behind it and ch 2, sc in ch sp. In next ch-3 sp, which falls directly behind a petal in rnd 2, make petal same as in rnd 2 except omit picots. Rep from * around alternating these 2 types of petals, turn. *(12 petals)*

Rnd 5 (WS): Working into backs of the petals of rnd 4, sl st into 2 double strand lps of the base of each of the next 3 tr, sc in 4th tr, [ch 3, sc in 4th tr of next petal] around, turn. *(12 ch sps)*

Rnd 6 (RS): Ch 3, 5 dc in same ch sp, work 6 dc in each rem ch sp around, join in top of beg ch-2, turn, do not fasten off. *(72 dc)*

Gusset & Strap

Rnd 7 (WS): Ch 1, **fpsc** *(see Stitch Guide)* around each dc, join in beg sc, for strap, ch 75, use care not to twist ch, sl st in 20th sc from beg of strap, turn, sc in next 75 chs of strap, place a marker in last sc of strap.

Rnd 8: Sc in next 53 sts of case and in each of next 75 sc of strap, do not join, move st marker. *(128 sc)*

Rnds 9 & 10: Rep rnd 8. At the end of rnd 10, do not fasten off.

Joining Front & Back

Rnd 11: With RS of Case Front and Back facing and with WS of Front piece facing, sl st into 3rd lp of hdc of rnd 6 of Back, [insert hook in top 2 lps of next sc of Gusset and into back 3rd lp of next hdc of Back, yo, draw through all sts on hook] around Gusset, then working in rem sts of Back that form part of bag opening, sl st into back 3rd lp of each hdc, sl st to beg of seam, do not fasten off, turn bag RS out to make Belt Lps.

Belt Loops

Sl st across 4 sts just worked, ch 8 to create a 2½-inch Belt Lp and attach with a sl st to the fptr made in rnd 3 that is 2 or 3 inches below bag opening, ch 3, turn, sl st to the nearest dc made in rnd 1, *dc in each ch of Belt Lp, at top of bag, sl st into 3rd hdc from the first start of Belt Lp*, sl st across next 5 sts along top of bag, ch 8, sl st to the dc made in row 1 that is directly 2 or 3 inches below bag opening, ch 3, sl st to nearest fptr made in row 3, rep from * to *, sl st along rem sts of bag opening, fasten off.

Stamen

With size E hook and 1 strand *(6 plies)* yellow rayon embroidery floss, leaving a 6-inch length at beg, ch 9, sc in first ch of ch-9, [ch 8, sc in same ch as first sc] 4 times,

ch 4, sl st into base of 3rd Stamen, leaving a 6-inch length, fasten off.

Pass the beg and ending lengths through center sts of rnd 1 of flower and tie ends in a secure knot behind flower.

Orange Center

Rnd 1: With size H hook, attach orange with a sl st to any dc post of rnd 1 of Case Front, [ch 3, sl st around post of next dc of rnd 1] around, fasten off.

Orange Trim

With Back facing, with size H hook, attach orange to 1 lp of seam ridge where Strap meets Gusset, working into this seam ridge all around bag, sl st loosely into top lp of every other st, draw up the lp of each sl st approximately ½ inch, continue in this manner along the edge of Strap to start of Orange Trim, then turn and add trim to edge of bag opening along Back, fasten off. Attach orange to the Case Front, on the ridge between the flower and Gusset, rep as for Back along Case Front, Strap and front opening, fasten off.

Deep Red Trim

With size H hook and a strand each of *(6 plies)* deep red cotton and metallic dark red, attach to lower edge of a petal made in rnd 2, work reverse sc *(see illustration on page 12)* along the edge of each petal, including around each picot of rnd 2, join in beg reverse sc, fasten off.

Finishing

Thread elastic through large-eyed yarn needle, weave elastic through the inside edge of bag opening. Draw elastic to desired tightness *(bag will not be closed, just snugly gathered)*, tie ends of elastic in a knot, weave in ends, fasten off.

Continued on page 26

Design by Belinda "Bendy" Carter

Little Jeweled Bag

This delightfully feminine little bag stitched in plastic canvas yarn and accented with sparkling jewels is the perfect size for just the bare necessities.

Gauge

Size H hook: 10 sc = 3 inches
Check gauge to save time.

Pattern Notes

Weave in loose ends as work progresses. Join rounds with a slip stitch unless otherwise stated.

Inside Lining

Rnd 1 (RS): With size H hook and white, ch 9, sc in 2nd ch from hook, sc in each of next 6 chs, 3 sc in last ch, working on opposite side of foundation ch, sc in next 6 chs, 2 sc in same ch as beg sc, join in beg sc. *(18 sc)*

Rnd 2: Working in **back lps** *(see Stitch Guide)* only, ch 1, sc in each st around, join in beg sc.

Rnd 3: Ch 1, sc in each sc around, join in beg sc.

Rep rnd 3 until from rnd 2 piece measures 5½ inches, fasten off.

Outer Mesh

Rnd 1: With size G hook, attach pink with a sl st in any rem free lp of rnd 1 of Inside Lining, [ch 5, sk next st, sl st in next st] 8 times *(8 ch-5 lps)*, 9th lp will be formed in next rnd.

Rnd 2: [Ch 5, sc in next ch-5 lp] around.

Rnds 3–10: Rep rnd 2.

Rnd 11: Pull Outer Mesh up to top edge of Inside Lining, ch 2, sl st in next sc on Inside Lining, [ch 2, sl st in next ch-5 lp, ch 2, sk next st on Inside Lining, sl st in next st] 8 times, ch 2, sk next st, sl st in beg sl st on Inside Lining.

Rnd 12: Ch 1, [2 sc in sk sc on Inside Lining, ch 1] 9 times, join in beg sc. *(18 sc; 9 ch-1 sps)*

Continued on page 29

EASY

Finished Size
3¼ x 6 inches, excluding handle

Materials
- Uniek Needloft plastic canvas nylon 2-ply medium (worsted) weight yarn (10 yds per skein): 3 skeins each white and pink
- Sizes G/6/4mm and H/8/5mm crochet hooks or size needed to obtain gauge
- Sewing needle
- White sewing thread
- 145-piece packet 5mm acrylic faceted stones #029 multi
- Tacky glue
- Small snap fastener

Design by Elizabeth Ann White

Dainty Flowers Headband

A charming little headband embellished with sweet flowers and dainty pearl beads will add a "dress up" touch to a special girl's favorite outfit.

EASY

Finished Size
One size fits most

Materials
- Elmore-Pisgah country cabled cotton fine (sport) weight yarn):
  1 oz/100 yds/28 g #G32 Capri blue
  ⅛ oz/12 yds/3½ g each #G25 bright yellow, #G11 shocking pink and #G5 purple
- Size 0/2.50mm steel crochet hook or size needed to obtain gauge
- Tapestry needle
- 10 inches ⅛-inch-wide elastic
- 5mm white pearl beads: 3
- Craft glue
- 2 small safety pins

Gauge
8 dc = 1 inch; 3 dc rows = 1 inch
Check gauge to save time.

Pattern Notes
Weave in loose ends as work progresses.
Join rounds with a slip stitch unless otherwise stated.

Special Stitches
Cross-stitch (cross-st): Sk next st, dc in next st, working behind st just made, dc in sk st.
Treble cluster (tr cl): Yo hook twice, insert hook in indicated st, yo, draw up a lp, [yo, draw through 2 lps on hook] twice, yo hook twice, insert hook in same st, yo, draw up a lp, [yo draw through 2 lps on hook] twice, yo, draw through all 3 lps on hook.

Headband
Rnd 1 (RS): With Capri blue, ch 6, sl st in first ch to form a ring, ch 1, 12 sc in ring, join in beg sc, turn. *(12 sc)*

Note: *Rnd 1 will be considered the first ring.*
Row 2: Now working in rows, ch 3 *(counts as first dc throughout)*, dc in same st as beg ch-3, 2 dc in each of next 4 sts, leaving rem sts unworked, turn. *(10 dc)*

Continued on page 28

Designs by Vicki Blizzard

Princess Pooch Scarf & Booties

Your dog will feel like Her Royal Highness when she steps out in style in this oh-so-chic scarf and set of matching boots stitched in soft, cozy yarns.

Gauge

Size H hook: 4 rnds = 1 inch; 5 sts = 1 inch
Size I hook: 7 rows = 1½ inches; 6 sts = 1½ inches
Check gauge to save time.

Pattern Notes

Weave in loose ends as work progresses.
Join rounds with a slip stitch unless otherwise stated.

Scarf

Row 1: With size I hook and MC, ch 105, sc in 2nd ch from hook, sc in each rem ch across, **changing color** *(see Stitch Guide)* to CC in last st, leaving a 12-inch length of MC, fasten off, turn. *(104 sc)*

Row 2: Ch 1, sc in each st across, changing to MC in last st, leaving a 12-inch length of CC, fasten off, turn.

Row 3: Ch 1, sc in each st across, changing to CC in last st, leaving a 12-inch length of MC, fasten off, turn.

Rows 4–7: Rep rows 2 and 3. At the end of row 7, leaving a 12-inch length of yarn, fasten off.

Finishing

On each end of Scarf, gather all

Continued on page 30

■■□□
EASY

Finished Size

Fits small 12–16-pound dogs (small poodles, small terriers, miniature pinschers, larger Chihuahuas)

Materials

• Red Heart Hokey Pokey medium (worsted) weight yarn: 2 oz/100 yds/ 57g #7108 tangerine *(MC)*
• Moda Dea Espree medium (worsted) weight yarn (1.76 oz/89 yds/50g per ball): 1 ball #2630 grassy *(CC)*
• Sizes H/8/5mm and I/9/5.5mm crochet hooks or sizes needed to obtain gauge
• Stitch marker

Design by Michele Wilcox

Cutie-Pie Sundress

Dress your little girl in cool, comfortable style on warm-weather days in this adorable little sundress featuring vertical stripes of delicious pastel colors.

EASY

Finished Size
Fits 6–12 months

Materials
- TLC Cotton Plus medium (worsted) weight yarn (3½ oz/186 yds/99g per ball):
  1 skein each #3001 white, #3752 hot pink, #3706 light rose, #3811 medium blue and #3645 mint
- Size G/6/4mm crochet hook or size needed to obtain gauge
- Tapestry needle

Gauge
4 sts = 1 inch; 2 dc rows = 1 inch; 4 sc rows = 1 inch
Check gauge to save time.

Pattern Notes
Weave in loose ends as work progresses.
Join rounds with a slip stitch unless otherwise stated.
Bodice and Skirt of sundress are crocheted vertically.

Bodice & Skirt
Row 1 (RS): Beg at center back, with white, ch 47, sc in 2nd ch from hook, sc in each of next 15 chs (bodice), dc in each of next 30 chs (skirt), turn. (16 sc; 30 dc)

Row 2 (WS): Ch 3 (counts as first dc throughout), working in **front lps** (see Stitch Guide) only, dc in each of next 29 dc, working in both lps, sc in each of next 16 sc, changing to hot pink in last sc, turn.

Row 3: Ch 1, working in both lps, sc in each of next 16 sc, working in **back lps** (see Stitch Guide) only, dc in each of next 30 dc, turn.

Row 4: Ch 3, working in front lps only, dc in each of next 29 dc, working in both lps, sc in each of next 16 sc, changing to mint in last sc, turn.

Row 5: Rep row 3.

Row 6: Ch 3, working in front lps only, dc in each of next 29 dc, working in both lps, sc in each of next 16 sc, changing to medium blue in last sc, turn.

Row 7: Rep row 3.

Row 8: Ch 3, working in front lps only, dc in each of next 29 dc, working in both lps, sc in each of next 16 sc, changing to light rose in last sc, turn.

Row 9: Rep row 3.

Row 10: Ch 3, working in front lps only, dc in each of next 29 dc, working in both lps, sc in each of next 16 sc, changing to white in last sc, turn.

Row 11: Rep row 3.

Row 12: Rep row 2.

Rows 13–70: Rep rows 3–12, ending last rep with row 10 (light rose). At the end of last row, leaving a length of yarn, fasten off. Thread tapestry needle with rem length of yarn, with RS facing, working in back lps only of row 70 and opposite side of foundation ch of row 1, sew center back seam.

Bottom Trim
Rnd 1 (RS): Attach white at center back with a sl st, ch 1, work 2 sc over post of each dc row around, join in beg sc. *(140 sc)*
Rnds 2–7 (RS): Ch 1, sc in each sc around, join in beg sc.
Rnd 8 (RS): Attach light rose at center back, ch 1, sc in same sc as beg ch-1, sk next 2 sc, 5 dc in next sc, sk next 2 sc, [sc in next sc, sk next 2 sc, 5 dc in next sc, sk next 2 sc] 22 times, sc in next sc, join in beg sc. *(23 groups 5-dc; 24 sc)*

Top Trim
Rnd 1 (RS): Attach white at center back with a sl st, ch 1, sc in same row as beg ch-1, sc in each of next 69 rows, join in beg sc. *(70 sc)*
Rnds 2–4 (RS): Ch 1, sc in each sc around, join in beg sc. At the end of rnd 4, fasten off.

Flower
Make 2.
Rnd 1: With hot pink, ch 2, 6 sc in 2nd ch from hook, join in beg sc. *(6 sc)*
Rnd 2: Ch 1, 2 sc in each sc around, join in beg sc. *(12 sc)*
Rnd 3: Ch 1, working in back lps only, *(sc, ch 1, dc) in next st, (dc, ch 1, sc) in next st, rep from * around, join in beg sc. *(6 petals)*
Rnd 4: Ch 1, working in rem front lps of rnd 2, *(sc, ch 1, hdc) in next st, (hdc, ch 1, sc) in next st, rep from * around, join in beg sc, fasten off. *(6 petals)*

Shoulder Strap
Make 2.
Row 1: With white, ch 31, sc in 2nd ch from hook, sc in each rem ch across, turn. *(30 sc)*
Rows 2–4: Ch 1, sc in each sc across, turn. At the end of row 4, fasten off.
Sew narrow end of Strap to back, count-

ing from center back sc, sew Strap to the 8th–11th sc sts. Counting sc sts from center back in opposite direction, sew 2nd Strap to the 8th–11th sc sts. *Sk 15 sc sts for underarm, sew front of Strap over next 4 sts, rep from * for rem front Strap.
Sew a Flower centered over Top Trim at the base of each front Strap. ✄

Baby Wrist Rattles

Designs by Kathleen Stuart

Baby will be thoroughly enchanted with these entertaining little animal rattles designed to fit comfortably on the wrist. They work up super-quick in medium weight yarn.

EASY

Finished Size

Animal heads 2 inches in diameter and strap opening 1½ inches in diameter

Materials

- Light (baby) weight yarn (1¾ oz/286 yds/ 50g per skein): 1 skein each pink and yellow 18 inches black
- Embroidery floss (8.75 yds per skein): 48 inches orange
- Size G/6/4mm crochet hook or size needed to obtain gauge
- Tapestry needle
- 9mm jingle bells: 4
- Fiberfill
- Stitch marker

Gauge

5 sc rnds = 1 inch; 5 sc = 1 inch
Check gauge to save time.

Pattern Notes

Weave in loose ends as work progresses.
Join rounds with a slip stitch unless otherwise stated.
Do not join rounds, use a stitch marker to mark rounds, move stitch marker as work progresses.

Piggie

Snout

Rnd 1 (RS): With pink, ch 2, 6 sc in 2nd ch from hook, place st marker. *(6 sc)*
Rnd 2: Working in **back lps** *(see Stitch Guide)* for this rnd only, sc in each st around.
Rnd 3: Sc in each sc around.

Head

Rnd 4: Working in back lps for this rnd only, 2 sc in each st around. *(12 sc)*
Rnd 5: [Sc in next sc, 2 sc in next sc] around. *(18 sc)*
Rnd 6: [Sc in each of next 2 sc, 2 sc in next sc] around. *(24 sc)*
Rnd 7: [Sc in each of next 3 sc, 2 sc in next sc] around. *(30 sc)*

Continued on page 31

Bee-autiful Rose Slippers

Design by Mary Layfield

Big, beautiful roses and fun bumblebee stripes of yellow and black give these warm and cozy slippers a whimsical look that's sure to make you smile!

Gauge

Size F hook: Rnds 1–4 = 1½ inches; 5 hdc = 1 inch
Check gauge to save time.

Pattern Notes

Weave in loose ends as work progresses. Join rounds with a slip stitch unless otherwise stated.

Special Stitch

V-stitch (V-st): (Dc, ch 3, dc) in indicated st.

Slipper

Make 2.

Rnd 1 (RS): With size F hook and black, ch 5, sl st in first ch to form a ring, ch 3 *(counts as first dc throughout)*, 17 dc in ring, join in 3rd ch of beg ch-3. *(18 dc)*

Rnd 2: Ch 2 *(counts as first hdc throughout)*, hdc in same st as beg ch-2, hdc in each of next 8 dc, 2 hdc in next dc, hdc in each of next 8 dc, join in 2nd ch of beg ch-2. *(20 hdc)*

Rnd 3: Ch 2, hdc in same st as beg ch-2, hdc in each of next 3 sts, [2 hdc in next st, hdc in each of next 3 sts] around, join in 2nd ch of beg ch-2. *(25 hdc)*

Finished Size
One size fits most
Sole: 9 inches
  unstretched

Materials
- Bernat Super Value
  medium (worsted)
  weight yarn:
  4 oz/200 yds/114 g
    #07421 black
  2 oz/100 yds/57 g
    #07445 yellow
- DMC Pearl Cotton
  size 5 crochet cotton
  80 yds #727 pale
    yellow
  15 yds #701 green
- DMC Cebelia size 10
  crochet cotton:
  2 oz #001 white
- Size 7/1.65mm steel
  crochet hook
- Size F/5/3.75mm
  crochet hook or
  size needed to
  obtain gauge
- Tapestry needle
- Straight pins

Rnd 4: Ch 2, hdc in same st as beg ch-2, [hdc in each of next 3 sts, 2 hdc in next st] around, join in 2nd ch of beg ch-2. *(32 hdc)*
Rnd 5: Ch 2, hdc in each st around, join in 2nd ch of beg ch-2.
Rnds 6 & 7: Rep rnd 5.
Rnd 8: Ch 2, hdc in same st as beg ch-2, [hdc in each of next 4 sts, 2 hdc in next st] 6 times, hdc in next st, turn. *(39 hdc)*
Rnds 9–12: Rep rnd 5.
Row 13: Now working in rows, ch 2, hdc in each hdc across, turn.
Rows 14–29: Ch 2, hdc in each hdc across, turn.
Row 30: With RS facing, fold row 29 flat across, ch 1, working through both thicknesses, sc in each of next 10 sc *(2 inches down back heel)*, fasten off. Fold rem sts of row 29 flat across so sts are equal on each side of crocheted seam, attach black, ch 1, working through both thicknesses, sc across edge, fasten off.

Striped Cuff
Make 4.
Row 1: With size F hook and pale yellow, ch 19, hdc in 5th ch from hook, hdc in each rem ch across, turn. *(16 hdc)*
Row 2: Ch 2, hdc in each of next 14 hdc, leaving rem 2 sts unworked, draw up a lp of black, fasten off pale yellow, turn. *(14 hdc)*
Row 3: With black, ch 2, hdc in each hdc across, turn.
Row 4: Ch 2, hdc in each of next 11 hdc, draw up a lp of pale yellow, fasten off black, turn. *(12 hdc)*
Row 5: With pale yellow, ch 2, hdc in each hdc across, turn.

Row 6: Ch 2, hdc in each hdc across, draw up a lp of black, fasten off pale yellow, turn.
Row 7: Rep row 3.
Row 8: Ch 2, hdc in each of next 10 hdc, draw up a lp of pale yellow, fasten off black, turn. *(11 hdc)*
Row 9: Rep row 5.
Row 10: Rep row 6.
Row 11: Rep row 3.
Row 12: Rep row 4.
Rows 13–20: Rep rows 9–12.
Row 21: Rep row 5.
Row 22: Ch 2, hdc in each st across, fasten off.
Row 23: Attach black in side edge of row 1, ch 1, sc in row 1, sc in row 2, sc in each rem row across, fasten off.
Rep row 23 on each rem Striped Cuff.
Sew 2 Striped Cuffs tog across row 22. Starting at center front of Slipper opening, positioning row 1 of Striped Cuff to front of Slipper, pin row 23 of Striped Cuff to top opening of Slipper. With tapestry needle sew Striped Cuff to Slipper.

Cuff Trim
Rnd 1: With size 7 steel hook, attach white crochet cotton at center front joining of Striped Cuffs, ch 1, sc in same st, [ch 10, sk next 2 sts, sc in next st] across to corner, ch 10, sc in same st as last sc at corner, [ch 10, sc in next seam of color change] around Striped Cuff, ending with sc in corner st at front, ch 10 sc in same st for corner, ch 10, sk next 2 sts, [sc in next st, ch 10 sk next 2 sts] across, ending with join in beg sc. *(34 ch-10 lps)*
Rnd 2: Ch 1, work 12 sc in each ch-10 lp around, join in beg sc, fasten off. *(408 sc)*
Thread tapestry needle with a length of pale yellow, at center back of Slipper, fold Striped Cuff in half and sew in place.

Rose

Make 2.

Inner petals

With size 7 steel hook and pale yellow, ch 6, sl st to join to form a ring.

Row 1: Ch 3 *(counts as first dc throughout)*, 5 dc in ring, turn. *(6 dc)*

Row 2: Ch 3, 2 dc in next st, dc in each of next 2 sts, 2 dc in next st, dc in next st, turn. *(8 dc)*

Row 3: Ch 3, dc in each of next 7 dc, turn. *(8 dc)*

Row 4: Ch 1, sc in first st, hdc in next st, dc in each of next 4 sts, hdc in next st, sc in next st, fasten off. *(8 sts)*

[Rep rows 1–4 in beg ch-6 ring] 4 times. *(5 petals)*

Middle petals

Rnd 5: Working between petals at back of Rose, attach pale yellow between petals, ch 1, sc in same st, ch 4, [sc between next 2 petals, ch 4] around, join in beg sc. *(5 ch-4 lps)*

Row 6: Now working in rows, sl st into next ch-4 lp, ch 3, 6 dc in same ch-4 lp, turn. *(7 dc)*

Row 7: Ch 3, [2 dc in next st, dc in next st] 3 times, turn. *(10 dc)*

Rows 8 & 9: Ch 3, dc in each dc across, turn.

Row 10: Ch 1, sc in first st, hdc in next st, dc in each of next 6 sts, hdc in next st, sc in next st, fasten off.

[Rep rows 6–10 in each rem ch-4 sp] 4 times.

Outer petals

Rnd 11: Rep rnd 5. *(5 ch-4 lps)*

Rnd 12: Sl st into next ch-4 lp, ch 3, 6 dc in same ch-4 lp, ch 1, [7 dc in next ch-4 lp, ch 1] 4 times, join in 3rd ch of beg ch-3. *(35 dc; 5 ch-1 sps)*

Rnd 13: Ch 4 *(counts as first dc, ch 1)*, [dc in next dc, ch 1] around, join in 3rd ch of beg ch-4. *(35 dc; 35 ch-1 sps)*

Row 14: Now working in rows, ch 3, [2 dc in next dc, dc in next dc] 3 times, turn. *(10 dc)*

Row 15: Ch 3, dc in same dc as beg ch-3, dc in each of next 8 dc, 2 dc in last dc, turn. *(12 dc)*

Row 16: Ch 1, sc in first dc, hdc in next dc, dc in each of next 2 dc, tr in each of next 4 dc, dc in each of next 2 dc, hdc in next dc, sc in next dc, fasten off.

Row 17: Attach pale yellow in next unworked dc of rnd 13, ch 3, [2 dc in next dc, dc in next dc] 3 times, turn. *(10 dc)*

Rows 18 & 19: Rep rows 15 and 16.

[Rep rows 17–19] 3 times.

To form the Rose, thread tapestry needle with a length of pale yellow, on Inner Petals, working with petals 2 and 4, fold first petal in half and 2nd petal around first, tack petals in place halfway up the petals, do not draw cotton tightly, just slightly to hold petal in place. Now fold rem petals 1, 3 and 5 one at a time around first and 2nd petals, tacking each in place as work progresses. Continue positioning and tacking rem 10 petals, but do not draw thread tight, shaping Rose as work progresses.

Leaves

Make 5.

Rnd 1: With Rose completed, working on the underside, with size 7 steel hook, attach green into center of Rose petal, ch 1, sc in same st, ch 5, [sc into center of next petal, ch 5] 4 times, join in beg sc. *(5 ch-5 lps)*

Row 2: Sl st in next ch-5 sp, ch 3, 5 dc in same ch-5 sp, turn. *(6 dc)*

Rows 3 & 4: Ch 3, dc in each dc across, turn.

Continued on page 30

Design by **Shirley Patterson**

Chain Waves Carryall

Decorate this roomy, easy-to-make bag with an interesting surface-stitch chevron pattern for an eye-catching carryall that's fashionable and functional.

Gauge
4 sc = 1 inch; 6 rows = 1½ inches
Check gauge to save time.

Pattern Notes
Weave in loose ends as work progresses. Join rounds with a slip stitch unless otherwise stated.

Special Stitch
Double treble cluster (dtr cl): Ch 5, [yo hook 3 times, insert hook in last sc, yo, draw up a lp, {yo, draw through 2 lps on hook} 3 times] twice, yo, draw through all 3 lps on hook.

Carryall Body
Make 2.

Note: Work the 2 body pieces in the following color sequence, 12 rows Windsor blue, 1 row black, 12 rows country rose, 3 rows black, 12 rows country blue, 1 row black and 12 rows medium sage.

Row 1 (WS): Ch 50, sc in 2nd ch from hook, sc in each rem ch across, turn. *(49 sc)*

Row 2: Ch 1, sc in each sc across, turn.

Row 3: Rep row 2.

Row 4: Rep row 2. At the end of row 4, draw up a lp, remove hook, do not fasten off.

Row 4A: Attach country club in first ch of opposite side of foundation ch, ch 1, sc in same ch as beg ch-1, [ch 9, sk next 7 chs of foundation ch, sc in next ch of foundation ch] across, fasten off. *(6 ch-9 lps)*

Row 5: With WS facing, pick up dropped lp of yarn from row 4, ch 1, sc in each of next 4 sc, *insert hook in next sc and under next ch-9 lp, complete sc**, sc in next 7 sc, rep from * across, ending last rep at **, sc in each of next 4 sc, turn.

Row 6: Ch 1, working in **back lp** *(see Stitch Guide)* only, sc in first st, [working in both lps of each st, sc in each of next 7 sts, sc in back lp only of next st] 6 times, draw up a lp, remove hook.

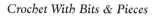

Row 6A: Attach country club in rem **front lp** *(see Stitch Guide)* of previous row, ch 1, sc in same st as beg ch-1, [ch 9, sk next 7 sts, sc in next rem front lp] 6 times, fasten off. *(6 ch-9 lps)*

Rows 7–10: Rep row 2.

Row 11: Rep row 5.

Rows 12–53: Maintaining color sequence, rep rows 6–11.

Edging

Row 1: With RS facing, attach black with a sl st to last sc at left edge, ch 1, 3 sc in same st as beg ch-1, working down side edge, sc in each row to bottom corner, 3 sc in corner st, sc in each st across bottom edge, 3 sc in corner st, working up side edge, sc in each row to top corner, 3 sc in end sc, fasten off.

Strap & Gusset

Row 1: With black, ch 8, sc in 2nd ch from hook, sc in each rem ch across, turn. *(7 sc)*

Row 2: Ch 1, sc in each sc across, turn. Rep row 2 until Strap measures approximately 70 inches.

Row 3: Takng care not to twist, holding last row to opposite side of foundation ch and working through both thicknesses, sl st across, draw up a lp, remove hook, do not fasten off. Position and pin Strap and Gusset to sides and bottom of body, having 3 or 4 rows at each bottom corner to allow for fullness. Pick up dropped lp, working through both thicknesses, sl st pieces tog, fasten off. Position 2nd body to Strap and Gusset, taking care to match sts so that body pieces are even, attach in same manner, do not fasten off.

Strap finishing

Row 1: Now working across rem of crocheted Strap and Gusset with black, at the junction of the top corner of body pieces, fold Gusset in half, sl st edges tog, ch 1, sc evenly sp to opposite end of Strap, ending at the junction of the top corner of body, fold in half, sl st in next st, turn.

Row 2: Ch 1, sc in first sc, [**dtr cl** *(see Special Stitch)* in last sc worked, sk next 4 or 5 sc, sc in next sc] 18 times across Strap, fasten off. *(18 dtr cl)*

Row 3: Attach country club with sl st in first sc of previous row, ch 1, sc over base of dtr cl st, *ch 7, remove hook from lp, insert hook under ch-5 of dtr cl, pick up dropped lp, draw through**, sc over base of next dtr cl, rep from * across, ending last rep at **, sl st in last sc, fasten off.

Top Opening Trim

Row 1 (RS): Working across front top opening, attach black at edge, ch 1, sc in same st as beg ch-1, [dtr cl in last sc worked, sk next 3 sc, sc in next sc] 12 times, fasten off.

Row 2 (RS): Attach country club with sl st in first sc of previous row, ch 1, sc over base of dtr cl st, *ch 7, remove hook from lp, insert hook under ch-5 of dtr cl, pick up dropped lp, draw through**, sc over base of next dtr cl, rep from * across, ending last rep at **, sl st in last sc, fasten off.
Turn bag around and rep rows 1 and 2 on back top opening of Carryall.

Button Loop

Attach sage with a sl st at back center of Carryall of row 52, ch 20, sl st around post of same sc as beg sl st, fasten off.
Sew button to row 52 at center front of Carryall.
To close Carryall, pass Button Lp around button. ✂

INTERMEDIATE

Finished Size

15 x 15 inches, excluding handle

Materials

- Red Heart Super Saver medium (worsted) weight yarn (8 oz/425 yds/ 226g per skein): 1 skein each #312 black, #380 Windsor blue, #374 country rose, #382 country blue and #632 medium sage
- Red Heart Super Saver medium (worsted) weight yarn (6 oz/327 yds/ 170g per skein): 1 skein #977 country club
- Size J/10/6mm crochet hook or size needed to obtain gauge
- Tapestry needle
- 1⅛-inch black shank button
- Straight pins

The Blues Belt
Continued from page 8

tion thickness. All ends to be completed on the bright navy blue Motif. Rep threading the opposite end of bright navy blue strand on next sc below center on each Motif end. The 3-threaded connection should be no wider than the width of the 3 pony beads. Knot ends to secure and weave into WS of bright navy blue Motif.

With sewing needle and silver thread, centered over rnd 1 on each end of each Motif, sew a 5mm silver bead.

Cornflower Blue Fringe
Make 4.

With size G hook and cornflower blue, leaving a 12-inch length at beg, ch 25, leaving a 12-inch length, fasten off.

On rcm 12-inch end, string pony beads into rem length [1 silver pony bead, 1 light blue pony bead] 7 times, ending with 1 silver pony bead *(15 beads)*, knot and trim end.

Bright Navy Blue Fringe
Make 2.

With size G hook and bright navy blue, leaving a 12-inch length at beg, ch 32, leaving a 12-inch length, fasten off.

On rem 12-inch end, string pony beads into rem length [3 silver pony beads, 1 light blue pony bead] 3 times, ending with 2 silver pony beads *(14 beads)*, knot and trim end.

Attaching Fringe

Thread rem beg length of Bright Navy Blue Fringe onto yarn needle, tie end in center sc of end Motif, knot end and weave into piece. Attach a Cornflower Blue Fringe in next sc to each side of the Bright Navy Blue Fringe in the same manner as Bright Navy Blue Fringe.

Attach Fringe in same manner on opposite end of belt. ✂

Mini Tech Totes
Continued from page 14

Beaded Bag

Gauge

Size H hook: 16 sc = 4½ inches
Check gauge to save time.

Pattern Notes

Weave in loose ends as work progresses.

Join rnds with slip stitch unless otherwise stated.

A number of brands of hemp cord are now widely available, the cord thickness is not standardized among brands and can vary with each ball. If substituting with another brand, try to choose a brand with similar thickness such as 20# Hungarian Hemp by Yaley Enterprises. The Elements cord looks equivalent to a sport weight or DK-weight yarn, and its stiffness makes it behave like worsted weight. The Camp Hoochee Coochee cord is highly recommended for this project because it's thin enough for stringing beads and the thickness does not vary too much within each hank. Substitute Coats & Clark Royale Classic Crochet Thread size 10 in linen color.

Special Stitches

Starting linked treble (sltr): Insert hook in 2nd ch from hook, yo, draw up a lp, insert hook in 3rd ch from hook, yo, draw up a lp, insert hook in first st of row, yo, draw up a lp *(4 lps on hook)*, [yo, draw through 2 lps on hook] 3 times.

Linked treble (ltr): Insert hook in first horizontal bar in previous treble, yo, draw up a lp, insert hook in 2nd horizontal bar in same treble, yo, draw up a lp, insert hook in next st of row, yo, draw up a lp *(4 lps on hook)*, [yo, draw through 2 lps on hook] 3 times.

Beaded chain stitch (bch): Push up a bead close to hook, insert hook in next st, yo, draw up a lp, yo, draw through 2 lps on hook, locking the bead in place with the sc st.

Beaded single crochet decrease (bsc dec): Push up a bead close to hook, [insert hook in next st, yo, draw up a lp] twice, yo, draw through all 3 lps on hook.

Bag

Row 1 (WS): With size H hook and thicker hemp *(Elements Hemp Jewelry Cord)*, ch 17, sc in bottom lp of the 2nd ch from hook, sc in bottom lp of each rem sc across, turn. *(16 sc)*

Row 2 (RS): Ch 4, work **sltr** *(see Special Stitches)*, work **ltr** *(see Special Stitches)* in each rem sc across, turn.

Row 3: Ch 1, sc in each ltr across, turn. *(16 sc)*

Rows 4–23: Rep rows 2 and 3. At the end of row 23, do not fasten off, attach a safety pin to the lp on hook.

Beaded Finishing

First tassel & seam

String a manageable amount of beads, about 26 inches, onto the thinner hemp. With WS facing, fold Bag in half widthwise. With size E hook, ch 1, 1 **bch** *(see Special Stitches)*, *draw up a 2-inch length of beads close to hook and make a ch that includes all of these beads loosely enough that it dangles nicely *(1 beaded lp)*, ch 1 tightly, 1 bch, rep from * twice, sl st into the first ch, *(1 beaded tassel is complete)*. Attach tassel with a sl st to the edge of the fold that is on the same side as the st holder. This is the back side of the Bag because the beads in the Seams will show on the backs of the sts.

When seaming Bag, place st into 1 strand from each edge that is being seamed tog, place 1 st into a sc row and 3 sts into a ltr row. A ltr row falls in the fold so begin Seam by catching 1 strand from the base of that row and 1 strand from the top of that row on the other side, sc into 1 strand from each side of Bag; 1 bch in the edges of the next row *(a sc row)*, *draw up approximately 6 beads *(¾-inch length or so of beads)* and make a bch that is ½ inch long, sk a st, sc tightly into next st, bsc in next st, rep from * to top of Bag where safety pin is attached.

Remove safety pin and change to H hook by inserting hook in the 2 free lps of both hemp strands.

Strap

[Push up 4 beads *(approximately ½-inch length of beads)* and firmly make a bch ½ inch long with both hemp strands] 64 times or to desired Strap length. When you need to add more beads to the strand, do not cut cord, just add from the other free end of the hank.

INTERMEDIATE

Finished Size

4½ x 6 inches

Materials

- Elements Hemp Jewelry Cord (100 yds/91.4m per ball): 1 ball #1890 natural
- Camp Hoochee Coochee Hemp Value Pack 20#: 2 hanks 10 yds each
- Sizes E/4/3.5mm and H/8/5mm crochet hooks or size needed to obtain gauge
- Bead needle
- 1 tube (30g) lime A/B craft glass aurora E beads
- 3-oz silver-lined rochelle beads #4997-ZE-001
- 33-piece flat AB mix green/yellow fashion glass beads
- 140 faceted glass beads color #BB3791-17
- 7 beads ranging in diameter from 7–10mm
- Safety pin

2nd tassel & seam

Beg 2nd Seam, making sure Strap is not twisted, sl st to 2 strands of corner of Bag, draw up a bead, bch, sc, end off only the thick hemp strand securely. Change to size E hook and Seam as for the first side. At bottom corner gold make 2nd Tassel, ch 1 tightly, then rep from * for other Tassel instructions 3 times and sl st into the first ch, fasten off.

Bag Opening & Closure

To make beaded button, *string onto the **bsc dec** (see Special Stitches) thin hemp 1 large bead (7mm or more) then 1 small 3.5mm, seed bead, rep from * 6 times. Leaving a 6-inch length at beg, ch 4, sl st to join in first ch to form a ring, ch 1, 8 sc in ring, ch 1, 1 bsc in each sc around (8 sts), [bsc dec in next 2 sts] 4 times (4 sts), [bsc dec in next 2 sts] twice (2 sts), leaving a 6-inch length, fasten off. Feed rem beg length down through center to ending length, tie firmly to upper center front of Bag 1½ inches from top edge.

Starting with a full hank of thin hemp cord, string 90 of the small 3.5mm seed beads onto hemp. With size E hook and front of Bag facing, attach cord with sl st to the center st of the top edge of the inside back of the Bag, st tightly and use only 1 bead per st, *1 bch, 1 bsc in next st at top of beg, rep from * to where Strap meets Seam, 1 bsc into Seam, rep from * around rem of Bag opening, treating other Seam as the first. At the sl st that began this rnd, make 25 bch tightly or number of bch that makes the best size lp for snugly surrounding the button to close Bag opening, sl st in first st to join at back edge of Bag, fasten off. ✄

Dainty Flowers Headband

Continued from page 16

Row 3: Ch 3, dc in each st across, turn.
Row 4: Ch 3, [**cross-st** (see Special Stitches) in next 2 sts] 4 times, dc in last st, turn. (dc; 4 cross-sts; dc)
Rows 5 & 6: Ch 3, dc in each st across, turn.
Row 7: Ch 3, [cross-st in next 2 sts] 4 times, dc in last st, turn.
Rows 8–37: Rep rows 5–7.
Row 38: Ch 3, dc in each st across, turn.
Row 39: Ch 2, dc in next st (beg dc dec), [**dc dec** (see Stitch Guide) in next 2 sts] 4 times, fasten off. (5 dc)
Rnd 40: With Capri blue, ch 6, sl st in first ch to form a ring, ch 1, 12 sc in ring, join in beg sc, leaving a length of yarn, fasten off. With tapestry needle sew 5 sc of rnd 40 to rem 5 dc of row 39.

Elastic Band

Attach a safety pin to each end of elastic. Attach Capri blue to elastic, working over elastic, ch 1, sc over elastic until elastic is covered completely, fasten off.
Place ends of elastic through rings at each end of Headband, sew ends of elastic tog.

Flower

Make 1 each bright yellow, shocking pink and purple.
Rnd 1: Ch 5, sl st to join to form a ring, (sl st, ch 3, **tr cl**—see Special Stitches—ch 3) 5 times in ring, join with sl st in first sl st, fasten off.
Sew Flowers to center top of Headband. Glue a pearl bead to center of each Flower. ✄

Rainbow Purse

Continued from page 9

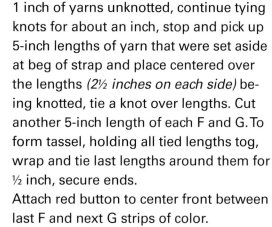

ending last rep at **, sc in each of next 4 sc, sl st in next sc, fasten off.

Purse Sides

Rnd 1 (RS): Working in back lps for this rnd only, attach B, ch 1, sc in each st around. *(64 sc)*

Rnd 2: Sc in each sc around, sl st in next st, fasten off.

Rnd 3: Attach C, ch 1, sc in each sc around.

Rnd 4: Sc in each sc around, sl st in next st, fasten off.

Rep rnds 3 and 4 in the following color sequence [D, E, F, G, B and C] twice.

Inside Bottom

Using Purse Bottom as a pattern, cut 2 pieces of plastic canvas the size of the Purse Bottom. Glue pieces tog. Cover plastic canvas with red felt, gluing felt to plastic canvas. Insert bottom into purse.

Closing Strap

Cut 5 lengths of F and G each 5 inches, set aside.

Cut 60-inch lengths of F and G. Attach F around center back st on last F rnd so that there are 30-inch lengths of yarn on each side of st. Attach G in same manner to last G rnd just above where F is attached. Holding the 2 F strands in one hand and the 2 G strands in the other hand, tie ends in loose knot, continue tying knots until there are 4½ inches of knots. Leaving next 1 inch of yarns unknotted, continue tying knots for about an inch, stop and pick up 5-inch lengths of yarn that were set aside at beg of strap and place centered over the lengths *(2½ inches on each side)* being knotted, tie a knot over lengths. Cut another 5-inch length of each F and G. To form tassel, holding all tied lengths tog, wrap and tie last lengths around them for ½ inch, secure ends.

Attach red button to center front between last F and next G strips of color.

Handle

Make 2.

Wrap D tightly around moon handle until entire handle is covered, glue ends to keep in place. Using D, attach a handle evenly centered to front and back of purse. ✄

Little Jeweled Bag

Continued from page 15

Rnd 13: Sl st into next ch-1 sp, [ch 5, sl st in next ch-1 sp] 9 times, fasten off.

Strap

Row 1: With size G hook and white, ch 40, fasten off.

Rnd 2: Now working in rnds, attach pink with sl st in first ch, [ch 3, sk next 2 chs, sl st in next ch] across ch, ch 3, working on opposite side of foundation ch, [ch 3, sk next 2 chs, sl st in next ch] across ch, ending with ch 3, sl st in same ch as beg sl st, fasten off.

Finishing

Sew snap fastener at center ½ inch down on inner edge of Inside Lining.

Glue 1 faceted stone, placing colors randomly on Inside Lining inside each diamond window opening created by Outer Mesh. ✄

Princess Pooch Scarf & Booties

Continued from page 17

12-inch ends tog and tie in an overhand knot, pushing knot as close to Scarf end as possible. Scarf end will gather tog. Cut ends of yarn to form a tassel. Scarf will twist naturally.

Booties
Make 4.
Rnd 1: With size H hook and MC, ch 2, 5 sc in 2nd ch from hook, do not join, place st marker in last st. *(5 sc)*
Rnd 2: 2 sc in each st around, do not join, move st marker. *(10 sc)*
Rnd 3: [Sc in next sc, 2 sc in next sc] around, do not join, move st marker. *(15 sc)*
Rnd 4: [Sc in each of next 2 sc, 2 sc in next sc] around, sl st to join in beg sc, do not turn. *(20 sc)*
Rnds 5–10: Ch 1, sc in each sc around, join in beg sc. At the end of rnd 10, draw up a lp of CC, drop MC to back of work, do not fasten off.

Rnd 11: Ch 1, sc in each sc around, join in beg sc, draw up a lp of MC, drop CC to back of work, do not fasten off.
Rnd 12: Ch 1 sc in each sc around, join in beg sc, draw up a lp of CC, drop MC to back of work, do not fasten off.
Rnds 13 & 14: Rep rnds 11 and 12. At the end of rnd 14, do not drop MC.
Rnd 15: With MC, ch 1, sc in same sc as beg ch-1, ch 1, [sc in next sc, ch 1] around, join in beg sc, draw up a lp of CC, fasten off MC.
Rnd 16: Ch 1, sc in each sc and each ch-1 sp around, join in beg sc, fasten off.

Tie
Make 4.
With size H hook and MC, ch 61, fasten off, trim ends. Starting at center front of Bootie, weave Tie through ch-1 sps of rnd 15.
To wear, gently place dog's foot down inside Bootie. Pull ends of Tie to tighten around dog's leg; tie ends in a bow. ✂

Bee-autiful Rose Slippers

Continued from page 23

Row 5: Ch 2, [yo, insert hook in next st, yo, draw up a lp, yo, draw through 2 lps on hook] twice, yo, draw through all 3 lps on hook, [yo, insert hook in next st, yo, draw up a lp, yo, draw through 2 lps on hook] 3 times, yo, draw through all 3 lps on hook, turn *(2 dc cl)*
Row 6: Ch 2, yo, insert hook in same st as beg ch-2, yo, draw up a lp, yo, draw through 2 lps on hook, yo, insert hook in next st, yo, draw up a lp, yo, draw through 2 lps on hook, yo, draw through all 3 lps on hook, fasten off. *(1 cl)*
Row 7: Attach green in next ch-5 sp of rnd 1, ch 3, 5 dc in same ch-5 sp, turn. *(6 dc)*
Rows 8–11: Rep rows 3–6.
[Rep rows 7–11] 3 times.
Tack Rose to center front of Slipper. ✂

Baby Wrist Rattles

Continued from page 20

Rnd 8: Sc in each of next 15 sc, working in **front lp** *(See Stitch Guide)* only of next st, (sc, hdc, ch 3, sl st in first ch, hdc, sc) all in same st *(for first ear)*, sc in each of next 6 sc, working in front lp only of next st, (sc, hdc, ch 3, sl st in first ch, hdc, sc) all in same st *(for 2nd ear)*, sc in each of next 7 sc.

Rnd 9: Sc in each of next 15 sc, sc in rem back lp of rnd 7 directly behind ear, sk ear sts, sc in each of next 6 sc, sc in rem back lp of rnd 7 directly behind ear, sk ear sts, sc in each of next 7 sc. *(30 sc)*

Rnd 10: Rep rnd 3.

Rnd 11: [Sc in each of next 3 sc, **sc dec** *(See Stitch Guide)* in next 2 sc] 6 times. *(24 sc)*

Rnd 12: [Sc in each of next 2 sc, sc dec in next 2 sc] 6 times. *(18 sc)*

Rnd 13: [Sc in next sc, sc dec in next 2 sc] 6 times. *(12 sc)*

Rnd 14: [Sc in each of next 2 sc, sc dec in next 2 sc] 3 times. *(9 sc)*

Stuff lightly with fiberfill and insert 2 jingle bells into center area of fiberfill.

Wrist Strap

Rnds 15–44: Sc in each sc around. At the end of rnd 44, sl st in next st, leaving a length of yarn, fasten off.

Fold rnd 44 flat across and sew to end of rnd 14.

Eyes

With tapestry needle and length of black, embroider eyes over rnd 5 with straight sts.

Duckie

Rnd 1: With yellow, ch 2, 6 sc in 2nd ch from hook, place st marker. *(6 sc)*

Rnd 2: 2 sc in each sc around. *(12 sc)*

Rnd 3: [Sc in next sc, 2 sc in next sc] 6 times. *(18 sc)*

Rnd 4: [Sc in each of next 2 sc, 2 sc in next sc] 6 times. *(24 sc)*

Rnd 5: [Sc in each of next 3 sc, 2 sc in next sc] 6 times. *(30 sc)*

Rnds 6–8: Sc in each sc around.

Rnd 9: [Sc in each of next 3 sc, sc dec in next 2 sc] 6 times. *(24 sc)*

Rnd 10: [Sc in each of next 2 sc, sc dec in next 2 sc] 6 times. *(18 sc)*

Rnd 11: [Sc in next sc, sc dec in next 2 sc] 6 times. *(12 sc)*

Rnd 12: [Sc in each of next 2 sc, sc dec in next 2 sc] 3 times. *(9 sc)*

Stuff lightly with fiberfill and insert 2 jingle bells into center area of fiberfill.

Wrist Strap

Rnds 13–42: Sc in each sc around. At the end of rnd 42, sl st in next st, leaving a length of yarn, fasten off.

Fold rnd 42 flat across and sew to end of rnd 12.

Beak

With orange, ch 4, sc in 2nd ch from hook, (hdc, dc, hdc) in next ch, 2 sc in last ch, working on opposite side of foundation ch, (hdc, dc, hdc) in next ch, sc in last ch, join in beg sc, leaving a 6-inch length, fasten off.

Sew beak to center front of head over rnd 1.

Eyes

With tapestry needle and length of black, embroider eyes over rnd 5 with straight sts. ✄

One of a Kind

It only takes one
ball or skein—or
less—of each yarn
to thread color used
to stitch the fun,
creative projects
included in this
chapter. You'll find
the handy yardage and weight
information included in each pattern
especially helpful when selecting yarn
or thread from quantities you already
have on hand.

Design by Tammy Hildebrand

Raspberry Fantasy Beaded Scarf

A fun, easy pattern worked in novelty coconut-style yarn makes this ultrachic scarf a must-have accessory. Simple beaded rows add an elegant touch.

EASY

Finished Size

20 inches in diameter
Pattern is written for
smallest size with
changes for larger
sizes in brackets.

Materials

- TLC Macaroon super bulky (super chunky) weight yarn (3 oz/115 yds/85g per ball): 1 ball #266024 raspberry
- Size J/10/6mm crochet hook or size needed to obtain gauge
- 6mm pearl beads: 55
- Tapestry needle

Gauge

4 dc = 1½ inches; 3 dc rows = 2½ inches
Check gauge to save time.

Pattern Notes

Weave in loose ends as work progresses.
String all beads onto yarn before beginning scarf.

Scarf

Row 1: Ch 13, dc in 4th ch from hook, dc in each rem ch across, turn. *(11 dc)*

Row 2: Ch 3 *(counts as first dc throughout)*, yo, insert hook in next st, yo, draw up a lp, yo, draw through 2 lps on hook, push up a bead next to hook, yo, draw through last 2 lps on hook *(beaded dc completed)*, dc in next st, [beaded dc in next st, dc in next st] 4 times, turn.

Continued on page 51

Designs by Belinda "Bendy" Carter

Jazzy Jewelry Head to Toe

From earrings and necklaces to a watch and ankle bracelet, you're stylish head to toe with this colorful collection of fun, funky jewelry stitched in metallic craft cord.

All-American Girl Watch

Gauge
Ch 4 = 1 inch
Check gauge to save time.

Pattern Note
Weave in loose ends as work progresses.

Watchband Side
Make 2.
Row 1: With red, ch 9 [10, 11, 12], fasten off.
Row 2: With blue, sl st in back ridge only of each ch across, fasten off.
Row 3: Hold piece so that blue ch is on top and red ch is on bottom, insert hook below first blue ch and above first red ch, draw up a lp of white/silver, sl st across working sl sts between blue ch and red ch so that a white/silver ch forms the middle, fasten off.

Finishing
Sew Watchband ends to watch face. Sew mini toggle rung to one end of band. To other end of band, sew 3 beads, then

sew toggle bar. If desired, apply glue to back of Watchband to secure ends.

Finished Size
Extra small [small, medium and large]
Each watchband side:
2¼ [2½, 2¾, 3] inches

Materials
- Uniek Needloft nylon blend craft cord (10 yds per skein):
  1 skein each red, blue, white/silver
- Size H/8/5mm crochet hook or size needed to obtain gauge
- Sewing needle
- Sewing thread
- Watch face cadran from Create A Craft
- Mini toggles from Create A Craft
- 4mm faceted beads:
  1 each red, white and blue
- Tacky glue

Finished Size

14 inches

Materials

- Uniek Needloft
  nylon blend craft
  cord (10 yds per
  skein):
  1 skein each
  solid gold and
  solid silver
- Size H/8/5mm
  crochet hook or
  size needed to
  obtain gauge
- Sewing needle
- Sewing thread
- Small barrel clasp:
  1 set
- Tacky craft glue

Finished Size

Circumference 9 inches

Materials

- Uniek Needloft nylon
  blend craft cord (10
  yds per skein):
  1 skein iridescent
  white
- Sizes H/8/5mm
  crochet hook or
  size needed to
  obtain gauge
- 6 x 9mm cool pearl
  pony beads: 12 each
  blue and turquoise
- 10 inches elastic
  thread
- Tacky glue

Silver & Gold Choker

Gauge

1 pattern rep = 2 inches
Check gauge to save time.

Pattern Note

Weave in loose ends as work progresses.

Choker

Row 1 (RS): Holding 1 strand gold and silver tog, with gold wrapped around hook above silver, ch 1, *drop lp from hook, insert hook in gold lp only *(gold lp should be to left of silver lp)*, ch 2, drop lp from hook, insert hook in silver lp only, ch 2, keeping silver lp on hook, insert hook in dropped gold lp, working with 1 strand each color, ch 1, drop lp from hook, insert hook in silver lp only *(silver lp should be to left of gold lp)*, ch 2, drop lp from hook, insert hook in gold lp only, ch 2, keeping gold lp on hook, insert hook in dropped silver lp, working with 1 strand each color, ch 1, rep from * until choker is 14 inches or desired length, fasten off.

Finishing

Sew end of small barrel clasp to each end of Choker. If desired, apply glue to back of Choker to secure ends.

Beaded Anklet

Gauge

Ch 4 = 1¼ inches
Check gauge to save time.

Pattern Notes

Weave in loose ends as work progresses.
Join rounds with slip stitch unless otherwise stated.

Beads

String beads onto elastic thread alternating 1 blue and 1 turquoise bead until all beads are on the elastic, tie ends in a knot so that elastic makes a 9-inch ring. There should be a sp of approximately 2½ inches of elastic showing with no beads.

Anklet

Rnd 1: Attach iridescent white to elastic, [ch 4, sk next 3 beads, sl st around elastic] 7 times, ch 4, sk next 3 beads, sl st in lp where iridescent white was attached.
Rnd 2: Turn work so that beads are now on top, draw unused iridescent white through center of anklet, working back across, [ch 4, sk next 3 beads, sl st in next sl st] 8 times, fasten off.
To secure ends, apply a small amount of glue to joining.

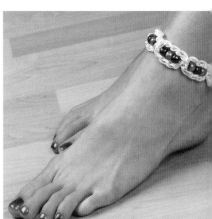

Pearl Drop Earrings

Gauge
1½ inches in diameter
Check gauge to save time.

Pattern Notes
Weave in loose ends as work progresses. Join rounds with a slip stitch unless otherwise stated.

Jeweled Pendant Necklace

Gauge
Rnd 1 of pendant = ¾ inch
Check gauge to save time.

Pattern Notes
Weave in loose ends as work progresses. Join rounds with slip stitch unless otherwise stated.

Earring
Make 2.
Rnd 1 (RS): With purple, [ch 3, sl st in 2nd ch from hook] 4 times, sl st to join in beg ch, fasten off.

Finishing
Thread needle with nylon thread, secure to beg sl st *(top of crocheted earring)*, string a pearl bead onto thread, secure with a knot to sl st at bottom of earring. Sew earring to fishhook ear wire. Secure pearl to center of thread with glue. With a drop of glue, secure thread ends.

Pendant
Rnd 1: With green, ch 4, sl st to join to form a ring, [ch 4, sl st in ring] 8 times. *(8 ch-4 sps)*
Rnd 2: Sl st to center of first ch-4 sp, [ch 3, sl st in 2nd ch from hook, ch 1, sl st in center of next ch-4 sp] 8 times, fasten off.

Neckline Chain
Holding 1 strand green and gold tog, ch 1, *yo with green only, draw through lp, yo with gold only, draw through lp, rep from * until neckline ch is 26 inches from beg, yo with green and gold. Draw through lp, sl st in beg ch, fasten off.

Finishing
Glue 9mm yellow stone to center of pendant and glue a 5mm yellow stone to each point. Attach jump ring to top of pendant point and to 1 each green and gold lp on neckline chain. ✂

BEGINNER

Finished Size
1½ inches in diameter

Materials
- Uniek Needloft nylon blend craft cord (10 yds per skein): 1 skein purple
- Size F/5/3.75mm crochet hook or size needed to obtain gauge
- Sewing needle
- 1 yd nylon thread
- 2 fishhook ear wire earrings
- 8mm pearl beads: 2
- Tacky craft glue

BEGINNER

Finished Size
3 inches in diameter

Materials
- Uniek Needloft nylon blend craft cord (10 yds per skein): 1 skein each green and gold
- Size H/8/5mm crochet hook or size needed to obtain gauge
- 5mm yellow acrylic faceted stones: 8
- 9mm yellow acrylic faceted stone: 1
- 1 gold spring and jump ring from Create A Craft
- Tacky glue

Design by Paula Gron

Collared Drawstring Purse

You'll be fashion-forward quick as a wink with this trendy bag that's easy to stitch and big on style. The optional eyelash yarn collar takes it from simple to sensational!

Gauge

Size I hook: 3 dc = 1 inch; 3 dc rnds = ¾ inch
Check gauge to save time.

Pattern Notes

Weave in loose ends as work progresses. Join rounds with a slip stitch unless otherwise stated.

Purse

Rnd 1 (RS): With size I hook and ombre yarn, ch 2, 6 sc in 2nd ch from hook, join in beg sc. *(6 sc)*

Rnd 2: Ch 1, 2 sc in each sc around, join in beg sc. *(12 sc)*

Rnd 3: Ch 1, [2 sc in next sc, sc in next sc] around, join in beg sc. *(18 sc)*

Rnd 4: Ch 1, [2 sc in next sc, sc in each of next 2 sc] around, join in beg sc. *(24 sc)*

Rnd 5: Ch 1, [2 sc in next sc, sc in each of next 3 sc] around, join in beg sc. *(30 sc)*

Rnd 6: Ch 1, [2 sc in next sc, sc in each of next 4 sc] around, join in beg sc. *(36 sc)*

Rnd 7: Ch 1, [2 sc in next sc, sc in each of next 5 sc] around, join in beg sc. *(42 sc)*

Rnd 8: Ch 1, [2 sc in next sc, sc in each of next 6 sc] around, join in beg sc. *(48 sc)*

Rnd 9: Ch 1, sc in each st around, join in beg sc, turn

Rnd 10 (WS): Working in **back lps** *(see Stitch Guide)* only, ch 1, draw up a lp in each of next

2 sts, yo, draw through 3 lps on hook, *draw up a lp in same place as last st and in next st, yo, draw through all 3 lps on hook, rep from * around, ending with draw up a lp in same place as last st and as first st, yo, draw through all 3 lps on hook, join, turn. *(48 sts)*

Rnd 11 (RS): Ch 3 *(counts as first dc throughout)*, dc in each st around, join in 3rd ch of beg ch-3. *(48 dc)*

Rnds 12–20: Rep rnd 11.

Rnd 21: Ch 4 *(counts as first dc, ch 1)*, sk next dc, ch 1, [dc in next dc, ch 1, sk next dc] around, join in 3rd ch of beg ch-4. *(24 dc; 24 ch-1 sps)*

Rnd 22: Ch 3, dc in next ch-1 sp, [dc in next dc, dc in next ch-1 sp] around, join in 3rd ch of beg ch-3. *(48 dc)*

Rnd 23: Rep rnd 11.

Rnd 24: Rep rnd 9.

Rnd 25 (WS): [Insert hook in next st, create a large lp over finger, catch the yarn that comes over the finger, draw both yarns through the st and onto the hook, drop lp from finger, yo, draw through all lps on hook] around, join in beg sc, fasten off.

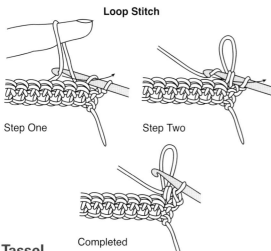

Loop Stitch

Step One

Step Two

Completed

Tassel
Cut 2 lengths of ombre yarn each 8 inches in length, set aside. Wrap ombre yarn around cardboard 10 times. Pass 8-inch length under strands at top edge, knot ends to secure. Cut bottom edge of strands. Wrap rem 8-inch length around bundle of strands approximately 1 inch down from top edge several times, secure and weave end into Tassel. Attach Tassel to center bottom of Purse.

Eyelash Embellishment
Rnd 1: With size E hook, attach eyelash yarn around post of any dc of rnd 21, ch 24, sk next dc of rnd 21, [**fpsc** *(see Stitch Guide)* around next dc, ch 24, sk next dc of rnd 21] around, join in beg sc, sl st to next sk dc of rnd 21.

Rnd 2: Ch 1, fpsc around same dc as beg ch-1, ch 36, [fpsc around next sk dc of rnd 21, ch 36] around, join in beg sc, fasten off.

Twisted Cord Handle
Measure out rem ombre yarn and divide into 2 long strands. Fold 1 strand in half and with 1 person on either end, twist strands to the right until they beg to curl. Fold the 2 ends tog and tie in a knot so they will not unravel. The folding causes the strands to twist themselves to make a stronger cord. Rep with rem strand of yarn. Using diagram as a guide, weave knotted ends of cord through drawstring opening of Bag in opposite directions for oppositional pull handles, knot ends tog, adjust knots so that they are within the ch-1 sps of rnd 21. ✂

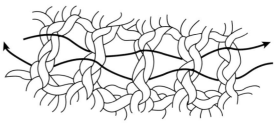

Cord Weave Diagram

INTERMEDIATE

Finished Size
6 inches in diameter; 10 inches deep, excluding handles

Materials
- Plymouth Encore colorspun bulky (chunky) weight yarn (143 yds/100g per ball): 1 ball #7128 dark green, dark red and gold ombre
- Filati Park bulky (chunky) weight eyelash yarn (44 yds/50g per ball): 1 ball rust print
- Sizes E/4/3.5mm and I/9/5.5mm crochet hooks or size needed to obtain gauge
- 6-inch piece cardboard

Design by **Shirley Patterson**

Little Miss Fingerless Mitts

Your little girl will feel oh so dressed up when she wears these dainty little gloves accented with ribbons and sequins with a pretty spring or summer outfit.

Gauge
7 dc cross-sts = 1½ inches in diameter;
4 dc cross-st rnds = 1 inch
Check gauge to save time.

Pattern Notes
Weave in loose ends as work progresses.
Join rounds with a slip stitch unless otherwise stated.

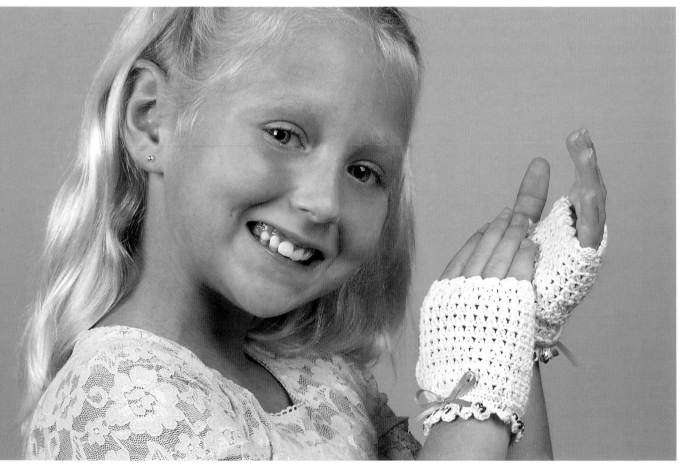

Unless otherwise stated, beginning chain-3 does not count as first double crochet. The first cross-stitch group will be worked with the last double crochet worked in the same stitch as beginning chain-3.

Special Stitches

Double crochet cross-stitch (dc cross-st): Sk next st, dc in next dc, dc in sk st.

Treble crochet cross-stitch (tr cross-st): Sk next st, tr in next st, tr in sk st.

Scallop: Sc in next st, [yo hook, insert hook in same st, yo, draw up a lp, yo, draw through 2 lps on hook] twice, yo, draw through all 3 lps on hook.

Mitt

Make 2.

Note: String alternating blue and gold sequins, string all sequins onto white crochet cotton and push sequins along thread until called for in rnd 13 [14].

Rnd 1 (RS): Ch 48 [56], taking care not to twist ch, join in first ch to form a ring, ch 1, sc in each ch around, join in beg sc. *(48 [56] sc)*

Rnds 2–4 [2–5]: Ch 3, **dc cross-st** *(see Special Stitches)* in each st around, join in top of first dc. *(24 [28] dc cross-sts)*

Rows 5 & 6 [6 & 7]: Now working in rows, ch 3, work 24 [28] dc cross-sts across, turn.

Rnd 7 [8]: Now working in rnds, ch 3, work 24 [28] dc cross-sts across, ch 4, sl st to join in first dc.

Rnd 8 [9]: Ch 4 *(does not counts as first tr)*, work 6 **tr cross-st** *(see Special Stitches)*, work 13 [17] dc cross-sts, work 5 tr cross-sts, work 2 tr cross-sts over ch-4 sp. *(26 [30] cross-sts)*

Rnd 9 [10]: Ch 3, dc cross-st 26 [30] times around, join in beg dc.

Rnd 10 [11]: Ch 2 *(counts as first hdc throughout)*, hdc in each st around, join in top of beg ch-2. *(52 [60] hdc)*

Rnd 11 [12]: Holding ponytail elastic next to previous rnd and working in sts and over elastic, ch 1, sc in each st around, join in beg sc.

Rnd 12 [13]: Ch 1, sc in same sc as beg ch-1, [ch 3, sk next sc, sc in next sc] around to last 2 sts, ch 1, sk next st, hdc in same st as beg sc, turn.

Rnd 13 [14]: Sl st into ch-3 sp, ch 1, beg in same ch-3 sp as beg ch-1, [insert hook in next ch-3 sp, yo, draw up a lp, push up a sequin next to hook, yo, draw through rem 2 lps of sc, yo, insert hook in next ch-3 sp, yo, draw up a lp, yo, draw through 2 lps on hook, yo, insert hook in same ch-3 sp, yo, draw up a lp, yo, draw through 2 lps on hook, push a sequin up next to hook, yo, draw through all 3 lps on hook] around, join in beg sc, fasten off.

Hand Edging

Rnd 1: Working on opposite side of foundation ch of Mitt, attach white in any st, ch 1, beg in same st as beg ch-1, [**scallop** *(see Special Stitches)* in next st, sk next 3 sts] around, join in beg sc, fasten off.

Thumb Edging

Rnd 1: Attach white in any st of thumb opening, ch 1, work 28 sc around opening, join in beg sc.

Rnd 2: Ch 1, beg in same st as beg ch-1, [scallop in next st, sk next 3 sts] 7 times, join in beg sc, fasten off.

Finishing

Cut ribbon in half. Working over rnd 11 [12], pass a strand of ribbon under center st at top of hand, tie ends in a bow. Attach 2nd length of ribbon on rem Mitt. ✂

INTERMEDIATE

Finished Size

Child's sizes 4–6 [6–8]

Palm width: 3 [3½] inches

Length: 3½ [4½] inches

Pattern is written for smallest size with changes for larger sizes in brackets.

Materials

- Aunt Lydia's Classic Crochet size 10 crochet cotton (350 yds per ball): 1 ball #1 white
- Size 5/1.90mm steel crochet hook or size needed to obtain gauge
- Sewing needle
- 16 inches ⅛-inch-wide light blue satin ribbon
- 26 [30] light blue sequins
- 26 [30] gold sequins
- 2 ponytail elastics approximately 3 inches in diameter

Design by Lori Zeller

Bodacious Beanbag Chair

Whether watching television or reading a favorite book, kids will love relaxing in this fun, colorful chair stitched in a rainbow of bright medium yarns.

Gauge
8 sc = 2 inches; 7 sc rows = 1½ inches
Check gauge to save time.

Pattern Notes
Weave in loose ends as work progresses. Join rounds with a slip stitch unless otherwise stated.

Beanbag Panel
Make 1 each deep violet, blue, green, gold, orange and burgundy.
Row 1: Ch 3, sc in 2nd ch from hook, sc in next ch, turn. *(2 sc)*

Row 2: Ch 1, 2 sc in each sc across, turn. *(4 sc)*

Row 3: Ch 1, sc in each sc across, turn.

Row 4: Ch 1, 2 sc in first sc, sc in each sc across to last sc, 2 sc in last sc, turn. *(6 sc)*

Rows 5–38: Rep rows 3 and 4. *(40 sc)*

Rows 39–113: Rep row 3.

Row 114: Ch 1, **sc dec** *(see Stitch Guide)* in next 2 sc, sc in each sc across to last 2 sc, sc dec in next 2 sc, turn. *(38 sc)*

Row 115: Ch 1, sc in each sc across, turn.

Rows 116–147: Rep rows 114 and 115. *(6 sc)*

Row 148: Ch 1, sc dec in next 2 sc, sc in each of next 2 sc, sc dec in next 2 sc, turn. *(4 sc)*

Row 149: Ch 1, [sc dec in next 2 sc] twice, turn. *(2 sc)*

Row 150: Ch 1, sc in each of next 2 sc. *(2 sc)*

Rnd 151: Now working in rnds. Ch 1, working around entire Panel, work 2 sc in end of last row, sc in end of each row to first row at bottom of Panel, 2 sc in end of first row, place a st marker in last sc made, working in unused lps of starting ch, sc in each of next 2 chs at bottom of Panel, 2 sc in end of first row, place a st marker in first sc of 2-sc group, sc in end of each row to last row at top of Panel, 2 sc in end of last row, place a st marker in last sc made,

EASY

Finished Size
Approximately
16 inches tall
loosely stuffed

Materials
- Medium (worsted)
  weight yarn (7
  oz/364 yds/198 g per
  skein):
  1 skein each deep
    violet, blue,
    green, gold,
    orange, burgundy
    and black
- Size G/6/4mm
  steel crochet hook
  or size needed to
  obtain gauge
- Tapestry needle
- Stitch markers
- Stuffing: beans,
  pellets or
  foam pieces

sc in each of next 2 sc of row 150, join in beg sc, fasten off.

Rnd 152: Attach black in marked sc of rnd 151, ch 1, 2 sc in same st as beg ch-1, [sc in each sc to next marked sc, 2 sc in marked sc] 3 times, sc in last 2 sc, join in beg sc, leaving a length of yarn, fasten off.

End Circle
Make 2.

Rnd 1: With black, ch 2, 8 sc in 2nd ch from hook, join in beg sc. *(8 sc)*

Rnd 2: Ch 1, 2 sc in each sc around, join in beg sc. *(16 sc)*

Rnd 3: Ch 1, [sc in next sc, 2 sc in next sc] 8 times, join in beg sc. *(24 sc)*

Rnd 4: Ch 1, [sc in each of next 3 sc, 2 sc in next sc] 6 times, join in beg sc, leaving a length of yarn, fasten off. *(30 sc)*

Assembly
With panels in rainbow order *(deep violet, blue, green, gold, orange and burgundy)*, sew end sts of each Panel to an end circle. Sew sides of Panels tog and fill as desired with beans, pellets or foam pieces. To close opening, sew opposite ends of Panels to rem end circle. ✀

Design by Katherine Eng

Citrus Party Mats

These quick and easy beaded table mats stitched in luscious lime and zesty orange add a cool, refreshing touch to a hot summertime picnic or outdoor party.

INTERMEDIATE

Finished Size
13 x 18½ inches

Materials
• Red Heart Hokey Pokey medium (worsted) weight yarn (4 oz/222 yds/ 113g per skein):
  1 skein each
    #7114 lime and
    #7108 tangerine
• TLC Wiggles light (sport) weight yarn (3.5 oz/250 yds/100g per skein):
  1 skein each #727 green and #209 orange
• Size H/8/5mm crochet hook or size needed to obtain gauge

Gauge
Rnds 1 and 2 = 1½ inches across widthwise; 3 sc and 2 ch-1 sps = 1½ inches
Check gauge to save time.

Pattern Notes
Weave in loose ends as work progresses.
Join rounds with a slip stitch unless otherwise stated.
One skein each lime and green will make 2 party mats and 1 skein each tangerine and orange will make 2 party mats.

Special Stitches
Small shell: 3 dc in indicated st.
Medium shell: 5 dc in indicated st.
Large shell: 7 dc in indicated st.

Mat
Rnd 1 (RS): With lime (tangerine), ch 18, (sc, ch 1, sc) in 2nd ch from hook, [ch 1, sk next ch, sc in next ch] 7 times, ch 1, sk next ch, ({sc, ch 1} twice, sc) in last ch, working on opposite side of foundation ch, [ch 1, sk next ch, sc in next ch] 7 times, ch 1, sk next ch, (sc, ch 1) in same ch as beg, join in beg sc, turn. *(20 sc; 20 ch-1 sps)*

Rnd 2 (WS): Ch 1, sc in next ch-1 sp, [ch 2, sc in next ch-1 sp] around, ch 2, join in beg sc, turn. *(20 ch-2 sps)*

Rnd 3 (RS): Ch 1, (sc, ch 2, sc) in next ch-2 sp, [ch 2, sc in next ch-2 sp] 9 times, ch 2, (sc, ch 2, sc) in next ch-2 sp, [ch 2, sc in next ch-2 sp] 9 times, ch 2, join in beg sc. *(22 ch-2 sps)*

Rnd 4 (WS): Ch 1, (sc, ch 2, sc) in next ch-2 sp, [ch 2, sc in next ch-2 sp] 8 times, [ch 2, (sc, ch 2, sc) in next ch-2 sp] 3 times, [ch 2, sc in next ch-2 sp] 8 times, [ch 2, (sc, ch 2, sc) in next ch-2 sp] twice, ch 2, join in beg sc, turn. *(28 ch-2 sps)*

Rnd 5 (RS): Ch 1, sc in next ch-2 sp, [ch 2, sc in next ch-2 sp] around, ch 2, join in beg sc, turn.

Rnd 6 (WS): Ch 1, (sc, ch 2, sc) in next ch-2 sp, [ch 2, sc in next ch-2 sp] 10 times, [ch 2, (sc, ch 2, sc) in next ch-2 sp] 4 times, [ch 2, sc in next ch-2 sp] 10 times, [ch 2, (sc, ch 2, sc) in next ch-2 sp] 3 times, ch 2, join in beg sc, turn.

Rnd 7 (RS): Rep rnd 5. *(36 ch-2 sps)*

Rnd 8 (WS): Rep rnd 5.

Rnd 9 (RS): Ch 1, (sc, ch 2, sc) in next ch-2 sp, [ch 2, (sc, ch 2, sc) in next ch-2 sp] 4 times, [ch 2, sc in next ch-2 sp] 13 times, [ch 2, (sc, ch 2, sc) in next ch-2 sp] 5 times, [ch 2, sc in next ch-2 sp] 13 times, ch 2, join in beg sc.

Rnd 10 (RS): Ch 1, sc in first ch-2 sp, **small shell** *(see Special Stitches)* in next ch-2 sp, [sc in next ch-2 sp, small shell in next ch-2 sp] around, join in beg sc, fasten off. *(23 small shells)*

Rnd 11 (RS): Draw up a lp of green (orange) in center dc of any small shell, ch 3 *(counts as first dc throughout)*, 4 dc in same st as beg ch-3, [**medium shell** *(see Special Stitches)* in center dc of next small shell] around, join in 3rd ch of beg ch-3, fasten off.

Rnd 12 (RS): Draw up a lp of lime (tangerine) in center dc of medium shell, ch 3, 6 dc in same st as beg ch-3, [**large shell** *(see Special Stitches)* in center dc of next medium shell] around, join in 3rd ch of beg ch-3, turn, sl st to center dc of large shell.

Rnd 13 (WS): Ch 1, sc in same dc as beg ch-1, ch 6, [sc in center dc of next large shell, ch 6] around, join in beg sc, turn.

Rnd 14 (RS): Ch 3, 6 dc in same st as beg ch-3, (sc, ch 3, sc) in next ch-6 sp, [large shell in next sc, (sc, ch 3, sc) in next ch-6 sp] around, join in beg sc, fasten off.

Rnd 15 (RS): Draw up a lp of green (orange) in any ch-3 sp, ch 1, (sc, ch 3, sc) in same ch-3 sp as beg ch-1, *ch 2, (sc, ch 3, sc) in center dc of next large shell, ch 2**, (sc, ch 3, sc) in next ch-3 sp, rep from * around, ending last rep at **, join in beg sc, fasten off.

With WS facing, block lightly. ✂

Designs by **Sue Childress**
Design by **Elizabeth Ann White**

Bootie Boutique

For a quick, last-minute baby shower gift, these simple yet sweet booties fit the bill perfectly. Make them in a rainbow of colors for a bootie bouquet!

Green V-Stitch
Design by Sue Childress

Gauge
2 V-sts = 1¼ inches; 6 hdc = 1¼ inches
Check gauge to save time.

Pattern Notes
Weave in loose ends as work progresses. Join rounds with a slip stitch unless otherwise stated.

Special Stitches
V-stitch (V-st): (Dc, ch 1, dc) in indicated st.
Beg V-stitch (beg V-st): Ch 4 *(counts as first dc and ch-1)*, dc in same st as beg ch-4.
Double treble decrease (dtr dec): *Yo hook 3 times, insert hook in ch-1 sp of next V-st, yo, draw up a lp, [yo, draw through 2 lps on hook] 3 times, rep from * 3 times *(5 lps on hook)*, yo, draw through all 5 lps on hook.

Bootie
Make 2.
Rnd 1 (RS): Beg with sole, ch 16, 2 hdc in 3rd ch from hook, hdc in each of next 11 chs, 2 dc in next ch, 3 dc in last ch, working on opposite side of foundation ch, 2 dc in

next ch, hdc in each of next 12 chs, join in top of beg ch. *(33 sts)*

Rnd 2: Ch 2 *(counts as first hdc throughout)*, hdc in same st as beg ch-2, 2 hdc in each of next 2 sts, hdc in each of next 10 sts, 2 dc in each of next 7 sts, hdc in each of next 12 sts, 2 hdc in next st, join in top of beg ch-2. *(44 sts)*

Rnd 3: Ch 3 *(counts as first dc)*, **bpdc** *(see Stitch Guide)* around each st around, join in 3rd ch of beg ch-3. *(44 bpdc)*

Rnd 4: Beg V-st *(see Special Stitches)* in first st, [sk next 2 sts, **V-st** *(see Special Stitches)* in next st] around, join in 3rd ch of beg ch-4. *(15 V-sts)*

Rnd 5: Sl st into ch-1 sp of V-st, beg V-st in same ch-1 sp, V-st in each of next 5 V-sts, **dtr dec** *(see Special Stitches)* in next 4 V-sts, V-st in each of next 5 V-sts, join in 3rd ch of beg V-st. *(11 V-sts; 1 dtr dec)*

Rnd 6: Sl st into ch-1 sp of V-st, beg V-st in same ch-1 sp, V-st in each of next 5 V-sts, V-st in top of dtr dec, V-st in each of next 5 V-sts, join in 3rd ch of beg V-st. *(12 V-sts)*

Rnd 7: Sl st into ch-1 sp of V-st, ch 1, sc in same ch-1 sp of V-st, 5 dc in ch-1 sp of next V-st, [sc in ch-1 sp of next V-st, 5 dc in ch-1 sp of next V-st] around, join in beg sc, fasten off.

Finishing

Cut green ribbon in half. Beg and ending at center front, weave over and under dc sts of rnd 6, tie ends in a bow at center front.

Blue Post-Stitch
Design by Sue Childress

Gauge

6 dc = 1¼ inches
Check gauge to save time.

Pattern Notes

Weave in loose ends as work progresses. Join rounds with a slip stitch unless otherwise stated.

Bootie

Make 2.

Rnd 1: Ch 14, dc in 4th ch from hook, hdc in each of next 8 chs, 2 dc in next ch, 5 dc in last ch, working on opposite side of foundation ch, 2 dc in next ch, hdc in each of next 8 chs, 2 dc in same ch as beg st, join in top of beg dc. *(29 sts)*

Rnd 2: Ch 2 *(counts as first hdc)*, 3 hdc in next st, hdc in each of next 9 sts, 2 dc in next 7 sts, hdc in next 10 sts, 3 hdc in last st, join in top of beg ch-2. *(40 sts)*

Rnd 3: Ch 2, **bphdc** *(see Stitch Guide)* around each st around, join in top of beg ch-2.

Rnd 4: Sk 2 top lps of bphdc and inserting hook into horizontal bar at back of sts, ch 2, hdc in each st around, join in top of beg ch-2.

Rnd 5: Ch 3 *(counts as first dc)*, 2 **fpdc** *(see Stitch Guide)* around same st as beg ch-3, sk next 2 sts, [3 fpdc around next st, sk next 3 sts] 9 times, sk next 2 sts, 3 fpdc around next st, join in top of beg ch-3. *(11 groups 3 fpdc sts)*

Rnd 6: Ch 1, sc in each of next 11 sts, [**dc dec** *(see Stitch Guide)* in next 3 sts] 3 times *(center front toe dec)*, sc in each of next 13 sts, join in beg sc. *(27 sts)*

Rnd 7: Ch 1, sc in each of next 10 sts, [insert hook in next st, yo, draw up a lp] 3 times, yo, draw through all 4 lps on hook *(toe dec)*, sc in each of next 11 sts, join in beg sc. *(24 sc)*

Rnd 8: Ch 1, **reverse sc** *(see illustration on page 12)* in each sc around, join in beg sc, fasten off.

Finished Size
4 inches long

Materials
- Fine (baby) weight yarn: 1 oz baby green
- Size E/4/3.5mm crochet hook or size needed to obtain gauge
- 40 inches ¼-inch-wide green satin ribbon

Finished Size
3½ inches long

Materials
- Fine (baby) weight yarn: 1 oz baby blue
- Size E/4/3.5mm crochet hook or size needed to obtain gauge
- 40 inches ¼-inch-wide baby blue satin ribbon

Finishing

Cut baby blue ribbon in half. Beg and ending at center front, weave ribbon over and under each sc of rnd 7, tie ends in a bow at center front.

Pink Love Knot

Design by Elizabeth Ann White

Gauge

Size B hook: 6 sts = 1 inch; 3 dc rows = 1 inch
Size C hook: 4 dc = 1 inch; 5 dc rows = 2 inches
Check gauge to save time.

Pattern Notes

Weave in loose ends as work progresses.

Join rounds with a slip stitch unless otherwise stated.

Use size B hook for 3½-inch foot and size C hook for 4½-inch foot.

Special Stitches

Love knot (lk): *(See illustration)* Draw up long lp in hook, yo, draw lp through, sc in back strand of long lp.

Love Knot Illustration

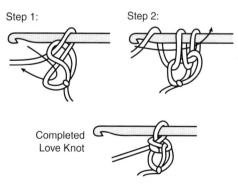

Step 1:   Step 2:

Completed Love Knot

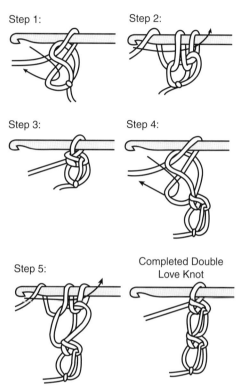**Double love knot (dlk):** *(See illustration)* [Draw up long lp on hook, yo, draw through, sc in back strand of long lp] twice.

Double Love Knot Illustration

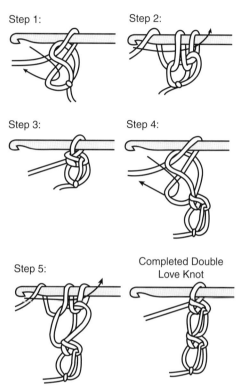

Step 1:   Step 2:

Step 3:   Step 4:

Step 5:   Completed Double Love Knot

Bootie

Make 2

Rnd 1 (RS): Beg at toe end of foot, ch 4, 11 dc in 4th ch from hook, join in top of beg ch. *(12 dc)*

Rnd 2: Ch 3 *(counts as first dc throughout)*, dc in same st as beg ch-3, 2 dc in each rem st around, join in 3rd ch of beg ch-3. *(24 dc)*

Rnds 3–5: Ch 3, dc in each dc around, join in 3rd ch of beg ch-3.

Row 6: Now working in rows, ch 3, dc in each of next 23 dc, turn. *(24 dc)*

Rows 7–11: Ch 3, dc in each dc across, turn.

Row 12: Fold row 11 in half, working through both thicknesses, work 12 sl sts across, fasten off.

Continued on page 51

![INTERMEDIATE]

Finished Size

3½ and 4½-inch foot

Materials

• Baby pompadour light (sport) weight yarn: ½ oz pink
• Sizes B/1/2.25mm and C/2/2.75mm crochet hooks or sizes needed to obtain gauge
• 40 inches ¼-inch-wide white satin ribbon

Pearls & Lace Wedding Cards

Designs by Lori Zeller

Add a unique touch to a bride's special day with these one-of-a-kind wedding cards that are easy to make with beads, thread crochet edgings and card stock.

Gauge

8 dc = ¾ inch
Check gauge to save time.

Pattern Notes

Weave in loose ends as work progresses.
Join rounds with a slip stitch unless otherwise stated.
Materials listed make both cards.

Special Stitches

V-stitch (V-st): (Dc, ch 1, dc) in indicated st.
Bead chain (bead ch): Push a bead up close to hook, ch 1 over bead.

Lace Oval

Row 1: String 30 pearl beads onto white cotton, ch 8, **bead ch** *(see Special Stitches)*, ch 2, dc in 6th ch from hook, dc in next ch, ch 2, sk next 2 chs, sc in each of next 2 chs, turn.
Row 2: Ch 1, sc in each of next 2 sc, ch 2, sc in each of next 2 dc, ch 2, bead ch, ch 2, turn.
Row 3: Dc in each of next 2 dc, ch 2, sk ch-2 sp, sc in each of next 2 sc, turn.
Rows 4–9: Rep rows 2 and 3.
Row 10: Rep row 2.

Finished Size
Each card 5 x 7 inches

Materials
- Royale Classic size 10 crochet cotton: 100 yds #201 white
- Size 6/1.80mm steel crochet hook or size needed to obtain gauge
- Tapestry needle
- Bead needle
- 1 yd ⅛-inch-wide white satin ribbon
- 3.5mm pearl beads: 30 for oval and 24 for circle
- 2 white blank 5 x 7-inch cards and envelopes
- Blue parchment card stock
- Blue card stock
- Craft glue

Row 11: Dc in each of next 2 dc, ch 2, sk next 2 chs, dc in each of next 2 sc, turn.

Row 12: Ch 3 *(counts as first dc throughout)*, dc in next dc, ch 2, sk next 2 chs, dc in each of next 2 dc, ch 2, bead ch, ch 2, turn.

Row 13: Dc in each of next 2 dc, ch 2, sk next 2 chs, dc in each of next 2 dc, turn.

Rows 14–19: Rep rows 12 and 13.

Row 20: Rep row 12.

Row 21: Dc in each of next 2 dc, ch 2, sk next 2 chs, sc in each of next 2 dc, turn.

Rows 22–39: Rep rows 2 and 3.

Row 40: Rep row 2.

Row 41: Rep row 11.

Rows 42–49: Rep rows 12 and 13.

Row 50: Rep row 12.

Row 51: Rep row 21.

Rows 52–59: Rep rows 2 and 3.

Row 60: Ch 1, sc in each of next 2 sc, ch 2, sk next 2 chs, dc in each of next 2 dc, leaving a length of cotton, fasten off.

Sew 6 sts of row 60 to opposite side of foundation ch.

Inner Oval Trim

Rnd 1: Attach white with a sc in any inner end st, work around inside of oval, work 1 sc around side of each sc and 2 sc around side of each dc, join in beg sc. *(80 sc)*

Rnd 2: Ch 2, sk next sc, [sl st in next sc, ch 2, sk next sc] around, sl st to join in base of first ch-2, fasten off.

Lace Circle

Row 1: String 24 pearl beads onto white cotton, ch 8, bead ch, ch 2, dc in 6th ch from hook, dc in next ch, ch 2, sk next 2 chs, sc in each of next 2 chs, turn.

Row 2: Ch 1, sc in each of next 2 sc, ch 2, sk next 2 chs, dc in each of next 2 dc, ch 2, bead ch, ch 2, turn.

Row 3: Dc in each of next 2 dc, ch 2, sk next 2 chs, sc in each of next 2 sc, turn.

Rows 4–47: Rep rows 2 and 3.

Row 48: Ch 1, sc in each of next 2 sc, ch 2, sk next 2 chs, dc in each of next 2 dc, leaving a length of cotton, fasten off.

Sew 6 sts of row 48 to opposite side of foundation ch.

Inner Circle Trim

Rnd 1: Attach white with sc in any inner end st, working around inside of oval, work 1 sc around side of each sc, join in beg sc. *(48 sc)*

Rnd 2: Ch 2, sk next sc, [sl st in next sc, ch 2, sk next sc] around, sl st to join in base of first ch-2, fasten off.

Heart

Make 5 for each card.

Rnd 1: With white, ch 4, sl st to join to form a ring, ch 1, [sc in ring, ch 3] 6 times, join in beg sc. *(6 ch-3 sps; 6 sc)*

Rnd 2: Sl st into ch-3 sp, ch 1, sc in same ch-3 sp *(sc at top center between lobes)*, ch 1, (dc, ch 1, {tr, ch 1} 4 times) in next ch-3 sp, **V-st** *(see Special Stitches)* in next ch-3 sp, ch 1, (sc, ch 3, sc) in next ch-3 sp *(center bottom of Heart)*, ch 1, V-st in next ch-3 sp, ch 1, ({tr, ch 1} 4 times, dc, ch 1) in next ch-3 sp, join in beg sc.

Rnd 3: Ch 2, [sc in next ch-1 sp, ch 2] 8 times, (sc, ch 3, sc) in next ch-3 sp, ch 2, [sc in next ch-1 sp, ch 2] around, join in beg sc, fasten off.

Card Assembly

Use photo as a guide for placement. Cut 4½ x 6½-inch piece of parchment card stock, center and glue to front of card. Cut 4 x 6-inch piece of blue card stock, center and glue to front of parchment. Cut oval or circle from parchment card stock and glue to front of blue. Weave ribbon through ch-2 sps on Lace Oval or Lace Circle, beg and ending at center bottom, tie ribbon ends in a bow, trim ends. Glue Lace Oval or Lace Circle to front outside edge of oval or circle. Glue a Heart centered within crocheted oval or circle. Glue a Heart to each front corner of card. With white ribbon, tie 2 small bows for each card. Glue a Bow at center top of card and glue a Bow to center of Heart at center of card. ✄

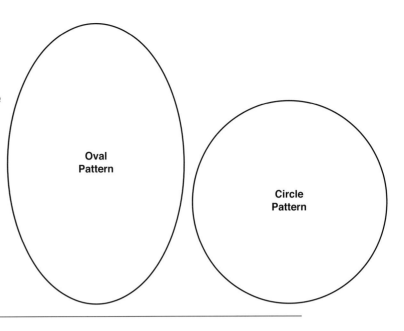

Oval Pattern

Circle Pattern

Raspberry Fantasy Beaded Scarf

Continued from page 34

Row 3: Ch 3, dc in each st across, turn.
Row 4: Ch 4 *(counts as first dc and ch-1 throughout)*, sk next st, dc in next st, [ch 1, sk next st, dc in next st] 4 times, turn.
Row 5: Ch 3, [dc in next ch-1 sp, dc in next dc] 5 times, turn.
Row 6: Rep row 4.
Row 7: Rep row 5.
Row 8: Rep row 2.
Row 9: Rep row 3.
Row 10: Rep row 4.

Row 11: Rep row 5.
Rows 12–63: Rep rows 6–11. At the end of row 63, ending with a row 3, fasten off.

Fringe

[Cut 2 lengths of yarn 16 inches long. Fold strands in half, insert hook in st, draw strands through at fold to form a lp on hook, draw cut ends through lp on hook, pull gently to secure] rep in each st across each end of scarf. Trim ends even. ✄

Bootie Boutique

Continued from page 48

Cuff

Rnd 1: Attach yarn at center back heel *(joining of row 12)*, ch 1, sc in same st as beg ch-1, work 35 sc evenly sp around ankle, join in beg sc. *(36 sc)*
Rnd 2: Ch 4 *(counts as first dc and ch-1)*, sk next sc, [dc in next sc, ch 1, sk next sc] around, join in 3rd ch of beg ch-4. *(18 dc; 18 ch-1 sps)*
Rnd 3: Sl st into next ch-1 sp ch 1, sc in same ch-1 sp, **dlk** *(see Special Stitches),*

[sc in next ch-1 sp, dlk] around, join in beg sc. *(18 sc; 18 dlk)*
Rnd 4: Lk *(see Special Stitches)*, sc in center of first dlk, dlk, [sc in center of next dlk, dlk] around, join, fasten off.

Finishing

Cut white ribbon in half. Beg and ending at center front, weave ribbon over and under dc sts of rnd 2 of Cuff, tie ends in a bow at center front. ✄

Retro Revisited

In today's fashion world, "hippie" is a style whose time has come again, updated with fresh colors and trendy new yarns. If you were part of the free-spirited '60s generation, you'll enjoy revisiting some of your old favorites in these fun, creative designs, and if you weren't, here's your chance to get a taste of what it was all about!

Groovy Beaded Curtain

Design by Vashti Braha

For the resident cool cat that likes to let it all hang out, this groovy beaded door curtain is the right-on accent for any hip, happening pad.

Gauge
Size E hook: Flower = 2 inches in diameter
Size L hook: 6–8 chs (stretch tautly, release, then measure) = 4 inches

Pattern Notes
Weave in loose ends as work progresses. Join rounds with a slip stitch unless otherwise stated.

Use a variety of beads of your choice that have holes large enough for hemp cord to pass through.

Beaded Fringe
Make 32 beaded strands in lengths approximately 18– to 73 inches.

Sort and rinse beads with water, allow beads to dry.

Run the last 4 inches of hemp cord through beeswax to aid in bead stringing; it will also make your starting and ending knots more secure. String beads onto hemp, approximately 5 beads for an 18-inch ch strand and 25 beads for a 73-inch ch strand.

If you encounter a thick spot in the hemp, trim it slightly with scissors; then run it through beeswax and twist it.

With size L hook and hemp, leaving a 4-inch length at beg, ch to desired length, incorporating a bead into the ch st at random intervals along the ch, ending with ch 12, sl st in 11th and 12th chs from hook *(hanging lp)*, leaving a 4-inch length of hemp, fasten off.

Flower Charm
Make 10.

Note: *Make 2 Flower Charms from each skein of embroidery floss. Do not separate plies.*

Rnd 1 (RS): With size E hook and embroidery floss, leaving a slight length at beg, ch 6, sl st to join to form a ring, ch 1, working over beg length, work 15 sc in ring, join in beg sc. *(15 sc)*

Rnd 2: [Ch 7, sk next 2 sts, sl st in next st] 5 times. *(5 petals)*

Rnd 3: Ch 1, [10 sc over next ch-7 sp, working over sl st of previous rnd, sc in sc of rnd 1] around, join in beg sc, fasten off. Dampen thoroughly with heavy spray starch, shape and place on a flat surface to dry.

Finishing
Tie Flower Charms onto end of some of the beaded strands. Pass dowel through hanging lps of Beaded Fringe, secure dowel above doorway. ✂

EASY

Finished Size
Strands range in length
from 21–73 inches,
including flowers

Materials
- Elements Hemp
  Jewelry Cord fine
  (string) cord (100 yds
  per ball):
  2 balls #1890 natural
- DMC cotton
  embroidery floss
  (8.7 yds per skein):
  1 skein each #444
    dark lemon, #996
    medium electric
    blue, #606 bright
    orange-red, #970
    light pumpkin and
    #552 medium violet
- Sizes E/4/3.5mm and
  L/11/8mm crochet
  hooks or sizes
  needed to obtain
  gauge
- Tapestry needle
- 22.58 oz/640g large
  glass red, white,
  yellow, green, plum
  and blue beads
  by Bead Solutions
  Beads by the Box/
  Beads Galore
- 360g mixed colors
  Rainbow Glass Beads
- 42g amethyst medium
  beads
- Heavy spray starch
- Bead reamer
- Beeswax
- Wooden dowel for
  hanging curtain

Design by Anne Halliday

Flower Power

Big, colorful flowers created with puffy clusters bring to mind the fanciful floral designs that artfully decorated the "peace mobile" vans of the free-spirited hippie era.

Gauge

Motif corner to corner = 5 inches; rnds 1 and 2 = 2½ inches

Pattern Notes

Weave in loose ends as work progresses.
Join rounds with a slip stitch unless otherwise stated.
Work the following color sequence and quantity of motifs:

Motif A: Make 50, rnds 1 and 2 with A, rnd 3 with MC, rnd 4 with A and rnd 5 with MC.

Motif B: Make 49, rnds 1 and 2 with B, rnd 3 with MC, rnd 4 with B and rnd 5 with MC.

Motif C: Make 40, rnds 1 and 2 with C, rnd 3 with MC, rnd 4 with C and rnd 5 with MC.

Motif D: Make 40, rnds 1 and 2 with D, rnd 3 with MC, rnd 4 with D and rnd 5 with MC.

Special Stitch

Cluster (cl): Ch 3, yo, insert hook in 3rd ch from hook, yo, draw up a lp, yo, draw through 2 lps on hook, yo, insert hook in same ch, yo, draw up a lp, yo, draw through 2 lps on hook, yo, draw through all 3 lps on hook.

Motif

Rnd 1 (RS): Ch 2, 6 sc in 2nd ch from hook, join in beg sc, turn.

Rnd 2 (WS): Ch 1, (sc, **cl**—*see Special Stitches*) in same sc as beg ch-1, [sc in next sc, cl] 5 times, join in beg sc, fasten off, turn. *(6 cls)*

Rnd 3 (RS): Attach MC with sl st in any sc of rnd 2, ch 4 *(counts as first dc, ch 1)*, working behind next cl, tr in sc on rnd 1 to left of sc on rnd 2, ch 1, [dc in next sc on rnd 2, ch 1, working behind next cl, tr in sc on rnd 1 to left of sc on rnd 2, ch 1] around, join in 3rd ch of beg ch-4, remove hook from lp, to hold lp, attach safety pin in dropped lp, turn. *(12 ch-1 sps)*

Note: *Keep MC and safety pin on WS.*

Rnd 4 (WS): Attach yarn with sc in same ch as joining, work cl, sk next ch, [sc in next st, work cl, sk next ch] around, join in beg sc, fasten off, turn. *(12 cls)*

Rnd 5 (RS): Remove safety pin, insert hook in dropped lp of MC, ch 2, sl st in sc in front of ch-2, ch 4 *(counts as first dc, ch 1)*, *working behind next cl, tr in ch-1 sp 1 rnd below cl, (tr, ch 1, tr) in next sc *(corner made)*, working behind next cl, tr in ch-1 sp 1 rnd below cl, ch 1**, dc in next sc, ch 1, rep from * around, ending last rep at **, join in 3rd ch of beg ch-4, fasten off. *(6 dc, 24 tr, 18 ch-1 sps)*

Finished Size
49 x 68 inches

Materials
- Red Heart Super
  Saver medium
  (worsted) weight
  yarn (8 oz/452 yds/
  226g per skein):
  3 skeins #312
     black (MC)
  1 skein each #774
     light raspberry
     (A), #342 light
     thyme (B), #322
     pale yellow
     (C) and #530
     orchid (D)
- Size I/9/5.5mm
  crochet hook or size
  needed to obtain
  gauge
- Yarn needle
- 2 safety pins

Half Motif

Make 16.

Row 1 (WS): With MC, ch 4, dc in 4th ch from hook, 5 dc in same ch, turn. *(7 dc)*

Row 2: Ch 2 *(counts as first hdc)*, hdc in same st as beg ch-2, 2 hdc in each of next 5 sts, hdc in last st, turn. *(13 hdc)*

Row 3: Ch 3 *(counts as first dc throughout)*, dc in same st as beg ch-3, [dc in next st, 2 dc in next st] 5 times, dc in each of next 2 sts, turn. *(19 dc)*

Row 4: Ch 3, dc in same st as beg ch-3, hdc in next st, sc in each of next 3 sts, hdc in next st, *(dc, ch 1, dc) in next st, hdc in next st, sc in each of next 3 sts, hdc in next st, rep from * once, 2 dc in last st, fasten off. *(23 st, 2 corner ch-1 sps)*

Assembly

When sewing Motifs tog, beg and end in corner ch-1 sps. When sewing Half Motifs, match first and last dc sts on rnd 4 to single corner ch sp on Motifs.

Using diagram as a guide for placement, thread yarn needle with a length of MC: whipstitch Motifs and Half Motifs tog to form horizontal strips; then whipstitch strips tog.

Edging

Rnd 1 (RS): Starting at point A as indicated on afghan diagram, attach MC with a sl st in tr to right of corner ch-1 sp, ch 3 *(counts as first dc, ch 1, mark this dc with safety pin)*, dc in next corner ch-1 sp, *ch 1, dc in next tr, ch 1, sk next st, [dc in next ch-1 sp, ch 1, sk next st] twice, dc in next tr, ch 1, dc in next corner ch-1 sp, ch 1, dc in next tr, ch 1, sk next st, [dc in next ch-1 sp, ch 1, sk next st] twice, dc in next tr, [**dc dec** *(see Stitch Guide)* in next 2 ch sps skipping seam bet, dc in next tr, ch 1, sk next st, {dc in next ch-1 sp, ch 1, sk next st} twice, dc in next tr, ch 1, dc in next corner ch-1 sp, ch 1, dc in next tr, ch 1, sk next st, {dc in next ch-1 sp, ch 1, sk next st} twice, dc in next tr] 10 times, ch 1, dc in next corner ch-1 sp, ch 1, dc in next tr, ch 1, sk next st, [dc in next ch-1 sp, ch 1, sk next st] twice, [dc in next tr, ch 1, working across next Half Motif and working around posts of sts at end of rows, {hdc in next row, ch 1} 8 times, working across next Motif, dc in next free tr, ch 1, sk next st, {dc in next ch-1 sp, ch 1, sk next st} twice] across to first corner of last motif**, dc in next tr, ch 1, dc in next corner ch-1 sp *(mark last dc made with safety pin for st placement)*, rep from * to **, join in 2nd ch of beg ch-3.

Rnd 2: Ch 1, sc in next ch-1 sp, ch 1, *sc in next dc, ch 1, [sc in next ch-1 sp, ch 1] 5 times, sc in next dc, [{ch 1, sc in next ch-1 sp} 4 times, sk next dc, sc in next dc dec, sk next dc, {sc in next ch-1 sp} 4 times, sc in next dc] 10 times, ch 1, [sc in next ch-1 sp, ch 1] 5 times, sc in next dc, ch 1, [sc in next ch-1 sp, ch 1] across to next marked dc, rep from * around, join in beg sc, remove safety pins.

Rnd 3: Ch 1, [sc in next ch-1 sp, ch 1] 11 times, sk next sc, sc in next sc, *ch 1, sk next sc, [{sc in next ch-1 sp, ch 1} 8 times, sk next sc, sc in next sc, ch 1, sk next sc] 9 times*, [sc in next ch-1 sp, ch 1] across to first sc of 3-sc group at point B, sk next sc, sc in next sc *(mark sc just made with safety pin)*, rep from * to * once, [sc in next ch-1 sp, ch 1] across to beg of rnd, join in beg sc.

Rnd 4: Sl st in next ch-1 sp, [ch 2, sl st in next ch-1 sp] 10 times, [sl st in next ch-1 sp, {ch 2, sl st in next ch-1 sp} 8 times] 9 times, sl st in next ch-1 sp, [ch 2, sl st in next ch-1 sp] across to marked st, [sl st in next ch-1 sp, {ch 2, sl st in next ch-1 sp} 8 times] 9 times, [sl st in next ch-1 sp, ch 2] across to beg of rnd, join in beg sl st, fasten off. ✄

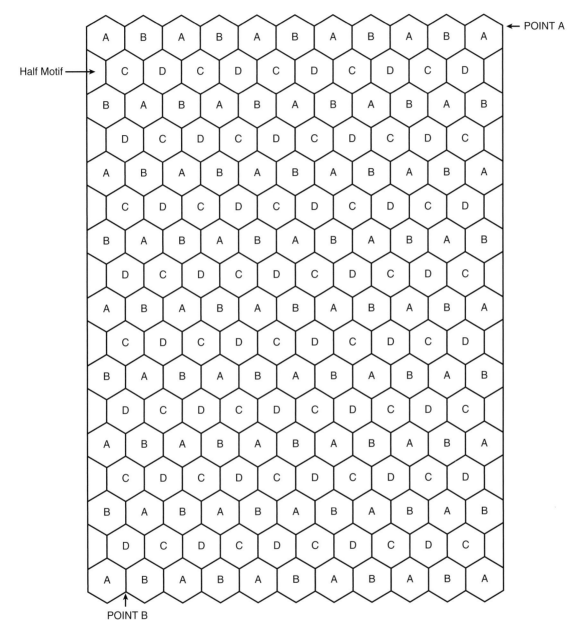

POINT A

Half Motif

POINT B

Flower Power

Design by **Sandy Abbate**

Free Spirit Poncho

From California dreamin' to a New York state of mind, this fun, colorful version of the classic cover-up is the perfect hippie-chic accessory for a casual, carefree wardrobe.

Gauge
Size K hook: square = 8½ inches; rnds 1 and 2 – 3 inches
Size N hook: 8 dc = 3 inches; 3 dc rnds = 2 inches

Pattern Notes
Weave in loose ends as work progresses.
Join rounds with a slip stitch unless otherwise stated.

Special Stitches
V-stitch (V-st): (Dc, ch 1, dc) in indicated st.
Beginning V-stitch (beg V-st): Ch 4 *(counts as first dc, ch 1)*, dc in same sp as beg ch-4.
Cluster (cl): [Yo hook, insert hook in indicated sp, yo, draw up a lp, yo, draw through 2 lps on hook] 4 times, yo, draw through all 5 lps on hook.
Beginning cluster (beg cl): Ch 2, [yo hook, insert hook in same sp as beg ch-2, yo, draw up a lp, yo, draw through 2 lps on hook] 3 times, yo, draw through all 4 lps on hook.

Neckband
Rnd 1 (RS): With size N hook and lavender, ch 90, sl st to join in first ch to form a ring, **beg V-st** *(see Special Stitches)* in same ch as joining, dc in each of next 44 chs, **V-st** *(see Special Stitches)* in next ch, dc in each of next 44 chs, join in 3rd ch of beg ch-4, fasten off. *(88 dc, 2 V-sts)*
Rnd 2: Attach pumpkin with a sl st in beg V-st, beg V-st in same ch-1 sp, dc in each dc to next ch-1 sp, V-st in next ch-1 sp, dc in each dc around, join in 3rd ch of beg ch-4, fasten off. *(92 dc, 2 V-sts)*
Rnd 3: With parakeet, rep rnd 2; set aside. *(96 dc, 2 V-sts)*

Square A
Make 2.
Rnd 1 (RS): With size K hook and lavender, ch 4, sl st to join to form a ring, ch 4 *(counts as first dc, ch 1)*, [dc in ring, ch 1] 7 times, join in 3rd ch of beg ch-4. *(8 ch-1 sps)*
Rnd 2: Sl st into ch-1 sp, **beg cl** *(see Special Stitches)* in same ch-1 sp, ch 3, [**cl** *(see Special Stitches)* in next ch-1 sp, ch 3] around, join in top of beg cl, fasten off.
Rnd 3: Attach lime in any ch-3 sp, ch 3

Finished Size
One size fits most

Materials
- Red Heart Classic medium (worsted) weight yarn (3½ oz/190 yds/99g per skein): 2 skeins #3 off-white 1 skein each #579 light lavender, #254 pumpkin and #513 parakeet
- Red Heart Super Saver medium (worsted) weight yarn (3 oz/170 yds/ 85g per skein): 1 skein #655 lime
- Sizes K/10½/6.5mm and N/13/9mm crochet hooks or sizes needed to obtain gauge
- Yarn needle

ch-2 sp, *(3 dc, ch 2, 3 dc) in corner ch-2 sp, ch 1, [3 dc in next ch-1 sp, ch 1] across to next corner ch-2 sp, rep from * twice, 3 dc in same corner ch-2 sp as beg ch-3, join in 3rd ch of beg ch-3, fasten off.

Rnd 6: Attach lavender in any corner ch-2 sp, rep rnd 5.

Rnd 7: Attach off-white in any corner ch-2 sp, rep rnd 5.

Square B
Make 2.
Rnds 1 & 2: With pumpkin, rep rnds 1 and 2 of Square A.
Rnd 3: With lime, rep rnd 3 of Square A.
Rnds 4 & 5: Rep rnds 4 and 5 of Square A.
Rnd 6: With pumpkin, rep rnd 6 of Square A.
Rnd 7: Rep rnd 7 of Square A.

Square C
Make 2.
Rnds 1 & 2: With parakeet, rep rnds 1 and 2 of Square A.
Rnd 3: With lime, rep rnd 3 of Square A.
Rnds 4 & 5: Rep rnds 4 and 5 of Square A.
Rnd 6: With parakeet, rep rnd 6 of Square A.
Rnd 7: Rep rnd 7 of Square A.

Assembly
Working in **back lps** (see Stitch Guide) only, using off-white, sew squares tog as indicated in diagram; sew sections tog as indicated.
Position rnd 3 of Neckband onto joined squares with a V-st at each center front and center back at V of junction of squares.

(counts as first dc throughout), 2 dc in same ch sp, ch 1, 3 dc in next ch-3 sp, ch 1, *(3 dc, ch 2, 3 dc) in next ch-3 sp, ch 1, 3 dc in next ch-3 sp, ch 1, rep from * twice, 3 dc in same ch-3 sp as beg ch-3, ch 2, join in 3rd ch of beg ch-3, fasten off.

Rnd 4: Attach off-white in any ch-2 sp, ch 3, 2 dc in same ch sp, ch 1, [3 dc in next ch-1 sp, ch 1] across to next corner ch-2 sp, *(3 dc, ch 2, 3 dc) in corner ch-2 sp, ch 1, [3 dc in next ch-1 sp, ch 1] across to next corner ch-2 sp, rep from * twice, 3 dc in same corner ch-2 sp as beg ch-3, join in 3rd ch of beg ch-3.

Rnd 5: Ch 3, 2 dc in same sp, ch 1, [3 dc in next ch-1 sp, ch 1] across to next corner

Continued on page 75

Design by Gina Carlson-Brown

Funky Helmet

A variety of trendy yarns gives a new, what's-happening-now look to the bohemian helmet hat from the 1960s and 1970s. Ear tassels add a touch of funky fun.

Gauge
2 sc = 1 inch

Pattern Notes
Weave in loose ends as work progresses.
Join rounds with a slip stitch unless otherwise stated.
Do not join rounds unless otherwise stated.

Use stitch marker to mark rounds, move as work progresses.

Helmet
Rnd 1 (RS): With MC, ch 4, sl st to join in first ch to form a ring, ch 1, place st marker in before next st, work 2 sc in each ch around. *(8 sc)*

Rnd 2: 2 sc in each sc around. *(16 sc)*

Rnd 3: Sc in each of next 7 sc, 2 sc in next sc, sc in each of next 8 sc, draw up a lp of CC, fasten off MC. *(17 sc)*

Rnd 4: 2 sc in each sc around. *(34 sc)*

Rnd 5: Sc in each of next 15 sc, 2 sc in next sc, sc in each of next 18 sc, draw up a lp of MC, fasten off CC. *(35 sc)*

Rnd 6: Sc in each of next 10 sc, 2 sc in next sc, sc in each of next 24 sc. *(36 sc)*

Rnd 7: Sc in each of next 20 sc, 2 sc in next sc, sc in each of next 15 sc. *(37 sc)*

Rnd 8: [Sc in each of next 10 sc, 2 sc in next sc] twice, sc in each of next 15 sc. *(39 sc)*

Rnd 9: Ch 2, sc in same st as beg ch-2, [dc in next st, sc in next st] around, draw up a lp of CC, fasten off MC. *(40 sts)*

Rnd 10: Sc in 2nd ch of ch-2, [dc in next sc, sc in next dc] around, draw up a lp of MC, fasten off CC.

Rnd 11: Dc in each st around.

Rnd 12: Sc in each st around. At the end of rnd 12, do not fasten off.

First Earflap
Row 13: Now working in rows, ch 1, sc in same st as beg ch-1, sc in each of next 7 sc, turn. *(8 sc)*

Rows 14–16: Ch 1, sc in each sc across, turn. At the end of row 16, fasten off.

Second Earflap
Row 13: Sk next 12 sts of rnd 12, attach MC in next sc, ch 1, sc in same sc as beg ch-1, sc in each of next 7 sc, turn. *(8 sc)*

Rows 14–16: Ch 1, sc in each sc across, turn.

EASY

Trim

Rnd 17: Now working in rnds, ch 1, sl st in each st around entire outer edge of Helmet and Earflaps, fasten off.

Fur Trim

Rnd 1 (RS): Attach CC1 around **post** *(see Stitch Guide)* of sc of rnd 3 of Helmet, ch 1, sc around post of same sc, sc around post of each of next 16 sc, join in beg sc, fasten off. *(17 sc)*

Rnd 2 (RS): Attach CC1 around post of sc of rnd 8, ch 1, sc around post of same sc, sc around post of each of next 38 sc, join in beg sc, fasten off. *(39 sc)*

Rnd 3 (RS): Working around bottom edge of Helmet sts of rnd 12 and outer edge around each Earflap, attach CC1, ch 1, sc around post of each st around entire outer edge, join in beg sc, fasten off.

Helmet Tie

Make 2.

Starting at about the middle on the WS of the Earflap *(row 14)* facing, attach CC, ch 1, sc over post of sc directly below, ch 15, sl st in 2nd ch from hook, sl st in each rem ch across, fasten off.

Helmet & Tie Tassels

Holding all rem strands of yarn tog, wrap all strands around the 4-inch cardboard. Cut bottom edge of strands. Set aside 8 strands of MC and 4 strands of CC1.

Take 1 strand of MC and place on a flat surface; take rem bundle of strands and place centered over single strand of MC, knot around bundle tightly to secure strands. Attach tassel to center top of Helmet.

Holding 4 strands of MC and 1 strand CC1, fold strands in half, insert hook into end of tie, draw strands through at fold to form a lp on hook, draw strands through lp on hook, pull ends gently to secure. ✂

Finished Size

Fits woman's head diameter 20–22 inches

Length from top to end of earpiece approximately 10 inches

Materials

- Plymouth Yukon super bulky (super chunky) weight yarn (3½ oz/60 yds/100g per skein): 1 skein #88 gray *(MC)*
- Gedifra Byzanz super bulky (super chunky) weight yarn (1¾ oz/33 yds/50g per skein): 1 skein #04 white, gray/tan *(CC)*
- Gedifra Chapello bulky (chunky) weight eyelash yarn (1¾ oz/33 yds/50g per skein): 1 skein #25 ecru *(CC1)*
- Size L/11/8mm crochet hook or size needed to obtain gauge
- Yarn needle
- Stitch marker
- 4-inch piece cardboard

Peace Garden Hat

Design by Katherine Eng

Wear this fun floral hat with your favorite hip-huggers or granny skirt and unleash your carefree, "flower child" personality!

BEGINNER

Size
Adult

Materials
• Red Heart Super
  Saver medium
  (worsted)
  weight yarn:
  3 oz #320 cornmeal
  2 yds each #381
    light blue, #358
    lavender and #373
    petal pink
• Sizes G/6/4mm
  and H/8/5mm
  crochet hooks or
  size needed to
  obtain gauge
• Yarn needle

Gauge
Size H hook: 3 sc rnds = 1 inch;
3 sc = 1 inch

Pattern Notes
Weave in loose ends as work progresses.

Join rounds with a slip stitch unless otherwise stated.

Check gauge to save time.

Special Stitches
Small shell: (2 dc, ch 2, 2 dc) in indicated st.
Beginning small shell (beg small shell): (Ch 3, dc, ch 2, 2 dc) in indicated st.
Large shell: (3 dc, ch 2, 3 dc) in indicated st.
Beginning large shell (beg large shell): [Ch 3, 2 dc, ch 2, 3 dc] in indicated st.

Bonnet
Rnd 1: With size H hook and cornmeal, ch 4, join to form a ring, ch 1, 8 sc in ring, join in beg sc. *(8 sc)*
Rnd 2: Ch 1, 2 sc in each sc around, join in beg sc. *(16 sc)*
Rnd 3: Ch 1, [sc in next sc, 2 sc in next sc] around, join in beg sc. *(24 sc)*
Rnd 4: Ch 1, [sc in each of next 2 sc, 2 sc in next sc] around, join in beg sc. *(32 sc)*
Rnd 5: Ch 1, [2 sc in next sc, sc in each of next 3 sc] around, join in beg sc. *(40 sc)*
Rnd 6: Ch 1, [sc in each of next 3 sc, 2 sc in next sc] around, join in beg sc. *(50 sc)*
Rnd 7: Ch 1, sc in each st around, join in beg sc.
Rnd 8: Ch 1, [sc in each of next 4 sc, 2 sc in next sc] around, join in beg sc. *(60 sc)*
Rnd 9: Rep rnd 7.
Rnd 10: Ch 1, sc in first st, *sk next 2 sc, **small shell** *(see Special Stitches)* in next sc, sk next 2 sc **, sc in next sc, rep from * around, ending last rep at **, join in beg sc. *(10 sc, 10 small shells)*
Rnd 11: Work **beg small shell** *(see Special Stitches)* in first sc, sc in ch-2 sp of each small shell and small shell in each sc around, join in 3rd ch of beg ch-3.
Rnd 12: Sl st into ch-2 sp, ch 1, sc in same ch-2 sp, small shell in each sc and sc in each ch-2 sp of each small shell, join in beg sc.
Rnds 13 & 14: Rep rnds 11 and 12.
Rnd 15: Rep rnd 11.

Rnd 16: Ch 2 *(counts as first hdc)*, *sc in next dc, sc in next ch-2 sp, sc in next dc, hdc in next dc, dc in next sc **, hdc in next dc, rep from * around, ending last rep at **, join in 2nd ch of beg ch-2. *(60 sts)*

Rnds 17 & 18: Rep rnd 7.

Brim

Rnd 19: Ch 1, sc in first st, *sk next 2 sc, **large shell** *(see Special Stitches)* in next sc, sk next 2 sc **, sc in next sc, rep from * around, ending last rep at **, join in beg sc. *(10 sc, 10 large shells)*

Rnd 20: Beg large shell *(see Special Stitches)* in same sc, *ch 1, sc in next ch-2 sp, ch 1 **, large shell in next sc, rep from * around, ending last rep at **, join in 3rd ch of beg ch-3.

Rnd 21: Sl st into ch-2 sp, ch 1, [sc in ch-2 sp of large shell, ch 1, large shell in next sc, ch 1] around, join in beg sc.

Rnd 22: Ch 1, (sc, ch 3, sc) in same sc as beg ch-1, *ch 1, sk next ch-1 sp, sk next dc, sc in next dc, ch 1, sk next dc, (sc, ch 3, sc) in next ch-2 sp of large shell, ch 1, sk next dc, sc in next dc, ch 1, sk next dc, sk next ch-1 sp **, (sc, ch 3, sc) in next sc, rep from * around, ending last rep at **, join in beg sc, fasten off.

Large Flower

Rnd 1: With size G hook and petal pink, ch 3, join to form a ring, ch 1, 6 sc in ring, join in beg sc, fasten off. *(6 sc)*

Rnd 2: Attach lavender in any sc, ch 1, (sc, ch 4, retaining last lp on hook, 2 tr in same sc, yo, draw through all 3 lps on hook, ch 4, sl st in same sc) in each sc around, join in beg sc, fasten off.

Small Flower

Make 2.

Rnd 1: Rep rnd 1 of Large Flower. *(6 sc)*

Rnd 2: Attach light blue in any sc, ch 1, (sc,

ch 3, retaining last lp of each st on hook, 2 dc in same sc, yo, draw through all 3 lps on hook, ch 3, sl st in same sc) in each sc around, join in beg sc, fasten off.

Sew Large Flower centered over rnds 17 and 18. Sew a Small Flower to each side of Large Flower. ✂

Design by **Vashti Braha**

Lunar Landscape Window Fringe

Sleep easy under the moon and stars and enjoy being at one with the universe with this novelty, fur-yarn window covering sparkling with silvery celestial accents.

Gauge

Size F hook: wishing star = 2½ inches in diameter; moon charm = 3½ inches long
Size P hook: 4 chs = 4 inches

Pattern Notes

Weave in loose ends as work progresses.
Join rounds with a slip stitch unless otherwise stated.
Size B hook is used for attaching jingle bells only.

Special Stitches

Chainless single crochet (csc): Insert hook into 2 sides of st just made, yo, draw up a lp, yo, draw through 2 lps on hook.

Chainless half double crochet (chdc): Yo, insert hook into 2 side lps of st just made, yo, draw up a lp, yo, draw through all 3 lps on hook.

Chainless double crochet (cdc): Yo, insert hook into 2 side lps of st just made, yo, draw up a lp, yo, draw through 2 lps on hook, yo, draw through rem 2 lps on hook.

Chainless treble crochet (ctr): Yo hook twice, insert hook into 2 side lps of st just made, yo, draw up a lp, [yo, draw through 2 lps on hook] 3 times.

Chainless double treble crochet (cdtr): Yo hook 3 times, insert hook into 2 side lps of st just made, yo, draw up a lp, [yo, draw through 2 lps on hook] 4 times.

Moon Charm

Row 1: With size F hook and 1 strand each 2-ply silver floss and 6-ply strand of white floss held tog, ch 17, sl st in 2nd ch from hook, sc in next ch, hdc in next ch, dc in next ch, 2 dc in next ch, dc in each of next 2 chs, 2 dc in next ch, dc in each of next 3 chs, 2 dc in next ch, dc in next ch, hdc in next ch, sc in next ch, sl st in last ch, turn. *(19 sts)*

Row 2: Sl st in sl st, sl st in next sc, sc in each of next 3 sts, 2 hdc in next st, dc in next st, 2 dc in each of next 2 sts, 2 tr in each of next 2 sts, 2 dc in next st, dc in each of next 2 sts, 2 hdc in next st, sc in each of

INTERMEDIATE

Finished Size
36 inches wide; length
16–36 inches

Materials
• Lion Brand Fun Fur
  bulky (chunky)
  weight eyelash yarn
  (1¾ oz/60yds/50g
  per ball):
  4 balls #153 black
  3 balls #109
    sapphire
  1 ball #191 violet
• DMC Metallic 6-ply
  embroidery floss
  (8¾ yds per skein):
  2 skeins #5283 silver
  1 skein #5272
    iridescent white
• DMC Metallic 2-ply
  pearl thread (27⅓
  yds per skein):
  1 skein #5283 silver
• Sizes B/1/2.25mm,
  F/5/3.75mm
  and P/15mm
  crochet hooks or
  sizes needed to
  obtain gauge
• Yarn needle
• Heavy spray starch
• 20mm jingle bells in
  assorted colors: 12
• Curtain rod or
  wooden dowel

next 3 sts, sl st in next st, ch 4, sl st in 4th ch from hook, turn. *(26 sts plus ch-4 lp)*

Row 3: Working across opposite side of foundation ch, sl st tightly in each ch across, ch 10, sl st in side of row 1 *(hanging lp)*, fasten off.

Wishing Star

Rnd 1: With size F hook, and 1 strand each 2-ply strand of silver floss and 3 plies of 6-ply strand of white floss held tog, ch 2, 5 sc in 2nd ch from hook, join in beg sc. *(5 sc)*

Rnd 2: Ch 1, 3 sc in each sc around, join in beg sc. *(15 sc)*

Rnd 3: Ch 6, ch 5 tightly, sl st in 6th ch from hook *(hanging lp)*, sc in next ch, hdc in next ch, dc in next ch, tr in each of next 2 chs, tr in st holding sl st, sk 2 sc, sl st in next sc, *ch 6, sc in 2nd ch from hook, hdc in next ch, dc in next ch, tr in each of next 2 chs, tr in st holding sl st, sk 2 sc, sl st in next sc, rep from * around, fasten off.

Large Star
Make 2.

Rnds 1–3: With size F hook and 6-ply strand of silver floss, rep rnds 1–3 of Wishing Star.

Continued on page 77

Designs by Vashti Braha

Far-Out Fur Accents

These totally rad window and lamp ponchos are definitely part of the solution for punching up a dull decor. The lamp design also makes a great cover-up for a small child.

■■□□
EASY

Finished Size

Window poncho will fit standard 36 x 36-inch window opening and stretch into a one size fits most poncho, cape or wrap

Lamp poncho will cover standard lamp shade diameter at top ranging from 22–32 inches and a length of 12–15 inches.

Gauge

Size F hook: rnd 1 of flower = 1 inch; completed flower = 2¾ inches

Size P hook: 2 rows of window poncho mesh (1 diamond) = 3 inches

Pattern Notes

Weave in loose ends as work progresses.

Join rounds with a slip stitch unless otherwise stated.

Window Poncho

Row 1: Beg at top of poncho, with size P hook and 2 strands of citrus held tog, ch 101, sc in 2nd ch from hook *(place a st marker in top 2 lps of this sc)*, [ch 6, sk next 4 chs, sc in next ch] 20 times, place a st marker in top 2 lps of last sc, turn. *(20 lps)*

Row 2: Taking care to keep foundation ch untwisted and at the bottom as work progresses, ch 8, sc in first ch-6 sp, [ch 6, sc in next ch-6 sp] across, ending with ch 3, dtr in sc holding first st marker, do not remove st marker, turn. *(21 ch sps)*

Row 3: Ch 1, sc in dtr, [ch 6, sc in next ch sp] across, turn. *(20 ch sps)*

Row 4: Ch 8, sc in first ch-6 sp, [ch 6, sc in next ch-6 sp] rep across, ending with ch 3, dtr in end sc, turn. *(21 ch sps)*

Rows 5–14: Rep rows 3 and 4. At the end of row 14, fasten off.

Collar reinforcement

Holding poncho with foundation ch at top, attach double strand of citrus in first sc of row 2 *(holds a st marker)*, with sl st, ch 1, sc in first ch sp 1 row below and around first sc as reinforcement, [4 sc around next 4 foundation chs, sc into next ch sp 1 row below and around next sc] across to last sc *(holding other st marker)*, remove st markers, fasten off.

Window Jeweled Flower

Make 4 bright canary;
3 each bright orange-red/bright red, dark electric blue and plum/dark plum;
2 each bright orange-red and very dark

Materials

- Lion Brand Fun Fur
  Prints bulky (chunky)
  eyelash yarn (1½ oz/57
  yds/40g per ball):
    6 balls #207 citrus
      (window poncho)
    4 balls #207 citrus
      (longer lamp poncho)
    2 balls #207 citrus
      (short lamp poncho)
- DMC cotton embroidery
  floss (8¾ yds per skein):
    12 skeins #973 bright
      canary
    6 skeins each #718
      plum and #606
      bright orange-red
    5 skeins each #995 dark
      electric blue and
      #333 very dark blue-
      violet
- DMC rayon embroidery
  floss (8¾ yds per skein):
    6 skeins each #30915
      dark plum and
      #30666 bright red
- DMC Metallic
  embroidery floss (8¾
  yds per skein):
    5 skeins each #5290
      electric blue and
      #5289 purple
- Sizes F/5/3.75mm and
  P/15mm crochet hooks
  or sizes needed to
  obtain gauge
- Yarn needle
- 18mm multicolored
  round rhinestones: 30
- Aleene's platinum super-
  bond fabric textile
  adhesive
- Curtain rod or wooden
  dowel
- 2 stitch markers

blue-violet/purple;

and 1 each plum, dark electric blue/ electric blue and very dark blue-violet.

Note: Use floss individually or with 2 colors held tog as indicated above.

Rnd 1: With size F hook, leaving a slight length at beg, ch 7, sl st to join in beg ch to form a ring, ch 1, working over beg length, work 18 sc in ring, join in beg sc. *(18 sc)*

Rnd 2: [Ch 7, sk 2 sc, sl st in next sc] 6 times. *(6 petals)*

Rnd 3: Ch 1, *(1 sc, 8 hdc, 1 sc) in next ch-7 sp, working over sl st of previous rnd, sc in next sc of rnd 1 directly below sl st, rep from * around, leaving a length, fasten off. Coat entire back of rhinestone with glue to protect mirrored backing, glue to center of flower and let dry a minimum of 4 hours. Set 2 flowers aside for Drawstring or Curtain Tieback. Glue rem 18 flowers as desired to Window Poncho

Drawstring or Curtain Tieback

With size P hook and 2 strands of citrus held tog, leaving a 5-inch length at beg, ch 100, leaving a 5-inch length at end, fasten off. Weave Drawstring through ch sps of row 1 for wearing as a cape and lace down the front to close cape into a poncho. To shorten length or wear as a collared cape, weave Drawstring through a different row of mesh. To cover window, weave a dowel through row 1 ch sps and use Drawstring as a curtain tieback.

Use rem tails to attach a flower to each end of Drawstring.

Lamp Poncho

Rnd 1: With size P hook and 2 strands citrus held tog, ch 45, sl st in 2nd ch from hook, sc in next ch [ch 5, sk next 2 chs, sc in next ch] across to last 3 chs, ch 5, sk next 2 chs, sc in last ch, taking care that row 1 is not twisted, sc in first ch to form a ring, ch 2, dc in next ch sp.

Rnd 2: Sc in ch sp just made, [ch 6, sc in next ch sp] around, ending with ch 2, tr in first sc.

Rnds 3 & 4: Rep rnd 2.

Rnd 5: Sc in ch sp just made, [ch 7, sc in next ch sp] around, ending with ch 3, tr in first sc.

Rnd 6: Rep rnd 5. End off to cover a 12-inch lamp shade or continue for longer shade.

Rnd 7: Sc in ch sp, [ch 8, sc in next ch sp] around, ending with ch 4, tr in beg sc.

Rnd 8: Rep rnd 7, fasten off.

Drawstring

With size P hook and 2 strands of citrus, ch 75, fasten off. Weave through row 1 or 2 of Lamp Poncho.

Lamp Jeweled Flower

Make 2 each bright canary and plum/ dark plum;

and 1 each dark plum, electric blue, bright orange-red/bright red, and very dark blue-violet/purple.

Note: Use floss individually or with 2 colors held tog as indicated above.

Rnds 1–3: Rep rnds 1–3 of Window Jeweled Flower.

Glue all 8 flowers as desired onto Lamp Poncho. ✄

Dig-It Flowerpot Cover

Design by Tammy Hildebrand

Dress up an inexpensive flowerpot with a simple, retro-style cover made from four large granny squares joined in a cylinder and finished with an easy single crochet edging. Cotton worsted yarn makes it durable and easy to care for.

Gauge

Rnd 1 of motif = 1½ inches; 7 sc = 2 inches

Pattern Notes

Weave in loose ends as work progresses.

Join rounds with a slip stitch unless otherwise stated.

Special Stitch

Cluster (cl): Yo, [insert hook in ring, yo, draw up a lp, yo, draw through 2 lps on hook] twice, yo, draw through all 3 lps on hook.

Cover

First motif

Rnd 1: With rose, ch 3, sl st in first ch to form a ring, ch 3 **cl** (see Special Stitch) in ring, ch 1, cl in ring, ch 2, [cl in ring, ch 1, cl in

Continued on page 76

EASY

Finished Size

Fits flowerpot 5½ inches tall x 5½ inches across bottom and 7½ inches across top

Materials

- Lion Brand Lion Cotton medium (worsted) weight yarn:
  5 oz #098 natural
  1 oz each #140 rose and #131 fern green
- Size I/9/5.5mm crochet hook or size needed to obtain gauge
- Tapestry needle

Go-Go Granny

Design by Darla Sims

The shimmer and shine practically dance off this glitzy updated version of the traditional granny-square afghan. A trendy mix of textured yarns creates a chic, luxurious throw.

Gauge
Size L hook: small square = 7½ inches square

Pattern Notes
Weave in loose ends as work progresses. Join rounds with a slip stitch unless otherwise stated.

Small Square
Make 24.

Note: Work Small Squares according to Small Square Color Sequence.

Rnd 1 (RS): With size L hook, ch 4, 11 dc in 4th ch from hook, join in 4th ch of beg ch-4, fasten off. *(12 dc)*

Rnd 2: Beg between any 2 dc sts, attach next color, ch 3 *(counts as first dc throughout)*, (2 dc, ch 2, 3 dc) in same sp as beg ch-3, *sk next 3 dc, (3 dc, ch 2, 3 dc) in next sp between dc, rep from * twice, join in 3rd ch of beg ch-3, fasten off. *(24 dc, 4 ch-2 sps)*

Rnd 3: Attach next color in any ch-2 sp, ch 3, 2 dc in same ch-2 sp, *dc in each of next 6 dc**, (3 dc, ch 2, 3 dc) in next ch-2 sp, rep from * around, ending last rep at **, 3 dc in same ch-2 sp as beg ch-3, ch 2, join in 3rd ch of beg ch-3, fasten off. *(48 dc, 4 ch-2 sps)*

Rnd 4: Attach next color in any ch-2 sp, ch 3, 2 dc in same ch-2 sp, *sk next 2 dc, dc in each of next 8 dc, sk next 2 dc**, (3 dc, ch 2, 3 dc) in corner ch-2 sp, rep from * around, ending last rep at **, 3 dc in same ch-2 sp as beg ch-3, ch 2, join in 3rd ch of beg ch-3, fasten off. *(56 dc, 4 ch-2 sps)*

Rnd 5: Attach A in corner ch-2 sp, ch 1, [3 sc in corner ch-2 sp, sc in each of next 14 sts] 4 times, join in beg sc, fasten off. *(68 sc)*

Large Square
Make 6.
Note: Work Large Squares according to Large Square Color Sequence.

Rnds 1–4: Rep rnds 1–4 of Small Square. *(56 dc, 4 ch-2 sps)*

Rnd 5: Attach next color in any ch-2 sp, ch 3, 2 dc in same ch-2 sp, *sk next 2 dc, dc in each of next 10 dc, sk next 2 dc**, (3 dc, ch 2, 3 dc) in corner ch-2 sp, rep from * around, ending last rep at **, 3 dc in same ch-2 sp as beg ch-3, ch 2, join in 3rd ch of beg ch-3, fasten off. *(64 dc, 4 ch-2 sps)*

Rnd 6: Attach next color in any ch-2 sp, ch 3, 2 dc in same ch-2 sp, *sk next 2 dc, dc in each of next 12 dc, sk next 2 dc**, (3 dc, ch 2, 3 dc) in next ch-2 sp, rep from * around, ending last rep at **, 3 dc in same ch-2 sp as beg ch-3, ch 2, join in 3rd ch of beg ch-3, fasten off. *(72 dc, 4 ch-2 sps)*

Rnd 7: Attach next color in any corner ch-2 sp, ch 3, 2 dc in same ch-2 sp, *sk next 3 dc, [3 dc in sp between sts, sk next 3 dc] 5 times**, (3 dc, ch 2, 3 dc) in corner ch-2 sp, rep from * around, ending last rep at **, 3 dc in same ch-2 sp as beg ch-3, ch 2, join in 3rd ch of beg ch-3, fasten off. *(84 dc, 4 ch-2 sps)*

Rnd 8: Attach next color in any corner ch-2 sp, ch 3, 2 dc in same ch-2 sp, *sk next 3 dc, [3 dc in sp between sts, sk next 3 dc] 6 times**, (3 dc, ch 2, 3 dc) in corner ch-2 sp, rep from * around, ending last rep at **, 3 dc in same ch-2 sp as beg ch-3, ch 2, join in 3rd ch of beg ch-3, fasten off. *(96 dc, 4 ch-2 sps)*

Rnd 9: Attach next color in any corner ch-2

sp, ch 3, 2 dc in same ch-2 sp, *sk next 3 dc, [3 dc in sp between sts, sk next 3 dc] 7 times**, (3 dc, ch 2, 3 dc) in corner ch-2 sp, rep from * around, ending last rep at **, 3 dc in same ch-2 sp as beg ch-3, ch 2, join in 3rd ch of beg ch-3, fasten off. *(108 dc, 4 ch-2 sps)*

Rnd 10: Attach A in corner ch-2 sp, ch 1, [3 sc in corner ch-2 sp, sc in each of next 27 dc] 4 times, join in beg sc, fasten off. *(120 sc)*

Joining
With size L hook and A, following diagram for placement of squares and working through **back lps** *(see Stitch Guide)* only, sl st squares tog.

Edging
Rnd 1: With RS facing, with size L hook, attach A in any sc, ch 1, sc in each sc around, working 3 sc in each center corner sc, join in beg sc.

Rnds 2 & 3: Ch 1, sc in each sc around, working 3 sc in each center corner sc, join in beg sc. At the end of last rep, fasten off.

Rnd 4: With WS facing, with size K hook, attach E in any sc, ch 1, sc in each sc around, working 3 sc in each center corner sc, join in beg sc.

Rnd 5: Ch 1, sc in each sc around, working 3 sc in each center corner sc, join in beg sc.

Rnd 6: Rep rnd 5, fasten off.

Small Square Color Sequence
Notes: Each rnd of each Small

INTERMEDIATE

Size
40 x 64 inches

Materials
• Lion Brand Homespun textured bulky (chunky) weight yarn (6 oz/185 yds/170g per skein):
  3 skeins #326 ranch *(A)*
  1 skein each #309 deco *(B)* and #311 rococo *(C)*
• Lion Brand Glitterspun medium (worsted) weight yarn (1¾ oz/115 yds/50g per skein):
  2 skeins #135 bronze *(D)*
• Lion Brand Fun Fur bulky (chunky) weight eyelash yarn (1¾ oz/60 yds/50g per ball):
  3 balls #126 chocolate *(E)*
  1 ball each #134 copper *(F)* and #124 champagne *(G)*
• Lion Brand Wool-Ease medium (worsted) weight yarn (3 oz/197 yds/85g per skein):
  1 skein each #124 caramel *(H)*, #127 mink *(I)*, #190 copper *(J)* and #128 espresso *(K)*
• Lion Brand Imagine medium (worsted) weight yarn (2.5 oz/222 yds/70g per skein):
  1 skein #99 fisherman *(L)*
• Lion Brand Microspun fine (sport) weight yarn (2.5 oz/168 yds/70g per skein):
  1 skein #124 mocha *(M)*
• Sizes K/10½/6.5mm and L/11/8mm crochet hooks or size needed to obtain gauge
• Yarn needle

Square is different; work each square following individual color sequence. For example, Square 1: rnd 1 is color I, rnd 2 is color M, rnd 3 is color A and rnd 4 is color F. Follow sequence given for each square in this manner. Rnd 5 of all Small Squares is worked as indicated within pattern.

```
┌──────┬───────┬──────┐
│      │ 23 │ 24 │      │
│  6   ├────┼────┤  5   │
│      │ 21 │ 22 │      │
├───┬──┼────┴──┬─┼───┬──┤
│20 │19│       │16│15│
│   │  │   4   │  │  │
│17 │18│       │13│14│
├───┴──┼──┬──┬─┼──┴──┤
│      │12│11│      │
│  3   ├──┼──┤  2   │
│      │10│ 9│      │
├───┬──┼──┴─┬┼───┬──┤
│ 8 │ 7│    ││ 4 │ 3│
│   │  │  1 ││   │  │
│ 5 │ 6│    ││ 1 │ 2│
└───┴──┴────┴┴───┴──┘
```

Placement of Squares

Square 1
1: I, 2: M, 3: A, 4: F

Square 2
1: C, 2: A, 3: L, 4: C

Square 3
1: A, 2: C, 3: K, 4: F

Square 4
1: B, 2: D, 3: C, 4: H

Square 5
1: A, 2: B, 3: M, 4: D

Square 6
1: F, 2: L, 3: A, 4: K

Square 7
1: K, 2: C, 3: L, 4: H

Square 8
1: D, 2: B, 3: E, 4: G

Square 9
1: E, 2: L, 3: F, 4: C

Square 10
1: H, 2: D, 3: C, 4: K

Square 11
1: L, 2: B, 3: I, 4: M

Square 12
1: C, 2: F, 3: A, 4: D

Square 13
1: D, 2: B, 3: E, 4: C

Square 14
1: C, 2: K, 3: H, 4: L

Square 15
1: J, 2: G, 3: A, 4: M

Square 16
1: F, 2: L, 3: D, 4: C

Square 17
1: L, 2: D, 3: J, 4: A

Square 18
1: A, 2: C, 3: A, 4: E

Square 19
1: M, 2: C, 3: I, 4: B

Square 20
1: H, 2: I, 3: F, 4: M

Square 21
1: G, 2: H, 3: B, 4: J

Square 22
1: C, 2: L, 3: D, 4: M

Square 23
1: M, 2: H, 3: B, 4: L

Square 24
1: B, 2: H, 3: A, 4: K

Large Square Color Sequence
Notes: Each rnd of each Large Square is different; work each square following individual color sequence in the same manner as Small Squares. Rnd 10 of all Large Squares is worked as indicated within pattern.

Square 1
1: F, 2: K, 3: B, 4: G, 5: A, 6: L, 7: H, 8: K, 9: B

Square 2
1: A, 2: K, 3: B, 4: D, 5: H, 6: C, 7: I, 8: A, 9: L

Square 3
1: C, 2: B, 3: I, 4: A, 5: F, 6: L, 7: M, 8: D, 9: C

Square 4
1: H, 2: C, 3: D, 4: K, 5: L, 6: A, 7: M, 8: C, 9: I

Square 5
1: K, 2: C, 3: D, 4: L, 5: F, 6: C, 7: E, 8: B, 9: I

Square 6
1: D, 2: I, 3: A, 4: L, 5: D, 6: C, 7: B, 8: J, 9: G. ✁

Free Spirit Poncho
Continued from page 61

With a length of off-white yarn, working in back lps only, sew Neckband to squares.

Poncho Bottom
Rnd 1: With size N hook, attach off-white in corner ch-2 sp at back bottom point, beg V-st in ch-2 sp, [dc in each dc, 2 dc at junction of each square and sk each ch-1 sp on each square] across to center front corner ch-2 sp, V-st in center front corner ch-2 sp, [dc in each dc, 2 dc at junction of each square and sk each ch-1 sp on each square] across to beg V-st, join in 3rd ch of beg ch-4. *(180 dc; 2 V-sts)*
Rnd 2: Sl st in ch-1 sp, beg V-st in ch-1 sp, dc in each dc to next ch-1 sp at center front, V-st in ch-1 sp of V-st, dc in each rem dc around, join in 3rd ch of beg ch-4.
Rnds 3–5: Rep rnd 2. At the end of rnd 5, fasten off.
Rnd 6: With parakeet, rep rnd 2.
Rnd 7: Rep rnd 2, fasten off.
Rnd 8: With pumpkin, rep rnd 2.
Rnd 9: Rep rnd 2, fasten off.
Rnd 10: With lavender, rep rnd 2.
Rnd 11: Rep rnd 2, fasten off.
Rnd 12: With size K hook, attach lime in any dc, ch 1, sc in same st as beg ch-1, sc in next st, ch 3, sc in 3rd ch from hook, [sc in each of next 2 sts, ch 3, sc in 3rd ch from hook] around, join in beg sc, fasten off.

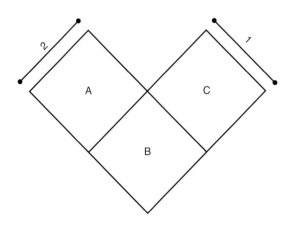

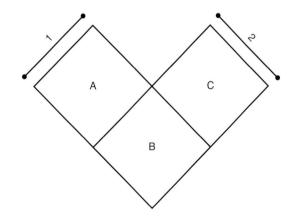

Assembly Diagram
Match up sides 1 and sides 2; sew together.

Neckline Trim

Rnd 1: With size K hook and working in opposite side of foundation ch, attach lime in any st, ch 1, sc in same st as beg ch-1, sc in next st, ch 3, sc in 3rd ch from hook, [sc in each of next 2 sts, ch 3, sc in 3rd ch from hook] around, join in beg sc, fasten off.

Tie

With size K hook and lavender, ch 200, fasten off.

Starting at center front, weave Tie through dc sts of rnd 1 of Neckband. Tie a knot in each end of Tie. Tie ends in a bow. ✄

Dig-It Flowerpot Cover
Continued from page 71

ring, ch 2] 3 times, join in top of beg ch-3, fasten off. *(8 cl)*

Rnd 2: Attach fern green in any ch-1 sp, ch 1, sc in same ch-1 sp, (3 dc, ch 3, 3 dc) in next ch-2 sp, *sc in next ch-1 sp, (3 dc, ch 3, 3 dc) in next ch-2 sp, rep from * around, join in beg sc, fasten off. *(4 ch-3 sps, 4 sc, 24 dc)*

Rnd 3: Attach natural with sl st in any ch-3 sp, ch 8 *(counts as first dc, ch 5)*, dc in same ch sp as beg ch-8, sk next st, (dc, ch 1, dc) in next st, sk next st, working over next sc, tr in ch-1 sp on rnd 1, sk next st, (dc, ch 1, dc) in next st, *(dc, ch 5, dc) in next ch-3 sp, sk next st, (dc, ch 1, dc) in next st, tr in next ch-1 sp on rnd 1, sk next st, (dc, ch 1, dc) in next st, rep from * twice, join in 3rd ch of beg ch-8. *(4 tr, 4 ch-5 sps, 8 ch-1 sps, 24 dc)*

Rnd 4: Ch 1, sc in first st, 5 sc in next ch-5 sp, sc in each st and in each ch-1 sp around with 5 sc in each ch-5 sp, join in first sc, fasten off. *(56 sc)*

Rnd 5: Attach fern green in center sc of any 5-sc group, ch 1, (sc, ch 3, sc) in same sc as beg ch-1, sc in each of next 13 sts, (sc, ch 3, sc) in next st, (ch 1, sc) in each of next 13 sts, ch 1, (sc, ch 3, sc) in next st, sc in each of next 13 sts, (sc, ch 3, sc) in next st, (ch 1, sc) in each of next 13 sts, ch 1, join, fasten off.

Joined motif

Rnds 1–4: Rep rnds 1–4 of First Motif.

Rnd 5: Attach fern green in center sc of any 5-sc group, ch 1, (sc, ch 3, sc) in same sc as beg ch-1, *sc in each of next 13 sts, sc in next st, ch 1, drop lp from hook, insert hook in corresponding ch-3 sp of Last Motif, draw dropped lp through, ch 1, sc in same st on working motif, [drop lp from hook, insert hook in corresponding ch-1 sp of Last Motif, draw dropped lp through, sc in next st on working motif] 13 times, drop lp from hook, insert hook in corresponding ch-1 sp of Last Motif, draw dropped lp through, sc, ch 1 in next st, drop lp from hook, insert hook in corresponding ch-3 sp of Last Motif, draw dropped lp through, ch 1, sc in same st on working motif, sc in each of next 13 sts, (sc, ch 3, sc) in next st, ch 1, (sc, ch 1) in each rem st, join in beg sc, fasten off.

Rep joined motif once for a total of 3 motifs.

Last motif

Rnds 1–4: Rep rnds 1–4 of First Motif.

Rnd 5: Attach fern green in center sc of any 5-sc group, ch 1, sc in same sc as beg ch-1, drop lp from hook, insert hook in corresponding ch-3 sp of First Motif, draw dropped lp through, ch 1, sc in same sc as beg ch-1, *sc in each of next 13 sts, sc, ch 1, sc in next st, drop lp from hook, insert hook in corresponding ch-3 sp of Last Motif, draw dropped lp through, ch 1, sc in same st as last sc on working motif, [drop lp from hook, insert hook in corresponding ch-1 sp of Last Motif, draw dropped lp through, sc in next st] 13 times, drop lp from hook, insert hook in corresponding ch-1 sp of last motif, draw dropped lp through*, sc in next st, ch 1, drop lp from hook, insert hook in corresponding ch-3 sp of Last Motif, draw dropped lp through, ch 1, sc in same st as last sc on working motif, rep from * to *, joining to First Motif, join in first sc, fasten off.

Bottom Edging
Rnd 1: Working around bottom edge in back lps (*see Stitch Guide*), attach natural in any st, ch 1, sc in same st, sc in each st around, join in beg sc.
Rnd 2: Ch 1, sc in each st around, join in beg sc, fasten off.

Top Edging
Rnd 1: Working around top edge in back lps, attach natural in any st, ch 1, sc in same st as beg ch-1, sc in each st around, join in beg sc.
Rnds 2 & 3: Ch 1, sc in each st around, join in beg sc. At the end of rnd 3, fasten off. ✂

Lunar Landscape Window Fringe
Continued from page 67

Small Star
Make 4.
Rnd 1: With size F hook and 2-ply strand of silver floss, ch 2, 5 sc in 2nd ch from hook, join in beg sc. *(5 sc)*
Rnd 2: Ch 1, 3 sc in each sc around, join in beg sc. *(15 sc)*
Rnd 3: Ch 5, ch 5 tightly, sl st in 6th ch from hook *(hanging lp)*, sc in next ch, hdc in next ch, dc in next ch, tr in next ch, tr in st holding sl st, sk next 2 sc, sl st in next sc, *ch 5, sc in 2nd ch from hook, hdc in next ch, dc in next ch, tr in next ch, tr in st holding sl st, sk next 2 sc, sl st in next sc, rep from * around, fasten off.

Window Strip
Make 20 in various lengths.
To make a strip approximately 30 inches long, feed 6-inch-long end of 1 strand of violet through a jingle bell, moon or star charm, using size B hook if desired, tie a sl knot 1 inch from charm, and with size P hook, ch 3, add 1 strand of sapphire, ch 3, add 1 strand of black, ch 3, sc in 2nd ch from hook, 2 **csc** (*see Special Stitches*), 3 **chdc** (*see Special Stitches*), 3 **cdc** (*see Special Stitches*), drop violet strand and add 2nd black strand, 3 **ctr** (*see Special Stitches*), 7 **cdtr** (*see Special Stitches*), ch 2, sl st around post of 6th cdtr from hook, ch 2, sl st in base of last cdtr made, fasten off.

To make strips of different lengths, vary the number of each kind of st in a free-form manner; for example, for a very short strip make 1 of each kind of sts instead of 3 of each kind; for the longer strip, make more than 3 of any st. There is no need to keep an exact count of sts made because each strand can differ from the rest.

Notes: *When making the chainless sts, pull up lps to 1 inch while working. This helps to keep the sts loose enough.*
Make a practice strip with smooth yarn and keep nearby to refer to while working. Use care to work in front of a bright lamp or sunlit window.

Finishing
Saturate moon and stars with heavy spray starch, air-dry for 24 hours and starch again if necessary. ✂

Fun With Color in Thread

Experimenting with color to find just the right combinations for your favorite crochet projects can be fun and rewarding. Some of us are drawn to bold, bright colors, some to softer pastels, while still others prefer a more subtle neutral palette. Whatever your preferences, don't be afraid to step out of your comfort zone and try something new!

Design by Shirley Patterson

Summer Garden Shadow Box

Colorful flowers and a busy bumblebee bring to mind a pretty summer garden in this creative design that makes a unique gift or decorative accent.

Gauge
Lavender flower = 1¾ inches in diameter; 5 trtr cl = 3 inches

Pattern Notes
Weave in loose ends as work progresses. Join rounds with a slip stitch unless otherwise stated.

Special Stitches
Triple treble cluster (trtr cl): *Yo 3 times, insert hook in indicated st, yo, draw up a lp,[yo, draw through 2 lps on hook] 3 times, rep from * twice, yo, draw through all 4 lps on hook.

Double crochet cluster (dc cl): [Yo hook, insert hook in indicated st, yo, draw up a lp, yo, draw through 2 lps on hook] 3 times, yo, draw through all 4 lps on hook.

Treble crochet cluster (tr cl): Yo twice, insert hook in indicated st, yo, draw up a lp, [yo, draw through 2 lps on hook] twice, yo hook twice, insert hook in same st, yo, draw up a lp, [yo, draw through 2 lps on hook] twice, yo, draw through all 3 lps on hook.

Lavender Flower
Rnd 1: With yellow, ch 2, 6 sc in 2nd ch from hook, join in beg sc. *(6 sc)*

Rnd 2: Ch 1, 2 sc in each st around, join in beg sc. *(12 sc)*

Rnd 3: Ch 1, (sc, ch 3, sc) in first st, ch 4, sk next st, [(sc, ch 3, sc) in next st, ch 4, sk next st] around, join in beg sc, fasten off.

Rnd 4: Attach lavender in any ch-4 sp, ch 1, (sc, hdc, 2 dc, hdc, sc) in same ch-4 sp as beg ch-1, sk next ch-3 sp, [(sc, hdc, 2 dc, hdc, sc) in next ch-4 sp, sk next ch-3 sp] around, join in beg sc.

Rnd 5: Ch 1, sc in each of first 4 sts, *2 sc in next st, 3 sc in next st, 2 sc in next st**, sc in each of next 8 sts, rep from * around, ending last rep at **, sc in each of next 4 sts, join in beg sc, fasten off.

Rnd 6: Attach aqua with sl st in any sk ch-3 sp of rnd 3, *ch 8, sl st in 2nd ch from hook *(tip of Leaf)*, sc in next ch, hdc in next ch, dc in next ch, tr in each of next 3 chs, ch 2, sc in next ch-3 sp, ch 2**, sl st in next ch-3 sp, rep from * around, ending last rep at **, join with sl st in beg sl st.

Rnd 7: Working on opposite side of ch-8, sc in each of first 6 chs, 3 sc in next ch, sc in each st and in each ch around with 3 sc in tip of each Leaf, join in beg sc, fasten off.

EASY

Finished Sizes

Bumblebee: 2 inches

Lavender flower: 2¼ inches including leaves

Yellow flower: 2 inches

Peach flower: 2¼ inches without leaves

Materials

- Size 10 crochet cotton:
  - 250 yds peach
  - 200 yds yellow
  - 100 yds aqua
  - 50 yds each lavender, green and black
- Size 5/1.90mm steel crochet hook or size needed to obtain gauge
- Tapestry needle
- 1 x 4 x 10-inch shadow box
- Pearl beads:
  - 3 white 6mm
  - 40 color of choice 4mm
- Fiberfill
- Tissue wrap
- Clear nail polish (optional)
- Craft glue

Sew or glue 6mm bead to center of Lavender Flower.

Yellow Flower

With yellow, form a small double lp, [ch 6, **trtr cl** *(see Special Stitches)* in lp, ch 5, sl st in top of trtr cl just made, ch 6, sl st in lp] 6 times, join with sl st in base of beg ch-6, fasten off. Sew or glue 6mm bead to center of Yellow Flower.

Leaf

Row 1: With green, ch 9, sc in 2nd ch from hook, sc in each ch across with 3 sc in last ch, working on opposite side of foundation ch, sc in each of next 5 chs, leaving rem chs unworked, turn.

Row 2: Ch 1, sc in each of first 6 sts, 3 sc in next st, sc in each of next 6 sts, leaving rem sts unworked, turn.

Row 3: Ch 1, sc in each of next 7 sts, 3 sc in next st, sc in each of next 5 sts, leaving rem sts unworked, turn.

Row 4: Ch 1, sc in each of first 8 sts, sl st in next st, leaving rem sts unworked, fasten off.

Rose

Center

Row 1: With peach, ch 16, 3 dc in 4th ch *(first 3 chs count as first dc)*, from hook and in each of next 3 chs, 3 tr in each of next 5 chs, 3 trtr in each ch across, turn.

Row 2: Ch 1, sc in first st, [ch 3, sc in next st] across, turn.

Rnd 3: Now working in rnds, fold or roll tog to shape Rose, working through all thicknesses, sl st in side, sl st at bottom, [ch 4, sl st] 6 times evenly sp around, join with sl st in beg sl st.

Petal

Rnd 4: Ch 1, (sc, hdc, 2 dc, 3 tr, 2 dc, hdc, sc) in each ch-4 sp around, join in beg sc.

Rnd 5: Working in back bar of sc, ch 6, [sl st in first sc of next Petal, ch 6] around, join with sl st in joining sl st.

Rnd 6: Ch 1, (sc, hdc, 2 dc, 5 tr, 2 dc, hdc, sc) in each ch-6 sp around, join in beg sc.

Rnd 7: Working in back bar of sc, ch 6, sl st in first sc of next Petal, fasten off.

Leaf

Rnd 8: Attach green with a sl st in ch-6 sp, ch 1, (sc, hdc, 2 dc, 7 tr, 2 dc, hdc, sc, sl st) in same ch sp, turn. *(17 sts)*

Rnd 9: Ch 4, **dc dec** *(see Stitch Guide)* in next 5 sts, ch 3, sl st in top of last st made, ch 4, sl st in same st as last st of dc dec, [ch 5, dc dec in next 5 sts, ch 3, sl st in top of last st made, ch 4, sl st in same st as last st of dc dec] twice, fasten off.

Sew or glue 6mm bead to center of Rose.

Bumblebee

Body & Head

Rnd 1: With yellow, leaving 12-inch length at beg, ch 2, 5 sc in 2nd ch from hook, join in beg sc. *(5 sc)*

Rnd 2: Ch 1, 2 sc in each st around, join in beg sc, drop yellow, do not fasten off. *(10 sc)*

Rnd 3: Attach black with sc in first st, sc in each of next 3 sts, 2 sc in next st, sc in each of next 4 sts, 2 sc in last st, join. *(12 sc)*

Rnd 4: Ch 1, sc in each st around, join in beg sc, drop black, do not fasten off.

Rnd 5: Draw up a lp of yellow, ch 1, sc in each of next 5 sts, 2 sc in next st, sc in each of next 5 sts, 2 sc in last st, join in beg sc. *(14 sc)*

Rnd 6: Ch 1, sc in each st around, join in beg sc, drop yellow.

Rnds 7 & 8: With black, ch 1, sc in each st around, join in beg sc. Lightly stuff with fiberfill.

Rnd 9: With yellow, ch 1, [sc in each of next 5 sts, **sc dec** *(see Stitch Guide)* in next 2 sts] twice, join in beg sc. *(12 sc)*

Rnd 10: Ch 1, [sc in each of next 4 sts, sc dec in next 2 sts] twice, join in beg sc. *(10 sc)*

Rnd 11: With black, ch 1, [sc in each of next 3 sts, sc dec in next 2 sts] twice, join in beg sc. *(8 sc)*

Rnd 12: Ch 1, [sc in each of next 3 sts, 2 sc in next st] twice, join in beg sc, fasten off black. *(10 sc)*

Rnd 13: With yellow, ch 1, [sc in each of next 4 sts, 2 sc in next st] twice, join in beg sc. *(12 sc)*

Rnds 14 & 15: Ch 1, sc in each st around. Lightly stuff with fiberfill.

Rnd 16: Ch 1, *[draw up a lp in each of next 3 sts, yo, draw through all 4 lps on hook] around, join in beg st, fasten off.

Stinger

With 12-inch length at beg of rnd 1 of Bumblebee, ch 3, sl st in 2nd ch from hook, sl st in next ch, leaving all of rem end, fasten off. Weave length inside of Body, pulling Stinger against Body. Secure end.

Continued on page 108

Dainty Handkerchiefs

Designs by Sue Childress

Pretty pastel handkerchiefs trimmed with charming lace edgings make a striking yet simple accent when tucked neatly into the pocket of a jacket or blouse.

Gauge
[Sc, ch 3] 5 times = 1½ inches in diameter; 5 sc = ½ inch

Pattern Notes
Weave in loose ends as work progresses. Join rounds with a slip stitch unless otherwise stated.

Green Handkerchief
Rnd 1 (RS): Attach green/white variegated in any corner hole on handkerchief, ch 1, sc in same hole as beg ch-1, sc in each handkerchief hole around outer

edge, join in beg sc.

Rnd 2: Ch 1, sc in same st as beg ch-1, ch 3, sk next 2 sts, [sc in next st, ch 3, sk next 2 sts] around, join in beg sc.

Rnd 3: Sl st into ch-3 sp, ch 1, (sc, hdc, sc) in same ch-3 sp, (sc, hdc, sc) in each ch-3 sp around, join in beg sc.

Rnd 4: Sl st into hdc, (ch 3—*counts as first dc*, 2 dc, ch 3, sl st in top of last dc, 3 dc) in same hdc, sc in next hdc, *(3 dc, ch 3, sl st in top of last dc, 3 dc) in next hdc, sc in next hdc, rep from * around, join in 3rd ch of beg ch-3, fasten off.

Blue Handkerchief
Rnd 1: Attach blue/pink variegated in any corner hole on handkerchief, ch 1, sc in same hole as beg ch-1, sc in each handkerchief hole around outer edge, join in beg sc.

Rnd 2: *(Ch 4, sc) 3 times in same sc, sc in each of next 5 sc, rep from * around, ending with sl st in same st as beg ch-4, fasten off. ✂

EASY

Finished Size
Green edging: 1 inch
Blue edging: ½ inch

Materials
- Size 10 crochet cotton:
  100 yds each green/ white variegated and blue/pink variegated
- Size 8/1.50mm steel crochet hook or size needed to obtain gauge
- 9½-inch square hemstitched handkerchiefs: 2

Design by Mindy Al-Aaraji

Double Triquetra Coaster

The Latin word "triquetra" is derived from an ancient religious symbol meaning "the power of three," which is beautifully rendered in this elegant coaster.

Gauge
Size 10 hook: Center and rnds 1–3 = 3 inches

Pattern Notes
Weave in loose ends as work progresses. Join rounds with a slip stitch unless otherwise stated.

Special Stitch
Double crochet cluster (dc cl): [Yo, insert hook in next dc, yo, draw up a lp, yo, draw through 2 lps on hook] 3 times, yo, draw through all 4 lps on hook.

Center
Cord A
Row 1: With size 10 hook and white, ch 2, sc in 2nd ch from hook, turn to left, **sc in vertical side of bars of sc** *(see illustration 1)*, [turn to left again and **sc in side of sc** *(see illustration 2)*] until cord measures 8 inches in length, fasten off.
Row 2: With size 12 hook, attach gold thread with sc in first side bar, [ch 1, sc in next bar] across side, fasten off. Weave into knot as shown in illustration A. Sew ends tog, tip to tip.

Cord B
Row 1: With size 10 hook and red, rep row 1 of Cord A until cord measures 9 inches in length, fasten off.
Row 2: Rep row 2 of Cord A. Weave into knot around Cord A as shown in illustration B. Sew ends tog, tip to tip.

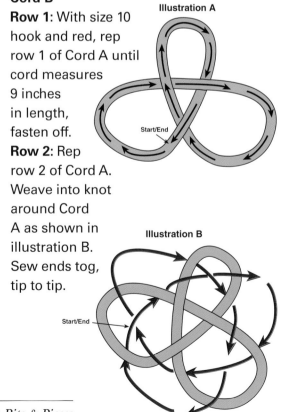

Illustration A

Illustration B

1.

2.

Crochet With Bits & Pieces

Coaster

Rnd 1: With size 10 hook, attach white with sc in ch-1 sp at center of 1 white lp on center, *ch 18, sc in ch-1 sp at center of next red lp**, ch 18, sc in ch-1 sp at center of next white lp, rep from * around, ending last rep at **, ending with ch 14, tr in beg sc forming last ch sp. *(6 ch lps)*

Rnd 2: Ch 3 *(counts as first dc)*, 2 dc in last ch sp made, 24 dc in each ch sp around, ending with 21 dc in same ch sp as first dc, join with sl st in top of beg ch-3, fasten off. *(144 dc)*

Rnd 3: With size 12 hook, attach gold with sc in first st, sc in each of next 10 sts, *[ch 1, sc in next st] 8 times, ch 1**, sc in each of next 16 sts, rep from * around, ending last rep at **, sc in each st across, join in beg sc, fasten off.

Rnd 4: With size 10 hook, attach red with sc in first st, *ch 3, sk next 4 sc, sc in next sc, [ch 5, sk next 3 sc, sc in next sc] twice, ch 5, sk next 2 sc, sc in next sc**, [ch 5, sk next 3 sc, sc in next sc] twice, rep from * around, ending last rep at **, ch 5, sk next 3 sc, join with ch 2, dc in beg sc forming last ch sp. *(36 ch sps)*

Rnd 5: Ch 1, sc in same ch sp as beg ch-1, *ch 3, (2 dc, ch 2, 2 dc) in next ch-3 sp, ch 3, sc in next ch sp**, [ch 5, sc in next ch sp] 4 times, rep from * around, ending last rep at **, [ch 5, sc in next ch sp] 3 times, join with ch 2, dc in beg sc.

Rnd 6: Ch 1, sc in same ch sp as beg ch-1, *ch 4, sk next ch sp, dc in each of next 2 dc, ch 2, 2 dc in next ch-2 sp, ch 2, dc in each of next 2 dc, ch 44, sk next ch sp**, [sc in next ch-5 sp, ch 5] 3 times, sc in next ch sp, rep from * around, ending last rep at **, [sc in next ch-5 sp, ch 5] twice, sc in next ch sp, join with ch 2, dc in beg sc.

Rnd 7: Ch 1, sc in same ch sp as beg ch-1, ch 5, sk next ch sp, *[dc in each of next 2 dc, ch 2, 2 dc in next ch-2 sp, ch 2] twice, dc in each of next 2 dc, ch 5, sk next ch sp**, [sc in next ch sp, ch 5] 3 times, sk next ch sp, rep from * around, ending last rep at **, sc in next ch sp, ch 5, sc in next ch sp, join with ch 2, dc in beg sc.

Rnd 8: Ch 1, sc in same ch sp as beg ch-1, *ch 6, sk next ch sp, [dc in next dc, 2 dc in next dc, ch 2] 4 times, dc in next dc, 2 dc in next dc, ch 6, sk next ch sp, sc in next ch sp**, ch 5, sc in next ch sp, rep from * around, ending last rep at **, join with ch 1, tr in beg sc.

Rnd 9: Ch 1, (sc, ch 3, sc) in same ch sp as beg ch-1, *ch 6, sk next ch sp, [dc in each of next 3 dc, ch 3] 4 times, dc in each of next 3 dc**, ch 6, sk next ch sp, (sc, ch 3, sc) in next ch sp, rep from * around, ending last rep at **, join with ch 3, tr in beg sc.

Rnd 10: Ch 11, sc in same ch sp as beg ch-1, ch 6, sc in next ch-6 sp, *[ch 6, **dc cl** *(see Special Stitch)* in next 3 sts] 5 times**, [ch 6, sc in next ch-6 sp] twice, rep from * around, ending last rep at **, ch 6, join in beg sc.

Rnd 11: Sl st in next ch sp, ch 1, 10 sc in same ch sp, 8 sc in each of next 6 ch sps, [10 sc in next ch sp, 8 sc in each of next 6 ch sps] around, join in beg sc, fasten off. ✂

Finished Size

5¾ inches across

Materials

• Size 20 crochet cotton:
  200 yds red
  100 yds white
• Metallic sewing thread:
  200 yds gold
• Sizes 12/1.00mm and 10/1.15mm steel crochet hooks or size needed to obtain gauge
• Sewing needle
• Sewing thread

Designs by Mary Layfield

Bold & Beautiful Necklaces

Add a bit of bold, bohemian style to your casual-chic outfit when you wear these elaborately fashioned necklaces embellished with lavish, eye-catching beads.

Finished Size
19 inches

Materials
- Size 5 pearl cotton
  (53 yds per ball):
  2 balls brown
- Size B/1/2.25mm
  crochet hook or size
  needed to obtain
  gauge
- Tapestry needle
- Sewing needle
- Sewing thread
- 4 cowrie shell beads
  by The Beadery
- 3 sliced drupa shells
  by The Beadery
- Neckline fastener

Seashells

Gauge
7 dc = 1 inch

Pattern Notes
Weave in loose ends as work progresses.
Work with 2 strands held together unless otherwise stated.

Necklace
Row 1: With 2 strands of brown, ch 119, dc in 5th ch from hook, dc in each of next 7 chs, 2 dc in next ch, [dc in each of next 8 chs, 2 dc in next ch] twice, dc in each of next 13 chs, 2 dc in next ch, dc in each of next 12 chs, 2 dc in next ch *(center front)*, dc in each of next 12 chs, 2 dc in next ch, dc in each of next 13 chs, 2 dc in next ch, [dc in each of next 8 chs, 2 dc in next ch] twice, dc in each of next 8 chs, leaving rem 8 chs of foundation ch unworked, ch 8, leaving a slight length of 1 strand of brown, fasten off. *(116 dc)*

Row 2: Attach 2 strands of brown in 42nd dc of row 1, (ch 4, 1 tr, ch 4, 1 dtr, ch 4, tr) in sp between 44th and 45th dc sts, ch 6, sc in 49th dc, sc in each of next 5 dc, (ch 6, tr, ch 4, dtr, ch 4, tr, ch 6) between 58th and 59th dc sts, sc in 63rd dc, sc in each of next 5 dc, ch 6, (tr, ch 4, dtr, ch 4, tr, ch 4) between 72 and 73 dc sts, sc in 76th dc, sc in each of next 2 dc, turn.

Row 3: Ch 1, [dc over ch-4 sp, ch 2] 3 times, dc over next ch-4 sp, ch 2, (dc, ch 2) 3 times in dtr, dc in next ch-4 sp, [ch 2, dc in next ch-6 sp] 3 times, ch 2, sk next sc, sc in each of next 3 sc, [ch 2, dc in next ch-6 sp] twice, ch 2, dc in next tr, ch 2, dc in next ch-4 sp, ch 2, [dc, ch 2] 3 times in dtr, dc in next ch-4 sp, ch 2, dc in next tr, [ch 2, dc in next ch-6 sp] twice, ch 2, sk next 2 sc, sc in each of next 3 sc, [ch 2, dc in next ch-6 sp] 3 times, ch 2, dc in next ch-4 sp, ch 2, (dc, ch 2) 3 times in dtr, dc in next ch-4 sp, [ch 2, dc in next ch-4 sp] 3 times, ch 1, sc in 39 dc of

row 1, fasten off 1 strand of brown, turn.

Row 4: Sc in last sc of row 3, hdc in next ch, 2 dc in next dc, [dc in each of next 2 chs, dc in next dc] 4 times, dc in each of next 2 chs, 3 dc in next dc, [dc in each of next 2 chs, dc in next dc] 5 times, dc in next ch, hdc in next ch, sk next sc, sc in next sc, sk next sc, [dc in each of next 2 chs, dc in next dc] 5 times, dc in each of next 2 chs, 3 dc in next dc, [dc in each of next 2 chs, dc in next dc] 5 times, dc in each of next 2 chs, sk next sc, sc in next sc, sk next sc, hdc in next ch, [dc in next ch, dc in each of next 2 chs] 5 times, 3 dc in next dc, [dc in each of next 2 chs, dc in next dc] 4 times, dc in each of next 2 chs, 2 dc in next dc, hdc in next ch, sc in next sc, fasten off.

First shell enclosure

Attach 1 strand of brown in first dc of row 3, ch 6, sl st in 36th dc of row 1, turn, [3 sc, ch 4, sl st in first ch of ch-4, 3 sc] over ch-6 sp, fasten off.

2nd shell enclosure

Attach 1 strand of brown in 40th st of row 3, ch 9, sl st in 31st of row 3, turn, [3 sc, ch 4, sl st in first ch of ch-4, 2 sc, ch 4, sl st in first ch of ch-4, 3 sc] over ch-9 sp, fasten off.

3rd shell enclosure

Attach 1 strand brown in 79th st of row 3, ch 9, sl st in 70th st of row 3, turn, (3 sc, ch 4, sl st in first ch of ch-4, 2 sc, ch 4, sl st in first ch of ch-4, 3 sc) over ch-9 sp, fasten off.

4th shell enclosure

Attach 1 strand of brown in 81st dc of row 1, ch 6, sl st in 110th st of row 3, turn, (3 sc, ch 4, sl st in first ch of ch-4, 3 sc) over ch-6 sp, fasten off.

With sewing needle and thread, sew a shell bead within the sp created by each of the Shell Enclosures.

Sew a sliced drupa bead to each of the dtr sts at center of each of the 3 points.

Fastener

At end of row 1, working with the 2 ch-8 sps, secure first end of neckline fastener to rem length of brown beyond rem ch-8, then secure rem ch-8 end into same end of fastener.

Sew to secure opposite end of neckline fastener to beg end of Necklace.

Antique Bone

Gauge

6 dc = 1 inch

Pattern Notes

Weave in loose ends as work progresses. Work with 2 strands of victory red held together throughout unless otherwise stated.

Special Stitch

Add bead to ch: To pull beads through onto crochet chain, use sewing needle and sewing thread, feed thread through bead and into crochet ch lp and back through bead, pull on both ends of thread to pull crochet cotton through bead, remove sewing thread, pick up dropped lp and continue.

Finished Size

19 inches

Materials

• South Maid size 10
  crochet cotton:
    150 yds #494
      victory red
• Size B/1/2.25mm
  crochet hook or size
  needed to obtain
  gauge
• Tapestry needle
• Sewing needle
• Sewing thread
• Black and white
  antique bone beads
  assortment by The
  Beadery:
    5 long
    12 round
• 4 black 6mm glass
  beads
• 8mm black glass
  bead

Necklace

Row 1: With 2 strands of victory red, ch 111, dc in 10th ch from hook *(closing lp)*, dc in each of next 49 chs, (dc, ch 2, dc) in next ch *(Necklace center)*, dc in each of next 50 chs, ch 18 leaving a length of cotton, fasten off. Pass ch-18 through a long antique bone bead, sew end of ch to first ch of ch-18, fasten off.

Row 2: Attach 2 strands of victory red with a sl st in 8th dc to the right of ch-2 sp at Necklace center, ch 3, sk next 3 dc, 2 dc in next dc, dc in next dc, ch 3, sk next 2 dc, (2 dc, ch 3, 2 dc) in ch-2 sp, sk next 2 dc, dc in next dc, 2 dc in next dc, ch 3, sk next 3 dc, sl st in next dc, fasten off.

Note: Thread antique bone beads onto cotton before beg next row, 1 round bead, 4 long beads, 11 round beads. The 5 glass beads are sewn into Necklace after completed.

Row 3: Attach 2 strands of victory red in 63rd dc of row 1, ch 1, sc in same dc as beg ch-1, ch 2, sk next dc of row 1, 2 dc in next dc, dc in next dc, ch 5, **add bead to ch** *(see Special Stitch)*, dc in each of next 3 dc, ch 4, add bead to ch, dc in each of next 2 dc, (dc, ch 5, dc) in next ch-3 sp, dc in each of next 2 dc, ch 4, add bead to ch, dc in each of next 3 dc, ch 5, add bead to ch, dc in 42nd dc of row 1, 2 dc in next dc, ch 2, sk next dc, sc in next dc, fasten off.

Row 4: Attach 2 strands of victory red in 65th dc of row 1, ch 1, sc in same st as beg ch-1, ch 4, add bead to ch, dc in each of next 3 dc, ch 7, add bead to ch, dc in each of next 3 dc, ch 5, add bead to ch, dc in each of next 3 dc, 5 dc over ch-5 sp, dc in each of next 3 dc, ch 5, add bead to ch, dc in each of next 3 dc, ch 7, add bead to ch, dc in each of next 3 dc, ch 4, add bead to ch, sk next dc of row 1, sc in each of next 2 dc, turn.

Row 5: Ch 5, add bead to ch, dc in each of next 3 dc, ch 9, add bead to ch, dc in each of next 3 dc, ch 9, add bead to ch, **dc dec** *(see Stitch Guide)* in first, 2nd and 3rd dc sts, ch 6, sl st in 3rd ch of ch-6, ch 3, dc dec in 3rd *(same dc as last dc of previous dc dec)*, 4th and 5th dc sts, ch 6, sl st in 3rd ch of ch-6, ch 3, dc dec in 5th, 6th and 7th dc sts, ch 6, sl st in 3rd ch of ch-6, ch 3, dc dec in 7th, 8th and 9th dc sts, ch 6, sl st in 3rd ch of ch-6, dc dec in 9th, 10th and 11th dc sts *(5 groups of dc dec)*, ch 9, add bead to ch, dc in each of next 3 dc, ch 9, add a bead to ch, dc in each of next 3 dc, ch 5, add a bead to ch, sk next dc of row 1, sc in next dc, fasten off.

First side trim

Row 6: Attach 2 strands of victory red in 70th dc of row 1, ch 4, dc in same dc as last sc of row 5, ch 7, [**sc dec** *(see Stitch Guide)* in next 3 dc, ch 10] twice, sc in top of next dc dec, turn.

Row 7: Ch 1, sc in each of next 4 chs, 2 sc in each of next 2 chs, sc in each of next 3 chs, ch 3, sk sc dec, sc in each of next 3 chs,

Continued on page 107

Pick a Pretty Pair

Designs by **Shirley Patterson**

For a friend or family member who delights in the written word, these beautifully refreshing rose bookmarks are the perfect solution for a special gift.

Rose & Pineapple

EASY

Gauge
Rose = 2 inches in diameter;
5 shells = 1½ inches

Pattern Notes
Weave in loose ends as work progresses.
Join rounds with a slip stitch unless otherwise stated.

Special Stitch
Shell: (2 dc, ch 2, 2 dc) in indicated st.

Rose
Row 1: With burgundy, ch 25, 3 dc in 4th ch from hook, [3 tr in next ch, 3 dc in next ch] across, sl st in last ch, turn.
Rnd 2: Now working in rnds, working around post of sts, [ch 4, sk next 3 sts, sl st around **post** *(see Stitch Guide)* of next st] 6 times, sl st to join in first sl st. *(6 ch-4 sps)*
Rnd 3: Ch 1, (sc, hdc, dc, 2 tr, 1 dtr, 2 tr, dc, hdc, sc) in each ch-4 sp around,

Finished Size
6 inches

Materials
- Acrylic nylon thread or size 10 crochet cotton:
   40 yds each rose
   30 yds burgundy
- Size 5/1.90mm steel crochet hook or size needed to obtain gauge
- Tapestry needle
- Sewing needle
- Sewing thread
- 1 yd ¼-inch-wide burgundy picot-edge ribbon
- 24 inches ⅛-inch-wide burgundy ribbon
- 8mm pearl oval bead
- 5mm pearl oval bead

join in beg sc. *(6 petals)*

Rnd 4: [Ch 4, sl st in sp between petals] 6 times.

Rnd 5: Ch 1, (sc, hdc, dc, 2 tr, 3 dtr, 2 tr, dc, hdc, sc) in each ch-4 sp around, join in beg sc, fasten off.

With a strand of burgundy, roll row 1 shaping to form center of Rose, sew to secure center.

Pineapple

Row 1: Attach Rose in sp between any 2 petals of rnd 5, (ch 3—*counts as first dc throughout*, dc, ch 2, 2 dc) in same st, ch 7, (2 dc, ch 3, 2 dc) in sp between next 2 petals, ch 7, **shell** *(see Special Stitch)* in sp between next 2 petals, turn.

Row 2: Ch 3, shell in ch-2 sp of shell, ch 5, 11 tr in next ch-3 sp, ch 5, shell in next ch-2 sp of shell, turn.

Row 3: Ch 3, shell in ch-2 sp of shell, ch 5, dc in first tr, [ch 1, dc in next tr] 10 times, ch 5, shell in ch-2 sp of next shell, turn.

Row 4: Ch 3, shell in ch-2 sp of shell, ch 5, sc in next ch-1 sp, [ch 3, sc in next ch-1 sp] 9 times, ch 5, shell in next ch-2 sp of next shell, turn.

Row 5: Ch 3, shell in ch-2 sp of shell, ch 5, sc in next ch-3 sp, [ch 3, sc in next ch-3 sp] 8 times, ch 5, shell in ch-2 sp of next shell, turn.

Row 6: Ch 3, shell in ch-2 sp of shell, ch 5, sc in next ch-3 sp, [ch 3, sc in next ch-3 sp] 7 times, ch 5, shell in ch-2 sp of next shell, turn.

Row 7: Ch 3, shell in ch-2 sp of shell, ch 5, sc in next ch-3 sp, [ch 3, sc in next ch-3 sp] 6 times, ch 5, shell in ch-2 sp of next shell, turn.

Row 8: Ch 3, shell in ch-2 sp of shell, ch 5, sc in next ch-3 sp, [ch 3, sc in next ch-3 sp] 5 times, ch 5, shell in ch-2 sp of next shell, turn.

Row 9: Ch 3, shell in ch-2 sp of shell, ch 5, sc in next ch-3 sp, [ch 3, sc in next ch-3 sp] 4

times, ch 5, shell in next ch-2 sp of shell, turn.

Row 10: Ch 3, shell in ch-2 sp of shell, ch 5, sc in next ch-3 sp, [ch 3, sc in next ch-3 sp] 3 times, ch 5, shell in next ch-2 sp of shell, turn.

Row 11: Ch 3, shell in ch-2 sp of shell, ch 5, sc in next ch-3 sp, [ch 3, sc in next ch-3 sp] twice, ch 5, shell in next ch-2 sp of shell, turn.

Row 12: Ch 3, shell in ch-2 sp of shell, ch 5, sc in next ch-3 sp, ch 3, sc in next ch-3 sp, ch 5, shell in next ch-2 sp of shell, turn.

Row 13: Ch 3, shell in ch-2 sp of shell, ch 5, sc in rem ch-3 sp, ch 5, shell in ch-2 sp of shell, draw up a lp, remove hook, leaving a 60-inch strand, fasten off; slide 8mm bead and then 6mm bead onto rem length.

Row 14: Ch 3, shell in ch-2 sp of shell, ch 5, sc in sc, slide 8mm bead up next to sc st, ch 1 over bead, ch 4, shell in ch-2 sp of next shell, turn.

Row 15: Ch 3, shell in ch-2 sp of shell, ch 3, shell in ch-2 sp of next shell, turn.

Row 16: Ch 3, shell in ch-2 sp of shell, ch 1, sc over next ch-3 sp, slide 6mm bead up next to last sc, ch 1, shell in ch-2 sp of next shell, fasten off.

Use photo as a guide. Thread tapestry needle with picot-edge burgundy ribbon, leaving a 12-inch length at beg for page marker, starting at ch-3 sp at center of row 1 of pineapple, weave ribbon through ch-5 sps down side edge and up opposite side edge, secure ends at center back.

Starting at center bottom of pineapple, weave ⅛-inch wide ribbon through ch-2 sps of shells around pineapple outer edge, tie ends in a bow at center bottom.

Fold a length of picot-edged ribbon into a bow and secure at center top edge of pineapple.

Fold a length of ⅛-inch wide burgundy ribbon into a small bow, attach bow top edge of pineapple.

Continued on page 109

Pot Holder Pizzazz

Design by Hazel Henry
Design by Mary Layfield
Design by Diane Stone

Brighten your kitchen and help take the drudgery out of necessary chores with our fun-to-make reversible pot holders stitched in colorful size 10 crochet cotton.

Pineapples & Picots
Design by Hazel Henry

Gauge
Rnds 1–3 = 1½ inches; 10 dc = 1 inch

Pattern Notes
Weave in loose ends as work progresses. Join rounds with a slip stitch unless otherwise stated.

Special Stitches
3-double crochet cluster (3-dc cl): [Yo, insert hook in next st, yo, draw up a lp, yo, draw through 2 lps on hook] 3 times, yo, draw through all 4 lps on hook.

Beginning 3-double crochet cluster (beg 3-dc cl): Ch 2, [yo, insert hook in next st, yo, draw up a lp, yo, draw through 2 lps on hook] twice, yo, draw through all 3 lps on hook.

Back
Rnd 1 (RS): With light blue, ch 7, sl st to join in first ch to form a ring, ch 3 *(counts as first dc throughout)*, 20 dc in ring, join in 3rd ch of beg ch-3. *(21 dc)*

Rnd 2: Ch 3, dc in same dc as beg ch-3, dc in each of next 2 dc, [2 dc in next dc, dc in each of next 2 dc] around, join in 3rd ch of beg ch-3. *(28 dc)*

Rnd 3: Ch 3, dc in same dc as beg ch-3, dc in next dc, [2 dc in next dc, dc in next dc] around, join in 3rd ch of beg ch-3. *(42 dc)*

Finished Size
7 inches

Materials
- Grandma's Best size 10 crochet cotton:
  60 yds #11 light blue
  50 yds #162 light yellow
- Size 7/1.65mm steel crochet hook or size needed to obtain gauge
- Tapestry needle

Rnd 4: Ch 3, dc in same dc as beg ch-3, dc in each of next 2 dc, [2 dc in next dc, dc in each of next 2 dc] around, join in 3rd ch of beg ch-3. *(56 dc)*

Rnd 5: Ch 3, dc in same dc as beg ch-3, dc in each of next 3 dc, [2 dc in next dc, dc in each of next 3 dc] around, join in 3rd ch of beg ch-3. *(70 dc)*

Rnd 6: Ch 3, dc in same dc as beg ch-3, dc in each of next 4 dc, [2 dc in next dc, dc in each of next 4 dc] around, join in 3rd ch of beg ch-3. *(84 dc)*

Rnd 7: Ch 3, dc in same dc as beg ch-3, dc in each of next 5 dc, [2 dc in next dc, dc in each of next 5 dc] around, join in 3rd ch of beg ch-3. *(98 dc)*

Rnd 8: Ch 3, dc in same dc as beg ch-3, dc in each of next 6 dc, [2 dc in next dc, dc in each of next 6 dc] around, join in 3rd ch of beg ch-3. *(112 dc)*

Rnd 9: Ch 3, dc in same dc as beg ch-3, dc in each of next 7 dc, [2 dc in next dc, dc in each of next 7 dc] around, join in 3rd ch of beg ch-3. *(126 dc)*

Rnd 10: Ch 3, dc in same dc as beg ch-3, dc in each of next 8 dc, [2 dc in next dc, dc in each of next 8 dc] around, join in 3rd ch of beg ch-3. *(140 dc)*

Rnd 11: Ch 3, dc in same dc as beg ch-3, dc in each of next 9 dc, [2 dc in next dc, dc in each of next 9 dc] around, join in 3rd ch of beg ch-3. *(154 dc)*

Rnd 12: Ch 3, dc in same dc as beg ch-3, dc in each of next 10 dc, [2 dc in next dc, dc in each of next 10 dc] around, join in 3rd ch of beg ch-3, fasten off. *(168 dc)*

Front

Rnd 1 (RS): With light yellow, ch 7, sl st to join in first ch to form a ring, ch 3, 20 dc in ring, join in 3rd ch of beg ch-3. *(21 dc)*

Rnd 2: Ch 3, dc in each of next 2 dc, ch 2, [dc in each of next 3 dc, ch 2] around, join in 3rd ch of beg ch-3. *(7 groups 3-dc, 7 ch-2 sps)*

Rnd 3: Ch 3, dc in same dc as beg ch-3, dc in next dc, 2 dc in next dc, ch 2, sk next ch-2 sp, *2 dc in next dc, dc in next dc, 2 dc in next dc, ch 2, sk next ch-2 sp, rep from * around, join in 3rd ch of beg ch-3. *(7 groups 5-dc, 7 ch-2 sps)*

Rnd 4: Sl st in next dc, **beg 3-dc cl** *(see Special Stitches)* in next 2 dc, *ch 3, sk next dc, 3 dc in next ch-2 sp, ch 3**, sk next dc, **3-dc cl** *(see Special Stitches)* in next 3 dc, rep from * around, ending last rep at **, join in top of beg 3-dc cl. *(7 cls, 7 groups 3-dc, 14 ch-3 sps)*

Rnd 5: Sl st into ch-3 sp, ch 3, 3 dc in same ch-3 sp, *ch 1, sk next 3 dc, 4 dc in next ch-3 sp, ch 1, sk next 3-dc cl**, 4 dc in next ch-3 sp, rep from * around, ending last rep at **, join in 3rd ch of beg ch-3.

Rnd 6: Sl st in each of next 3 dc, sl st into next ch-1 sp, ch 3, 2 dc in same ch-1 sp, *ch 5, sk next 4 dc, sc in next ch-1 sp, ch 5, sk next 4 dc**, 3 dc in next ch-1 sp, rep from * around, ending last rep at **, join in 3rd ch of beg ch-3. *(21 dc, 7 sc, 14 ch-5 sps)*

Rnd 7: Ch 3, dc in same dc as beg ch-3, dc in next dc, 2 dc in next dc, *ch 2, 2 dc in next ch-5 sp, ch 1, 2 dc in next ch-5 sp, ch 2**, 2 dc in next dc, dc in next dc, 2 dc in next dc, rep from * around, ending last rep at **, join in 3rd ch of beg ch-3. *(63 dc)*

Rnd 8: Ch 3, dc in same dc as beg ch-3, *dc in each of next 3 dc, 2 dc in next dc, ch 3, sk next ch-2 sp, 3 dc in next ch-1 sp, ch 3, sk next ch-2 sp**, 2 dc in next dc, rep from * around, ending last rep at **, join in 3rd ch of beg ch-3. *(70 dc)*

Rnd 9: Sl st in next dc, ch 3, dc in each of next 4 dc, *ch 4, sk next dc, sk next dc, sk next ch-3 sp, 2 dc in next dc, dc in next dc, 2 dc in next dc, ch 4, sk next ch-3 sp, sk next dc**, dc in each of next 5 dc, rep from * around, ending last rep at **, join in 3rd ch of beg ch-3.

Rnd 10: Sl st in next dc, beg 3-dc cl in next 3 sts, *ch 9, sk next ch-4 sp, sk next dc**, 3-dc cl over next 3 dc, rep from * around, ending last rep at **, join in beg 3-dc cl. *(14 cls)*

Rnd 11: Sl st into ch-9 sp, ch 3, 9 dc in same ch sp, ch 1, sk next 3-dc cl, [10 dc in next ch-9 sp, ch 1, sk next 3-dc cl] around, join in 3rd ch of beg ch-3. *(140 dc)*

Rnd 12: Ch 1, sc in same dc as beg ch-1, sc in each of next 9 dc, ch 2, sk next ch-1 sp, [sc in each of next 10 dc, ch 2, sk next ch-1 sp] around, join in beg sc.

Rnd 13: Ch 3, dc in each of next 9 sc, 2 dc in next ch-2 sp, [dc in each of next 10 sc, 2 dc in next ch-2 sp] around, join in 3rd ch of beg ch-3. *(168 dc)*

Joining

Rnd 14: Holding WS of Front and Back tog, with Front facing and working through both thicknesses, ch 1, sc in each st around, join in beg sc, fasten off.

Edging

Rnd 1: With Front facing, attach light blue in any sc, ch 3, dc in each of next 3 sc, *ch 2, sk next sc, dc in next sc, ch 2, sk next sc**, dc in each of next 4 sc, rep from * around, ending last rep at **, join in 3rd ch of beg ch-3.

Rnd 2: Sl st in next dc, ch 1, sc in same dc, *ch 3, sc in next dc, ch 2, sk next dc, 3-dc cl in next ch-2 sp, ch 5, sl st in 4th ch from hook, ch 1, 3-dc cl in next ch-2 sp, ch 2, sk next dc**, sc in next dc, rep from * around, ending last rep at **, join in beg sc, fasten off.

Patriotic Garden
Design by Hazel Henry

Gauge

Rnds 1–6 of rose = 2 inches; 8 dc = 1 inch

Pattern Notes

Weave in loose ends as work progresses.

Join rounds with a slip stitch unless otherwise stated.

Front

Rnd 1 (RS): With red, ch 5, sl st in first ch to form a ring, ch 6 *(counts as first dc and ch-3)*, [dc in ring, ch 3] 5 times, join in 3rd ch of beg ch-6. *(6 ch-3 sps)*

Rnd 2: Ch 1, sc in same st as beg ch-1, (sc, hdc, dc, hdc, sc) in next ch sp, *sc in next dc, (sc, hdc, dc, hdc, sc) in next ch sp, rep from * around, join in beg sc. *(6 petals)*

Rnd 3: Working behind petals, ch 4, [sl st in next sc between petals, ch 4] around, join with sl st in same sc as first ch-4. *(6 ch-4 sps)*

Rnd 4: Ch 1, sc in same st as beg ch 1, *(sc, hdc, 3 dc, hdc, sc) in next ch sp**, sc in next st between ch sps, rep from * around, ending last rep at **, join in beg sc.

Rnd 5: Working behind petals, ch 6, [sl st in next sc between petals, ch 6] around, join with sl st in same st as beg ch-6.

Rnd 6: Ch 1, sc in same st as beg ch-1, *(sc, hdc, 2 dc, 2 tr, 2 dc, hdc, sc) in next ch sp**, sc in st between ch sps, rep from * around, ending last rep at **, join in beg sc.

Rnd 7: Working behind petals, ch 8, [sl st in next sc between petals, ch 8] around, ending with sl st in same st as beg ch-8, fasten off. *(6 ch-8 sps)*

Rnd 8: Attach white with a sl st in any ch-8 sp, ch 3 *(counts as first dc throughout)*, 7 dc in same ch sp, ch 2, [8 dc in next ch sp, ch 2] around, **change color** *(see Stitch Guide)* to blue, join in 3rd ch of beg ch-3.

Finished Size

6½ inches

Materials

- Size 10 crochet cotton:
  75 yds white
  25 yds blue
  15 yds red
- Size 7/1.65mm steel crochet hook or size needed to obtain gauge
- Tapestry needle

Rnd 9: (Ch 3, dc) in first st, dc in each dc across to st before next ch-2 sp, 2 dc in next st, ch 2, [2 dc in next st, dc in each st across to st before next ch-2 sp, 2 dc in next st, ch 2] around, change color to white in last ch, join in 3rd ch of beg ch-3.

Rnd 10: (Ch 3, dc) in first st, dc in each st across to st before next ch-2 sp, 2 dc in next st, ch 2, [2 dc in next st, dc in each st across to st before next ch-2 sp, 2 dc in next st, ch 2] around, change color to blue in last ch, join in 3rd ch of beg ch-3.

Rnds 11–14: Rep rnds 9 and 10.

Rnd 15: Rep rnd 9, fasten off. *(22 dc between each ch-2 sp)*

Back

Rnd 1: With white, ch 6, sl st in first st to form ring, ch 3, dc in ring, ch 2, [2 dc in ring, ch 2] 5 times, join in 3rd ch of beg ch-3. *(12 dc, 6 ch-2 sps)*

Rnd 2: (Ch 3, dc) in first dc, 2 dc in next dc, ch 2, [2 dc in each of next 2 dc, ch 2] around, join in 3rd ch of beg ch-3.

Rnd 3: (Ch 3, dc) in first dc, dc in each of next 2 dc, 2 dc in next dc, ch 2, [2 dc in next dc, dc in each of next 2 dc, 2 dc in next dc, ch 2] around, join in 3rd ch of beg ch-3.

Rnds 4–9: (Ch 3, dc) in first dc, dc in each dc across to st before next ch-2 sp, 2 dc in next dc, ch 2, [2 dc in next dc, dc in each st across to st before next ch-2 sp, 2 dc in next st, ch 2] around, join in 3rd ch of beg ch-3.

Rnd 10: (Ch 3, dc) in first dc, dc in each st across to st before next ch-2 sp, 2 dc in next st, ch 3, [2 dc in next dc, dc in each dc across to st before ch-2 sp, 2 dc in next dc, ch 3] around, join in 3rd ch of beg ch-3.

Rnd 11: (Ch 3, dc) in first dc, dc in each dc across to st before next ch-3 sp, 2 dc in next dc, ch 3, [2 dc in next dc, dc in each dc across to st before next ch-3 sp, 2 dc in next dc, ch 3] around, join in 3rd ch of beg ch-3, fasten off. *(6 ch-3 sp, 22 dc between each ch sp)*

Joining & Trim

Rnd 12: Holding Front and Back WS tog with Front facing, matching sts and working through both thicknesses, attach white with sc in any st, sc in each st around with 3 sc in each ch-3 sp around, join in beg sc, fasten off.

Rnd 13: Attach red with sc in center st of any 3-sc group, ch 18 *(hanging lp)*, sc in next st, ch 2, sk next 2 sts, 4 dc in next st, [ch 2, sk next 2 sts, sc in next st, ch 2, sk next 2 sts, 4 dc in next st] 3 times, ch 2, *sc in center st of next 3-sc group, ch 3, sc in next st, ch 2, sk next 2 sts, 4 dc in next st, [ch 2, sk next 2 sts, sc in next st, ch 2, sk next 2 sts, 4 dc in next st] 3 times, ch 2, rep from * around, join in beg sc, work 18 sc over ch-18 hanging lp, sl st in next sc, fasten off.

Winter Rose
Design by Hazel Henry

Gauge
Rnds 1 and 2 of Back = 2 inches in diameter; 3 dc = ½ inch

Pattern Notes
Weave in loose ends as work progresses.
Join rounds with a slip stitch unless otherwise stated.
Work with 2 strands of cotton held together throughout.

Hanging Loop
Attach 2 strands of forest green to plastic ring, ch 1, 24 sc over ring, join in first sc, fasten off. Set aside.

Front
Rose
Rnd 1 (RS): Working with 2 strands of cardinal held tog, ch 5, sl st to join in first ch to form a ring, ch 3 *(counts as first dc)*, 9 dc in ring, join in 3rd ch of beg ch-3. *(10 dc)*

Rnd 2: Ch 1, sc in each dc around, join in beg sc.

Rnd 3: Ch 2, (2 dc, ch 2, sl st) in same st as beg ch-2, sk next sc, *(sl st, ch 2, 2 dc, ch 2, sl st) in next sc, sk next sc, rep from * around, do not join. *(5 petals)*

Rnd 4: Ch 3, [sc in **back lp** *(see Stitch Guide)* only of rem sk sc of rnd 2, ch 3] around, to join sl st in first ch of beg ch-3. *(5 lps)*

Rnd 5: Sl st into ch-3 sp, (ch 2, 4 dc, ch 2, sl st) in same ch-3 sp, *(sl st, ch 2, 4 dc, ch 2, sl st) in next ch-3 sp, rep from * around, do not join. *(5 petals)*

Rnd 6: Working at back of petals between dc sts of previous rnd, ch 1, insert hook at center between 4-dc of petal and sc over ch-3 sp, ch 5, [insert hook at center between 4 dc of next petal and sc over ch-3 sp, ch 5] around, ending with sl st in first ch of ch-5 of first lp. *(5 ch-5 lps)*

Rnd 7: Sl st into ch-5 sp, (ch 2, 6 dc, ch 2, sl st) in same ch sp, *(sl st, ch 2, 6 dc, ch 2, sl st) in next ch-5 sp, rep from * around, do not join. *(5 petals)*

Rnd 8: Working at back of petals between dc sts of previous rnd, ch 2, insert hook at center between 6-dc of petal and sc over ch-5 sp, ch 5, [insert hook at center between 6-dc of petal and sc over ch-5 sp, ch 5] around, ending with sl st in first ch of ch-5, fasten off.

Rnd 9: Attach 2 strands of forest green in any ch-5 sp, ch 3, 7 dc in same ch-5 sp, 8 dc in each of next 4 ch-5 sps, join in 3rd ch of beg ch-3, fasten off. *(40 dc)*

Rnd 10: Attach 2 strands of black in 3rd ch of beg ch-3 of previous rnd, ch 7 *(counts as first dc, ch 4)*, dc in same st as beg ch-7, sk next 3 dc, [(dc, ch 4, dc) in next dc, sk next 3 dc] around, join in 3rd ch of beg ch-7. *(10 ch-4 sps, 20 dc)*

Rnd 11: Sl st into ch-4 sp, ch 1, 7 sc in same ch-4 sp, sl st between next 2 dc, [7 sc in next ch-4 sp, sl st between next 2 dc] around, join in beg sc, fasten off.

Rnd 12: Attach 2 strands of natural in 4th sc of 7-sc group, ch 1, sc in same sc, ch 3, dc in 3rd dc on rnd 9, ch 3, *sc in 4th sc of next 7-sc group of rnd 11, ch 3, sk next 3 dc of rnd 9, dc in next dc, ch 3, rep from * around, join in beg sc. *(10 dc, 10 sc, 20 ch-3 sps)*

Rnd 13: Sl st in next ch, ch 3, 2 dc in next ch, dc in next ch, sk next dc, dc in next ch, 2 dc in next ch, dc in next ch, sk next sc, *dc in next ch, 2 dc in next ch, dc in next ch, sk next dc, dc in next ch, 2 dc in next ch, dc in next ch, sk next sc, rep from * around, join in 3rd ch of beg ch-3. *(80 dc)*

Rnd 14: Ch 3, dc in each of next 3 dc, 2 dc in next dc, [dc in each of next 4 dc, 2 dc in next dc] around, join in 3rd ch of beg ch-3, fasten off. *(96 dc)*

Back

Rnd 1 (RS): With 2 strands of natural held tog, ch 5, sl st to join in first ch to form a ring, ch 3, 19 dc in ring, join in 3rd ch of beg ch-3. *(20 dc)*

Rnd 2: Ch 3, dc in same dc as beg ch-3, 2 dc in each rem dc around, join in 3rd ch of beg ch-3. *(40 dc)*

Rnd 3: Ch 4 *(counts as first tr)*, 2 tr in next dc, [tr in next dc, 2 tr in next dc] around, join in 4th ch of beg ch-4. *(60 tr)*

Rnd 4: Ch 3, dc in next tr, 2 dc in next tr, [dc in each of next 2 tr, 2 dc in next tr] around, join in 3rd ch of beg ch-3. *(80 dc)*

Rnd 5: Ch 3, dc in each of next 3 dc, 2 dc in next dc, [dc in each of next 4 dc, 2 dc in next dc] around, join in 3rd ch of beg ch-3, fasten off. *(96 dc)*

Continued on page 109

Finished Size

6¼ inches

Materials

- Size 10 crochet cotton:
  150 yds natural
  75 yds black
  30 yds each cardinal and forest green
- Size 1/2.25mm steel crochet hook or size needed to obtain gauge
- Tapestry needle
- 1-inch plastic ring

Design by **Brenda Stratton**

Sweet Scents Jar

Stitch an elegant lace cover to fit a recycled or canning jar filled with sweet-smelling potpourri to add a pretty touch and fresh, clean fragrance to your home.

Gauge
8 dc = 1 inch; 4 dc rnds = 1 inch

Pattern Notes
Weave in loose ends as work progresses. Join rounds with a slip stitch unless otherwise stated.

Special Stitches
Shell: (2 dc, ch 2, 2 dc) in indicated st.
Beginning shell (beg shell): (Ch 3, dc, ch 2, 2 dc) in indicated st.
4-double crochet shell (4-dc shell): (4 dc, ch 2, 4 dc) in indicated st.
6-double crochet shell (6-dc shell): (6 dc, ch 2, 6 dc) in indicated st.
Beginning joining shell (beg joining shell): 2 dc, ch 1, sl st in previous shell, ch 1, 2 dc in same sp as previous 2 dc sts.
End joining shell: 2 dc, ch 1, sl st in shell at beg of rnd, ch 1, 2 dc in same sp as previous 2 dc sts.
Inverted decrease (inverted dec): Retaining last lp of each st on hook, dc in next dc, [tr in next ch-2 sp of next shell] twice, dc in next dc, yo, draw through all 5 lps on hook.

Jar Cover
Rnd 1 (RS): Beg at bottom of jar with sky blue, ch 6, sl st to join to form a ring, ch 3 *(counts as first dc throughout)*, 17 dc in ring, join in 3rd ch of beg ch-3. *(18 dc)*
Rnd 2: Ch 4 *(counts as first dc, ch 1 throughout)*, [dc in next dc, ch 1] 17 times, join in 3rd ch of beg ch-4. *(18 dc, 18 ch-1 sps)*
Rnd 3: Ch 3, 2 dc in next ch-1 sp, [dc in next dc, 2 dc in next ch-1 sp] around, join in 3rd ch of beg ch-3. *(54 dc)*
Rnd 4: Ch 4, sk next dc, [dc in next dc, ch 1, sk next dc] around, join in 3rd ch of beg ch-4. *(27 dc, 27 ch-1 sps)*
Rnd 5: Ch 3, [2 dc in next ch-1 sp, dc in next dc] around, ending with 3 dc in last ch-1 sp, join in 3rd ch of beg ch-3. *(82 dc)*
Rnd 6: Ch 4, sk next dc, [dc in next dc, ch 1, sk next dc] around, join in 3rd ch of beg ch-4. *(41 dc, 41 ch-1 sps)*
Rnd 7: Ch 3, dc in next ch-1 sp, [dc in next dc, dc in next ch-1 sp] around, join in 3rd ch of beg ch-3. *(82 dc)*
Rnd 8: Ch 4, sk next dc, [dc in next dc, ch 1, sk next dc] around, join in 3rd ch of beg ch-4. *(41 dc, 41 ch-1 sps)*
Rnds 9–26: Rep rnds 7 and 8.

INTERMEDIATE

Size

Fits 36 oz mayon-
naise jar

Materials

• Caron Grandma's
Best size 10 crochet
cotton (2 oz/400
yds/56.7g per ball):
1 ball #21 white

• Caron Grandma's
Best size 10 crochet
cotton (1½ oz/300
yds/44g per ball):
1 ball #165 sky blue

• Size 7/1.65mm steel
crochet hook or size
needed to obtain
gauge

• Tapestry needle

• 36-oz recycled
mayonnaise jar or
canning jar

• 18 inches ½-inch-
wide light pink satin
ribbon

• 11 light pink ribbon
flowers with white
pearl centers

• Hot-glue gun

• Dried potpourri, bath
beads or scented
soaps

Rnd 27: Sl st into next ch-1 sp, ch 1, 2 sc in same ch-1 sp, [2 sc in next ch-1 sp] around, join in beg sc, fasten off. *(82 sc)*

Lace trim

Rnd 1: Holding jar cover with top opening facing and working on the side farthest away, attach white at back *(seam side)* of jar cover in any skipped dc of rnd 23, ch 1, sc in same dc as beg ch-1, *ch 3, dc in top of sc, ch 3, dc in sp between dc and ch-3, [ch 3, dc in sp between dc and ch-3] until there are 23 open sps formed **, sk next 7 sps on rnd 23 of jar cover, inserting hook from back of work to front, sc in the next sk dc on rnd 23, rep from * around, ending last rep at **, ending with sk 8 sps, join in beg sc. *(115 open lps)*
Note: The open lps of Rnd 1 form the foundation for Lace Trim.

Rnd 2: Ch 1, sc in first lp, **shell** *(see Special Stitches)* in next lp, sc in next lp, [shell in next lp, sc in next lp] 4 times, **4-dc shell** *(see Special Stitches)* in next lp, [sc in next lp, shell in next lp] 5 times, **sc dec** *(see Stitch Guide)* in next 2 lps, ***beg joining shell** *(see Special Stitches)* in next lp, sc in next lp, [shell in next lp, sc in next lp] 4 times, 4-dc shell in next lp **, [sc in next lp, shell in next lp] 5 times, sc dec in next 2 lps, rep from * around, ending last rep at **, [sc in next lp, shell in next lp] 4 times, **end joining shell** *(see Special Stitches)* in next lp *(this joins last shell to first shell of rnd)*, draw up a lp in last lp, sl st to join in beg sc.

Continued on page 106

Designs by Lori Zeller

My Friend Wendy

Your favorite little girl will be wide-eyed with wonder when you crochet this adorable little doll and wardrobe as a special surprise just for her!

Gauge

Size B hook: With size 5 cotton, 9 sc = 1 inch; 9 sc rnds = 1 inch
Size 5 steel hook: With size 10 cotton, 10 sc = 1 inch; 10 sc rows = 1 inch
Check gauge to save time.

Pattern Notes

Weave in loose ends as work progresses.
Join rounds with a slip stitch unless otherwise stated.
Ch-3 counts as first dc throughout.

Special Stitches

Shell: (2 dc, ch 2, 2 dc) in indicated st.
Beginning shell (beg shell): (Ch 3, dc, ch 2, 2 dc) in indicated st.
Double shell: ({2 dc, ch 2} twice and 2 dc) in indicated st.
Bead single crochet (bead sc): Insert hook in indicated st, yo, draw up a lp, push a bead up close to hook, yo, draw through 2 lps on hook.

Wendy

Head & Body

Rnd 1 (RS): With size B hook and ecru, ch 2,

Crochet With Bits & Pieces

6 sc in 2nd ch from hook, join, turn. *(6 sc)*

Rnd 2: Ch 1, 2 sc in each sc around, join, turn. *(12 sc)*

Rnd 3: Ch 1, [sc in next sc, 2 sc in next sc] around, join, turn. *(18 sc)*

Rnd 4: Ch 1, [sc in each of next 2 sc, 2 sc in next sc] around, join, turn. *(24 sc)*

Rnd 5: Ch 1, sc in each sc around, join.

Rnd 6: Ch 1, [sc in each of next 3 sc, 2 sc in next sc] around, join, turn. *(30 sc)*

Rnds 7–9: Rep rnd 5.

Rnd 10: Ch 1, sc in each of next 10 sc, [**sc dec** *(see Stitch Guide)* in next 2 sc] twice, sc in each of next 2 sc, [sc dec in next 2 sc] twice, sc in each of next 10 sc, join, turn. *(26 sc)*

Rnd 11: Rep rnd 5.

Rnd 12: Ch 1, sc in each of next 8 sc, 2 sc in each of next 4 sc, sc in each of next 2 sc, 2 sc in each of next 4 sc, sc in next 8 sc, join, turn. *(34 sc)*

Rnds 13–15: Rep rnd 5.

Rnd 16: Ch 1, sc in each of next 9 sc, [sc dec in next 2 sc] 3 times, sc in each of next 4 sc, [sc dec in next 2 sc] 3 times, sc in each of next 9 sc, join in beg sc, turn. *(28 sc)*

Rnd 17: Ch 1, [sc in each of next 2 sc, sc dec in next 2 sc] around, join, turn. *(21 sc)*

Rnd 18: Ch 1, [sc in next sc, sc dec in next 2 sc] around, join, turn. *(14 sc)*

Stuff Head with fiberfill.

Rnd 19: Ch 1, sc in each of next 2 sc, [sc dec in next 2 sc] 5 times, sc in next 2 sc, join, turn. *(9 sc)*

Rnds 20 & 21: Rep rnd 5.

Rnd 22: Rep rnd 2.

Rnd 23: Ch 1, sc in each of next 3 sc, 2 sc in each of next 3 sc, sc in each of next 6 sc, 2 sc in each of next 3 sc, sc in each of next 3 sc, join, turn. *(24 sc)*

Rnd 24: Ch 1, [sc in each of next 3 sc, 2 sc in next sc] around, join, turn. (30 sc)

Rnds 25–37: Rep rnd 5.

Rnd 38: Ch 1, [sc in each of next 3 sc, sc dec in next 2 sc] around, join, turn. *(24 sc)*

Rnds 39–42: Rep rnd 5.

Rnd 43: Ch 1, [sc in each of next 2 sc, sc dec in next 2 sc] around, join, turn. *(18 sc)*

Stuff Body with fiberfill.

Rnd 44: Ch 1, [sc in next sc, sc dec in next 2 sc] around, join, turn. *(12 sc)*

Rnd 45: Ch 1, [sc dec in next 2 sc] 6 times, join, leaving a length of thread, fasten off. *(6 sc)*

Sew opening at bottom of Body closed.

Leg
Make 2.

Rnd 1: With size B hook and ecru, ch 4, 2 sc in 2nd ch from hook, sc in next ch, 4 sc in last ch, working on opposite side of foundation ch, sc in next ch, 2 sc in same ch as beg 2-sc, join, turn. *(10 sc)*

Rnd 2: Ch 1, 2 sc in each sc around, join, turn. *(20 sc)*

Rnd 3: Ch 1, sc in each of next 8 sc, 2 sc in each of next 4 sc, sc in each of next 8 sc, join, turn. (24 sc)

Rnd 4: Ch 1, sc in each sc around, join, turn.

Rnd 5: Rep rnd 4.

Rnd 6: Ch 1, sc in each of next 8 sc, [sc dec in next 2 sc] 4 times, sc in each of next 8 sc, join, turn. *(20 sc)*

Rnd 7: Ch 1, sc in each of next 6 sc, [sc dec in next 2 sc] 4 times, sc in each of next 6 sc, join, turn. *(16 sc)*

Rnd 8: Ch 1, sc in each of next 6 sc, [sc dec in next 2 sc] twice, sc in next 6 sc, join, turn. *(14 sc)*

INTERMEDIATE

Size
9½ inches tall

Materials
• Size 5 crochet cotton: 150 yds ecru
• Size 10 crochet cotton:
  200 yds bright pink,
  100 yds each pastels, brown and navy
  50 yds each white, light blue, dark green and light green
  1 yd each red and blue
• Size B/1/2.25mm crochet hook or size needed to obtain gauge
• Size 5/1.90mm steel crochet hook or size needed to obtain gauge
• Tapestry needle
• Sewing needle
• Matching sewing threads
• Fiberfill
• 201 white 4mm pearl beads
• 14 inches ⅛-inch-wide white ribbon
• Powder blush
• Cotton swab
• 9 small snap fasteners
• Stitch marker

Rnds 9–11: Rep rnd 4.

Rnd 12: Ch 1, 2 sc in first sc, sc in each of next 12 sc, 2 sc in next sc, join, turn. *(16 sc)*

Rnds 13–15: Rep rnd 4.

Rnd 16: Ch 1, 2 sc in first sc, sc in each of next 14 sc, 2 sc in next sc, join, turn. *(18 sc)*

Rnd 17: Rep rnd 4.

Rnd 18: Ch 1, 2 sc in first sc, sc in each of next 5 sc, sc dec in next 2 sc, sc in each of next 2 sc, sc dec in next 2 sc, sc in each of next 5 sc, 2 sc in next sc, join, turn. *(18 sc)*

Rnd 19: Rep rnd 4.

Rnd 20: Ch 1, sc in each of next 7 sc, 2 sc in next sc, sc in each of next 2 sc, 2 sc in next sc, sc in next 7 sc, join, turn. *(20 sc)*

Rnds 21 & 22: Rep rnd 4.

Rnd 23: Ch 1, sc in each of next 7 sc, 2 sc in next sc, sc in each of next 4 sc, 2 sc in next sc, sc in each of next 7 sc, join, turn. *(22 sc)*

Rnd 24: Ch 1, sc dec in next 2 sc, sc in each of next 18 sc, sc dec in next 2 sc, join, turn. *(20 sc)*

Rnds 25–27: Rep rnd 4.

Rnd 28: Ch 1, sc in each of next 6 sc, sc dec in next 2 sc, sc in each of next 4 sc, sc dec in next 2 sc, sc in next 6 sc, join, turn. *(18 sc)*

Rnd 29: Ch 1, 2 sc in first sc, sc in each of next 16 sc, 2 sc in next sc, join, turn. *(20 sc)*

Rnd 30: Ch 1, sc in each of next 5 sc, 2 sc in next sc, sc in next 8 sc, 2 sc in next sc, sc in each of next 5 sc, join, turn. *(22 sc)*

Rnds 31–33: Rep rnd 4.

Rnd 34: Ch 1, 2 sc in first sc, sc in each of next 20 sc, 2 sc in next sc, join, turn. *(24 sc)*

Rnd 35: Rep rnd 4.

Rnd 36: Ch 1, sc in each of next 6 sc, 2 sc in next sc, sc in each of next 10 sc, 2 sc in next sc, sc in each of next 6 sc, join, turn. *(26 sc)*

Rnds 37–42: Rep rnd 4.

Rnd 43: Ch 1, sc in each of next 6 sc, sc dec in next 2 sc, sc in each of next 10 sc, sc dec in next 2 sc, sc in each of next 6 sc, join, turn. *(24 sc)*

Rnds 44 & 45: Rep rnd 4.

Rnd 46: Ch 1, [sc in each of next 2 sc, sc dec in next 2 sc] around, join, turn. *(18 sc)*

Stuff Leg with fiberfill.

Rnd 47: Ch 1, [sc in next sc, sc dec in next 2 sc] around, join, turn. *(12 sc)*

Rnd 48: Ch 1, [sc dec in next 2 sc] around, join, leaving a length of thread, fasten off. *(6 sc)*

Sew Leg opening closed.

Arm

Make 2.

Rnd 1: With size B hook and ecru, ch 2, 6 sc in 2nd ch from hook, join, turn. *(6 sc)*

Rnd 2: Ch 1, 2 sc in each sc around, join, turn.

Rnd 3: Ch 1, [sc in each of next 2 sc, 2 sc in next sc] around, join, turn. *(16 sc)*

Rnd 4: Ch 1, sc in each sc around, join, turn.

Rnds 5–12: Rep rnd 4.

Rnd 13: Ch 1, sc dec in next 2 sc, sc in each of next 12 sc, sc dec in next 2 sc, join, turn. *(14 sc)*

Rnds 14 & 15: Rep rnd 4.

Rnd 16: Ch 1, sc in each of next 6 sc, 2 sc in each of next 2 sc, sc in next 6 sc, join, turn. *(16 sc)*

Rnd 17: Rep rnd 13. *(14 sc)*

Rnds 18–20: Rep rnd 4.

Rnd 21: Ch 1, sc in each of next 3 sc, sc dec in next 2 sc, sc in each of next 4 sc, sc dec in next 2 sc, sc in each of next 3 sc, join, turn. *(12 sc)*

Rnds 22 & 23: Rep rnd 4.

Rnd 24: Ch 1, [sc in each of next 2 sc, sc dec in next 2 sc] around, join, turn. *(9 sc)*

Rnd 25: Rep rnd 4.

Rnd 26: Ch 1, [sc in each of next 2 sc, 2 sc in next sc] around, join, turn. *(12 sc)*

Rnd 27: Ch 1, sc in each of next 6 sc, ch 3 *(for thumb)*, sc in 2nd ch from hook, sc in next ch, sc in each of next 6 sc, join, turn.

Rnd 28: Ch 1, sc in each of next 6 sc, sk thumb sts, sc in each of next 6 sc, join, turn. *(12 sc)*

Rnd 29: Rep rnd 4.

Stuff Arm with fiberfill.

Crochet With Bits & Pieces

Rnd 30: Ch 1, [sc in next 4 sc, sc dec in next 2 sc] twice, join, turn. *(10 sc)*

Rnd 31: Rep rnd 4, leaving a length of thread, fasten off.

Fold rnd 31 flat and sew opening closed.

Hair

Scalp

Rnd 1: With size 5 steel hook and brown, ch 19, 2 sc in 2nd ch from hook, sc in each of next 16 chs, 4 sc in last ch, working on opposite side of foundation ch, sc in each of next 16 chs, 2 sc in same ch as beg 2-sc, join. *(40 sc)*

First side

Row 2: Ch 1, working in **back lps** *(see Stitch Guide)* for this row only, sc in each of next 19 sts, turn. *(19 sc)*

Row 3: Ch 1, sc in each of next 5 sc, [sc dec in next 2 sc, sc in each of next 5 sc] twice, turn. *(17 sc)*

Row 4: Ch 1, sc in each sc across, turn.

Row 5: Ch 1, sc in each of next 4 sc, sc dec in next 2 sc, sc in each of next 5 sc, sc dec in next 2 sc, sc in each of next 4 sc, turn. *(15 sc)*

Row 6: Rep row 4.

Row 7: Ch 1, sc in each of next 4 sc, sc dec in next 2 sc, sc in each of next 9 sc, turn. *(14 sc)*

Row 8: Ch 1, sc in each of next 8 sc, sc dec in next 2 sc, sc in each of next 4 sc, turn. *(13 sc)*

Row 9: Ch 1, sc in each of next 3 sc, [sc dec in next 2 sc] twice, sc in next 6 sc, turn. *(11 sc)*

Row 10: Ch 1, sc in each of next 3 sc, [sc dec in next 2 sc] 3 times, sc in each of next 2 sc, turn. *(8 sc)*

Row 11: Ch 1, sc in first sc, [sc dec in next 2 sc] 3 times, sc in last sc, turn. *(5 sc)*

Row 12: Ch 1, sc in next sc, [sc dec in next 2 sc] twice, turn. *(3 sc)*

Row 13: Ch 1, sk first 2 sc, sc in last sc, fasten off.

2nd side

Row 2: Sk next 2 sc of rnd 1, working in back lps for this row only, attach brown in next st, ch 1, sc in same st as beg ch-1, sc in each of next 18 sts, turn. *(19 sc)*

Rows 3–12: Rep rows 3–12 of First Side. *(3 sc)*

Row 13: Ch 1, sk first 2 sc, sc in last sc, turn.

Edging & bangs

Rnd 1: Ch 1, work 24 sc across bottom back of Scalp, 12 sc across first side of front, sc in back lp only of each of next 2 unworked sc of rnd 1, 12 sc across 2nd Side of front, join. *(50 sc)*

Rnd 2: Ch 1, working in back lp only, sc in same st as joining, ch 4, [sc in next st, ch 4] around, join in beg sc, leaving a length of yarn, fasten off.

Hair Tie

Make 2.

With size 5 steel hook and desired color, ch 76, fasten off.

Note: *If desired, make hair ties to match each outfit.*

Assembly

To attach Legs, thread tapestry needle with a long length of ecru, with foot pointing forward position a Leg at each side of Body, leaving several inches of ecru at beg, pass needle through rnd 42 of first Leg and out opposite side, through rnd 45 of Body from side to side and through rnd 42 of 2nd Leg, pass needle back through 2nd Leg, through Body and through first Leg, secure ends, weave ends into Leg.

Attach Arms in same manner, passing needle through rnd 5 of Arms and rnd 26 of Body.

Sew Scalp to top of Head. Cut 96 strands of brown each 13 inches long. Fold a strand in half, insert hook in rem free lp of rnd 1, draw strand through at fold to form a lp on hook, draw cut ends through lp on hook, pull gently to secure. Continue to rep attaching strands of brown in each rem free lp on Scalp. Separate strands of Hair into 2 ponytails and attach a Hair Tie to each ponytail and tie ends in a bow. Trim Hair as desired.

Thread a length of ecru onto tapestry needle, sew nose in center front of rnd 11 in satin st. Embroider eyes with blue slightly above and to either side of nose. Embroider smiling mouth with red centered below nose. Using cotton swab, dab a bit of powder blush onto cheeks.

Clothing

Panties

Row 1: Beg with waistband ribbing, with size 5 steel hook and white, ch 4, sc in 2nd ch from hook, sc in each of next 2 chs, turn. *(3 sc)*

Rows 2–38: Ch 1, working in back lps only, sc in each of next 3 sc, turn.

Row 39: Ch 1, holding last row to opposite side of foundation ch and working through both thicknesses, sl st in each st across, turn RS out.

Rnd 40: Now working in rnds in ends of ribbing rows, ch 3, dc in same st as beg ch-3, dc in each ribbing row, join in 3rd ch of beg ch-3. *(40 dc)*

Row 41: Now working in rows, ch 1, sc in same st as beg ch-1, sc in each of next 19 sts, turn, leaving rem 20 sts unworked. *(20 sc)*

Rows 42–49: Ch 1, sc dec in next 2 sc, sc in each sc across to last 2 sc, sc dec in next 2 sc, turn. *(4 sc)*

Row 50: Ch 1, [sc dec in next 2 sc] twice, turn. *(2 sc)*

Rows 51–58: Ch 1, sc in each of next 2 sc, turn.

Row 59: Ch 1, 2 sc in each of next 2 sc, turn. *(4 sc)*

Rows 60–67: Ch 1, 2 sc in first sc, sc in each sc across to last sc, 2 sc in last sc, turn. *(20 sc)* At the end of row 67, leaving a length, fasten off. Sew the 20 sc to rem 20 sc of rnd 40. Place Panties on doll.

Dress

Row 1: Starting at neckline with size 5 steel hook and pastels, ch 21, sc in 2nd ch from hook, sc in each rem ch across, turn. *(20 sc)*

Row 2: Ch 3, dc in same st as beg ch-3, 2 dc in each st across, turn. *(40 dc)*

Row 3: Ch 3, dc in each of next 5 dc, [2 dc in next dc] 8 times, dc in each of next 12 dc, [2 dc in next dc] 8 times, dc in each of next 6 dc, turn. *(56 dc)*

Row 4: Ch 3, dc in each of next 5 dc, [2 dc in each of next 2 dc, dc in each of next 12 dc] 3 times, 2 dc in each of next 2 dc, dc in each of next 6 dc, turn. *(64 dc)*

Row 5: Ch 3, dc in each of next 5 dc, [2 dc in each of next 4 dc, dc in each of next 12 dc] 3 times, 2 dc in each of next 4 dc, dc in each of next 6 dc, turn. *(80 dc)*

Row 6: Ch 3, dc in each of next 7 dc, ch 4, sk next 24 dc *(sleeve)*, dc in each of next 16 dc, ch 4, sk next 24 dc *(sleeve)*, dc in each of next 8 dc, turn. *(32 dc, 2 ch-4 sps)*

Row 7: Ch 3, dc in each dc and each ch across, turn. *(40 dc)*

Rows 8 & 9: Ch 1, sc in each st across, turn. *(40 sc)*

Skirt

Row 1: Ch 1, sc in first sc, [ch 2, sc in next sc] rep across, turn. *(40 sc, 30 ch-2 sps)*

Row 2: Change to hook size B, ch 1, sc in first ch-2 sp, [3 dc in next ch-2 sp, sc in next ch-2 sp] across, turn. *(20 sc, 19 groups 3-dc)*

Row 3: Ch 3, dc in same sc as beg ch-3, [sk next dc, sc in next dc, sk next dc, 3 dc in next sc] across, ending with 2 dc in last sc, turn.

Row 4: Ch 1, sc in first dc, [sk next dc, 3 dc in next sc, sk next dc, sc in next dc] across, turn.

Rows 5 & 6: Rep rows 3 and 4.

Row 7: Rep row 3.

Rnd 8: Ch 1, sc in first dc, [sk next dc, 3 dc in next sc, sk next dc, sc in next dc] across, join in beg sc, turn.

Rnd 9: Ch 3, 2 dc in same sc as beg ch-3, sk next dc, sc in next dc, sk next dc, [3 dc in next sc, sk next dc, sc in next dc, sk next dc] around, join in 3rd ch of beg ch-3, turn.

Rnds 10–17: Sl st in first sc, ch 3, 2 dc in same st as beg ch-3, sk next dc, sc in next dc, sk next dc, [3 dc in next sc, sk next dc, sc in next dc, sk next dc] around, join in 3rd ch of beg ch-3, turn.

Rnd 18: Sl st into first sc, ch 3, 2 dc in same st as beg ch-3, sk next dc, (sc, ch 3, sc) in next dc, sk next dc, [3 dc in next sc, sk next dc, (sc, ch 3, sc) in next dc, sk next dc] around, join in 3rd ch of beg ch-3, fasten off. Sew a snap fastener at each neckline and waistline.

Beaded Dress

Note: Thread 201 pearl beads onto pink cotton.

Row 1: With size 5 steel hook and pink, ch 32, sc in 2nd ch from hook, sc in each of next 3 chs, ch 2, sc in each of next 8 chs, ch 2, sc in each of next 7 chs, ch 2, sc in each of next 8 chs, ch 2, sc in each of next 4 chs, turn. *(31 sc, 4 ch-2 sps)*

Row 2: Ch 3, dc in each of next 3 sc, **shell** *(see Special Stitches)* in next ch-2 sp, dc in each of next 8 sc, shell in next ch-2 sp, dc in each of next 7 sc, shell in next ch-2 sp, dc in each of next 8 sc, shell in next ch-2 sp, dc in each of next 4 sc, turn. *(31 dc, 4 shells)*

Row 3: Ch 1, sc in each of next 6 dc, (sc, ch 2, sc) in next ch-2 sp of shell, sc in each of next 12 dc, (sc, ch 2, sc) in next ch-2 sp, sc in each of next 2 dc, [**bead sc** *(see*

Special Stitches) in next dc, sc in next dc] 4 times, sc in next dc, (sc, ch 2, sc) in next ch-2 sp, sc in each of next 12 dc, (sc, ch 2, sc) in next ch-2 sp, sc in each of next 6 dc, turn.

Row 4: Ch 3, dc in each of next 6 sc, (dc, ch 2, 3 dc) in next ch-2 sp, dc in each of next 14 sc, (3 dc, ch 2, dc) in next ch-2 sp, dc in each of next 13 sc, (dc, ch 2, 3 dc) in next ch-2 sp, dc in each of next 14 sc, (3 dc, ch 2, dc) in next ch-2 sp, dc in each of next 7 sc, turn.

Row 5: Ch 1, sc in each of next 8 dc, (sc, ch 2, sc) in next ch-2 sp, sc in each of next 20 dc, (sc, ch 2, sc) in next ch-2 sp, sc in each of next 3 sc, [bead sc in next dc, sc in next dc] 5 times, sc in each of next 2 dc, (sc, ch 2, sc) in next ch-2 sp, sc in each of next 20 dc, (sc, ch 2, sc) in next ch-2 sp, sc in each of next 8 dc, turn.

Row 6: Ch 3, dc in each of next 8 sc, dc in next ch-2 sp, ch 3, sk next 22 sc, dc in next ch-2 sp, dc in each of next 17 sc, dc in next ch-2 sp, ch 3, sk next 22 sc, dc in next ch-2 sp, dc in each of next 9 sc, turn.

Row 7: Ch 1, sc in each of next 10 dc, sc in each of next 3 chs, dc in each of next 5 dc, [bead sc in next dc, sc in next dc] 5 times, sc in each of next 4 dc, sc in each of next 3 chs, sc in each of next 10 dc, turn. *(45 sc)*

Row 8: Ch 3, dc in each sc across, turn. *(45 dc)*
Row 9: Ch 4 *(counts as first dc, ch 1)*, sk next dc, dc in next dc, [ch 1, sk next dc, dc in next dc] across, turn. *(23 dc, 22 ch-1 sps)*

Skirt
Row 1: Change to size B hook, **beg shell** *(see Special Stitches)* in first ch-1 sp, dc in next ch-1 sp, [shell in next ch-1 sp, dc in next ch-1 sp] across, turn. *(11 shells, 11 dc)*
Row 2: Beg shell in first dc, bead sc in next ch-2 sp, [sk next 2 dc, shell in next dc, bead sc in next ch-2 sp] across, turn.
Row 3: Beg shell in first sc, ch 1, sc in next ch-2 sp, ch 1, [sk next 2 dc, shell in next sc, ch 1, sc in next ch-2 sp, ch 1] across, turn.
Row 4: Beg shell in first sc, bead sc in next ch-2 sp, [**double shell** *(see Special Stitches)* in next sc, bead sc in next ch-2 sp] across, turn.
Row 5: Beg shell in first sc, [ch 1, sc in next ch-2 sp] twice, [ch 1, shell in next sc, {ch 1, sc in next ch-2 sp} twice] across, ending with ch-1 sc in last dc, turn.
Row 6: Beg shell in first sc, ch 1, shell in next sc, bead sc in next ch-2 sp, [shell in next sc, ch 1, shell in next sc, bead sc in next ch-2 sp] across, turn.
Rnd 7: Now working in rnds, beg shell in first sc, sc in next ch-2 sp, shell in next ch-1 sp, sc in next ch-2 sp, [shell in next sc, sc in next ch-2 sp, shell in next ch-1 sp, sc in next ch-2 sp] 10 times, join in 3rd ch of beg ch-3, turn. *(22 shells)*
Rnd 8: Sl st into first sc, beg shell in same sc, bead sc in next ch-2 sp, [shell in next sc, bead sc in next ch-2 sp] around, join in 3rd ch of beg ch-3.
Rnd 9: Sl st in next sc, beg shell in same sc, sc in next ch-2 sp, [shell in next sc, sc in next ch-2 sp] around, join in 3rd ch of beg ch-3, turn.
Rnds 10–19: Rep rnds 8 and 9.
Rnd 20: Rep rnd 8.

Rnd 21: Sl st into first sc, ch 1, (sc, ch 3, sc) in same sc as beg ch-1, ch 1, (sc, ch 3, sc) in next ch-2 sp, ch 1, [(sc, ch 3, sc) in next sc, ch 1, (sc, ch 3, sc) in next ch-2 sp, ch 1] around, join in beg sc, fasten off.
Sew a snap fastener at back neckline and waistline. Starting at center back, weave white ribbon through waistline, tie ends in a bow at center front.

Shoe
Make 2.
Row 1: With size 5 steel hook and pink, starting at front of sole, ch 4, sc in 2nd ch from hook, sc in each of next 2 chs, turn. *(3 sc)*
Row 2: Ch 1, 2 sc in first sc, sc in next sc, 2 sc in last sc, turn. *(5 sc)*
Rows 3–5: Ch 1, sc in each sc across, turn.
Row 6: Ch 1, sc in each of next 2 sc, sk next sc, sc in each of next 2 sc, turn. *(4 sc)*
Row 7: Ch 1, sc in first sc, sc dec in next 2 sc, sc in next sc, turn. *(3 sc)*
Row 8: Ch 1, sc in each sc across, turn.
Row 9: Ch 1, sc in first sc, sk next sc, sc in last sc, turn. *(2 sc)*
Rnd 10: Ch 1, working around outer edge of sole, work 28 sc evenly sp around, join. *(28 sc)*
Rnd 11: Ch 3, working in back lps only, dc in each st around, join in 3rd ch of beg ch-3.
Rnd 12: Ch 3, dc in each dc around, join in 3rd ch of beg ch-3.
Rnd 13: Ch 1, sc in each of next 8 dc, place a marker in last sc, sc in next dc, [sc dec in next 2 dc] 7 times, sc in next dc, ch 6, sl st in marked st, turn, sl st in each ch across, sl st in last sc made, sc in each of next 4 sc, join in beg sc, fasten off.

Shorts
Row 1: Beg with waistband with size 5 steel hook and dark green, ch 5, sc in 2nd ch from hook, sc in each rem ch across, turn. *(4 sc)*

Rows 2–37: Ch 1, working in back lps only, sc in each st across, turn.
Row 38: Ch 1, working in back lps only, sc across, do not turn.

Body
Row 1: Working in ends of ribbing rows, ch 3, work 47 dc evenly sp across, turn. *(48 dc)*
Row 2: Ch 3, dc in each dc across, sl st in 4th dc at beg of row leaving first 3 sts unworked to form fly of Shorts.
Rnd 3: Ch 3, dc in each of next 3 dc, 2 dc in next dc, [dc in each of next 4 dc, 2 dc in next dc] around, join in 3rd ch of beg ch-3. *(54 dc)*
Rnd 4: Ch 3, dc in each dc around, join in 3rd ch of beg ch-3.
Rnd 5: Rep rnd 4.

First leg
Rnd 6: Ch 4, sk next 26 dc, sl st in next st, ch 3, dc in each of next 26 dc, dc in each of next 4 chs, join in 3rd ch of beg ch-3.
Rnd 7: Ch 3, dc in each dc around, join in 3rd ch of beg ch-3, fasten off.

2nd leg
Rnd 6: Attach dark green in joining at back in rnd 5, ch 3, dc in each rem dc around, working 1 dc in each ch of ch-4, join in 3rd ch of beg ch-3.
Rnd 7: Ch 3, dc in each dc around, join in 3rd ch of beg ch-3, fasten off.
Sew a snap fastener over back waistband.

Top
Bottom ruffle
Row 1: With size 5 steel hook and light green, ch 8, sc in 5th ch from hook, sc in each rem ch across, turn.
Row 2: Ch 1, sc in each sc across, turn.
Note: Ch-4 is the bottom of ruffle.
Row 3: Ch 4, sc in each sc across, turn.
Rows 4–71: Rep rows 2 and 3.

Bodice
Row 1: Working in ends of rows across top of ruffle, ch 1, work 36 sc across, turn.
Rows 2–7: Ch 1, sc in each sc across, turn.
Right back
Row 8: Ch 1, sc in each of next 7 sc, turn.
Rows 9–16: Ch 1, sc in each of next 7 sc, turn.
Row 17: Ch 1, sc in each of next 4 sc, turn.
Row 18: Ch 1, sc in each of next 4 sc, leaving a length of cotton, fasten off.

Front
Row 8: Sk next 4 sc of row 7, attach light green in next sc, ch 1, sc in same sc as beg ch-1, sc in each of next 13 sc, turn. *(14 sc)*
Rows 9–13: Ch 1, sc in each of next 14 sc, turn.

First shoulder shaping
Row 14: Ch 1, sc in each of next 4 sc, turn.
Rows 15–18: Ch 1, sc in each of next 4 sc, turn. At the end of Row 18, fasten off.

2nd shoulder shaping
Row 14: Sk next 6 sc on row 13 of front, attach light green in next sc, ch 1, sc in same sc as beg ch-1, sc in each of next 3 sc, turn. *(4 sc)*
Rows 15–18: Ch 1, sc in each of next 4 sc, turn. At the end of row 18, fasten off.

Left back
Row 8: Sk next 4 sc of row 7, attach light green in next sc, ch 1, sc in same sc as beg ch-1, sc in each of next 6 sc, turn. *(7 sc)*
Rows 9–16: Ch 1, sc in each sc across, turn.
Row 17: Sl st in each of next 4 sts, ch 1, sc in same st as beg ch-1, sc in each of next 3 sc, turn.
Row 18: Ch 1, sc in each of next 4 sc, leaving a length of cotton, fasten off.
Sew shoulder seams. Sew a snap fastener at each back neckline and waistline.

Sandal
Make 2.
Sole bottom
Row 1: With size 5 steel hook and brown, rep row 1 of Shoe. *(3 sc)*
Rows 2–9: Rep rows 2–9 of Shoe. *(2 sc)*
Rnd 10: Ch 1, work 28 hdc evenly sp around outer edge of sole, join in beg hdc, fasten off.

Sole top
Rows 1–9: Rep rows 1–9 of Sole Bottom.
Rnd 10: Ch 1, work 28 hdc evenly sp around outer edge of sole, join in beg hdc, do not fasten off.
Rnd 11: Holding Sole Bottom and Top tog and working through both thicknesses, sl st in each st around, fasten off.

Strap
Row 1: With size 5 steel hook and brown, ch 16, sc in 2nd ch from hook, sc in each rem ch across, turn. *(15 sc)*
Row 2: Sl st in each of first 3 sc of row 1, ch 14, sk next 9 sc of row 1, sl st in each of next 3 sc of row 1, leaving a length of cotton, fasten off.
Sew ends of row 1 to sole so that Sandal will fit on foot. ✀

Sweet Scents Jar
Continued from page 97

Continued from page 97

Rnd 3: Sl st to the ch-2 sp at center of 2nd shell, **beg shell** *(see Special Stitches)* in same ch-2 sp, dc in next sc, [shell in next shell, dc in next sc] 3 times, **6-dc shell** *(see Special Stitches)* in ch-2 sp of 4-dc shell, [dc in next sc, shell in next shell] 4 times, **inverted dec** *(see Special Stitches)*, *[shell in next shell, dc in next sc] 4 times, 6-dc shell in ch-2 sp of 4-dc shell, [dc in next sc, shell in next shell] 4 times, inverted dec, rep from * around, join in 3rd ch of beg ch-3, fasten off.
Using photo as a guide, glue each 6-dc shell point of rnd 3 evenly sp around to rnd 9 of jar cover. Glue a light pink flower to each top and bottom point of lace trim.

Tie

With sky blue, make a ch 24 inches long, sl st in 2nd ch from hook, sl st in each rem ch across, fasten off.

Beg at center back, weave tie through ch sps of rnd 26. Place cover over jar and tie ends in a bow.

Lid Cover

Rnds 1–6: Rep rnds 1–6 of Jar Cover. *(41 dc, 41 ch-1 sps)*

Rnd 7: Ch 3, [2 dc in next ch-1 sp, dc in next dc] around, ending with 3 dc in last ch-1 sp, join in 3rd ch of beg ch-3. *(124 dc)*

Rnd 8: Ch 4, sk next dc, [dc in next dc, ch 1, sk next dc] around, join in 3rd ch of beg ch-4.

Rnd 9: Ch 1, sc in same st as beg ch-1, sc in next ch-1 sp, [sc in next dc, sc in next ch-1 sp] around, join in beg sc. *(124 dc)*

Rnd 10: Ch 1, sc in same sc as beg ch-1, ch 3, sk 2 sc, [sc in next sc, ch 3, sk next 2 sc] around, join in beg sc, fasten off.

Rnd 11: Attach white in first sc of previous rnd, ch 1, sc in same sc as beg ch-1, shell in next ch-3 sp, [sc in next sc, shell in next ch-3 sp] around, join in beg sc.

Rnd 11: Ch 3, shell in next shell, [dc in next sc, shell in next shell] around, join in 3rd ch of beg ch-3, fasten off.

Weave light pink ribbon through ch-1 sps of rnd 8. Glue a light pink flower over rnd 1 of lid cover.

With ribbon ends at center front, place lid cover onto jar cover, draw ribbon ends tightly and tie ends in a bow.

Fill jar as desired with potpourri, bath beads or scented soaps. ✂

Bold & Beautiful Necklaces
Continued from page 88

2 sc in each of next 2 chs, sc in each of next 3 chs, ch 3, sk sc dec, sc in each of next 2 chs, 2 sc in next ch, sc in each of next 2 chs, ch 3, sk next dc, sc in each of last 3 chs, sc in next st, fasten off.

2nd side trim

Row 6: Attach 2 strands of victory red in top of first dc dec of row 5, ch 1, sc in same st as beg ch-1, [ch 10, sc dec in next 3 dc] twice, ch 7, dc in same dc as first sc of row 5, ch 4, sc in 32nd dc of row 1, turn.

Row 7: Ch 1, sc in each of next 3 chs, ch 3, sk next dc, sc in next 2 chs, 2 sc in next ch, sc in each next 2 chs, ch 3, sk next sc dec, sc in next 3 chs, 2 sc in each of next 2 chs, sc in each of next 3 chs, ch 3, sk next sc dec, sc in each of next 3 sc, 2 sc in each of next 2 chs, sc in each of next 4 chs, join in beg sc, fasten off.

First neckline trim

Attach 2 strands victory red in 31st dc of row 1, sc in same st, sc in each of next 6 sts, [2 sc in next st, sc in each of next 5 sts] 4 times, fasten off.

2nd neckline trim

Attach 2 strands of victory red in last dc of row 1, ch 1, sc in same st as beg ch-1, sc in each of next 4 dc, [2 sc in next dc, sc in each of next 5 dc] 4 times, 2 sc in next dc, sc in each of next 2 dc, fasten off.

Finishing

Use photo as a guide for bead placement. With sewing needle and thread, sew 8mm black glass bead to center of row 3 in ch-5 sp. Sew 6mm black glass beads in ch sps at center of row 5. ✂

Summer Garden Shadow Box
Continued from page 82

Leg
Make 6.
With black, ch 6, sc in 2nd ch from hook, sl st in each ch across, fasten off.
Optional: To stiffen Legs, dip each Leg into clear nail polish.
Using photo as a guide, sew or glue Legs to black stripes on each side of Body.

Antennae
For first Antenna, attach black with sl st to base of rnd 14, ch 4, sl st in 2nd ch from hook, sl st in each ch across, sl st in same st as ch-4, fasten off.
For 2nd Antenna, sk next 3 sts, rep first Antenna.
Optional: To stiffen Antennae, coat with clear nail polish.

Facial features
With black, embroider small straight sts for eyes and mouth.

Small wing
Make 2.
Row 1: Attach black at base of rnd 11, just behind Antenna, ch 4, 5 dc in same st, turn.
Row 2: Ch 3, dc dec in first 5 sts, ch 3, sl st in top of last st made, ch 3, sl st in same st on rnd 11, fasten off.
For 2nd Small Wing, rep on other side of rnd 11, beg behind other Antenna.

Large wing
Make 2.
Row 1: Attach black with sl st 1 row directly behind first Small Wing, ch 4, 7 tr in same st, turn.
Row 2: Ch 1, sc in each st across, ch 4, sl st in same st as first ch-4 of row 1, fasten off.
For 2nd Large Wing, rep first Large Wing on other side of Body opposite previous Wing.

Leaf Spray
With yellow, [ch 4, **dc cl** *(see Special Stitches)* in 4th ch from hook] 40 times, fasten off.

Beaded Trim
Thread 3mm beads *(40)* onto aqua thread, [ch 5, **tr cl** *(see Special Stitches)*, in 5th ch from hook, push up a bead] 40 times, join with sl st in first ch of first ch-5, fasten off.

Assembly
Using photo as a guide, glue Beaded Trim around top of display box.
Cover backing of display case with tissue paper.
Arrange and glue Leaf Spray to tissue paper.
Arrange and glue Flowers and Bumblebee over Leaf Spray.
Place back on display case and secure. ✄

Pick a Pretty Pair

Continued from page 90

Rose & Lace

Gauge
5 shells = 1½ inches

Pattern Notes
Weave in loose ends as work progresses.
Join rounds with a slip stitch unless
otherwise stated.

Special Stitch
Shell: (2 dc, ch 2, 2 dc) in indicated st.

Rose
Row 1: With rose, rep row 1 of Rose of
Rose and Pineapple.

Rnds 2–5: Rep rnds 2–5 of Rose of Rose
and Pineapple.

Lace
Row 1: Attach white in sp between any 2
petals, (ch 3—*counts as first dc through-
out*, dc, ch 2, 2 dc, ch 9, **shell**—*see Special
Stitch*), in sp between next 2 petals, turn.
Row 2: Ch 3, shell in ch-2 sp of shell, ch 9,

shell in ch-2 sp of next shell, turn.
Row 3: Ch 3, shell in ch-2 sp of
shell, ch 2, working over ch-9
sp of previous row and into 5th
ch of ch-9 below, (dc, ch 5, sl st
in 3rd ch from hook, ch 2, dc) in
same 5th ch, ch 2, shell in ch-2 sp
of shell, turn.
Rows 4 & 5: Rep row 2.
Row 6: Rep row 3.
Rows 7–18: [Rep rows 4–6]
4 times.
Starting at back of Lace,
weave ribbon through ch-2
sps of shells to bottom, weave
through to center sp at bottom,
leaving a 6-inch length of
ribbon, fasten off. Leaving a
11-inch length at beg for page marker,
weave ribbon down opposite edge
of Lace through ch-2 sps of shells to
bottom, leaving a 6-inch length of ribbon,
fasten off. Tie ends in a bow.
Weave rem 11-inch length through and
around a post at center back of Rose. ✂

■□□
EASY

Finished Size
7¼ inches

Materials
• Acrylic nylon thread
  or size 10 crochet
  cotton:
  30 yds each white
  and rose
• Size 5/1.90mm steel
  crochet hook or
  size needed to
  obtain gauge
• Tapestry needle
• Sewing needle
• Sewing thread
• 1 yd ⅛-inch-wide
  rose ribbon

Pot Holder Pizzazz
Continued from page 95

Joining
Rnd 1: Holding Front and Back with WS
tog and Front facing, working through
both thicknesses, attach 2 strands of black
in first dc of previous rnd, ch 7, dc in same
st as beg ch-7, sk next 3 dc, *(dc, ch 3,
dc) in next dc, sk next 3 dc, rep from *
around, join in 3rd ch of beg ch-7.

Rnd 2: Sl st into ch-4 sp, ch 1, 7 sc in
same ch-4 sp as beg ch-1, sl st between
next 2 dc, pick up hanging lp, sl st in first
sc on plastic ring, [ch 1, sc in next sc]
rep around hanging lp, sl st in top of last
sl st, [7 sc in next ch-4 sp, sl st between
next 2 dc] around, join in beg sc, fasten
off. ✂

Fun With Color in Thread   **109**

From Scraps to Sensational

Turn leftover scrap yarn into creative works of art for your home and wardrobe! Blend high-end fashion yarns with ordinary medium weight acrylic to create exciting new looks in fashion that are just as much fun to make as they are to wear or display. So, gather up your scrap yarn and favorite hooks and crochet something sensational!

Design by Katherine Eng

Fluorescent Fun Shawl

Add a spectacular shawl worked in eye-catching horizontal stripes to your wardrobe! A lush variety of scrumptious textures and bold colors make it fun and fanciful.

Gauge
Size H hook: Rows 1 and 2 = ¾ inch; 3 sc and 2 ch-2 sps = 1½ inch
Check gauge to save time.

Pattern Notes
Except for copper rows, always leave a 7-inch length of yarn at beginning and ending of each row when attaching and fastening off yarn.
Shawl is crocheted from center outward on each side of foundation chain.
Work in **front loops** *(see Stitch Guide)* of single crochet stitches only.

Shawl
First Half
Row 1 (RS): With size H hook and fuchsia, ch 263, sc in 2nd ch from hook, [ch 2, sk next 2 chs, sc in next ch] 87 times, fasten off, turn. *(88 sc; 87 ch-2 sps)*
Row 2 (WS): Draw up a lp of copper in first sc, ch 1, sc in same sc as beg ch-1, [ch 2, sk next ch-2 sp, sc in next sc] across, fasten off, turn.
Row 3: Draw up a lp of black in first sc, ch 1, sc in same sc as beg ch-1, [ch 2, sk next ch-2 sp, sc in next sc] across, turn.

Row 4: Ch 1, sc in first sc, [ch 2, sk next ch-2 sp, sc in next sc] across, turn.
Rows 5–7: Rep row 4. At the end of row 7, fasten off, turn.
Row 8: Rep row 2.
Rows 9 & 10: With turquoise, rep rows 3 and 4. At the end of row 10, fasten off, turn.
Rows 11 & 12: Rep rows 3 and 4. At the end of row 12, fasten off, turn.
Rows 13 & 14: With purple, rep rows 3 and 4. At the end of row 14, fasten off, turn.
Rows 15 & 16: Rep rows 3 and 4. At the end of row 16, fasten off, turn.
Row 17: With mango, rep row 3, fasten off.
Row 18: Rep row 2.
Rows 19–23: Rep rows 3–7.
Row 24: Rep row 2.
Rows 25 & 26: With fuchsia, rep rows 3 and 4.
Row 27: With size G hook, ch 3, sl st in next sc, [ch 3, sk next ch-2 sp, sl st in next sc] across, fasten off.

2nd Half
Row 1 (RS): With size H hook and working in opposite side of foundation ch, draw up a lp of fuchsia, ch 1, sc in same ch as

BEGINNER

Finished Size

16 x 68 inches,
    excluding fringe

Materials

- Lion Brand Wool-
  Ease medium
  (worsted) weight
  yarn (3 oz/197 yds/
  85g per skein):
  2 skeins #153 black
  1 skein each #137
      fuchsia and
      #147 purple
- Lion Brand Micro-
  Spun light (sport)
  weight yarn:
  1 oz/100 yds/28.35g
      #148 turquoise
  ½ oz/50 yds/14.18g
      #186 mango
- Lion Brand Fun
  Fur bulky (chunky)
  weight eyelash yarn
  (1¾ oz/60yds/50g
  per ball):
  2 balls #134 copper
- Sizes G/6/4mm
  and H/8/5mm
  crochet hooks or
  size needed to
  obtain gauge
- Tapestry needle

beg ch-1, [ch 2, sk next 2 chs, sc in next ch] across, fasten off, turn. *(88 sc; 87 ch-2 sps)*
Rows 2–27: Rep rows 2–27 of First Half.

Finishing

Weave copper yarn into WS and sew down ends.

Cut 14-inch lengths of yarn; use 2 lengths to add fringe to end of each row, except copper. Draw lengths through end of rows, fold in half and tie in an overhand knot, with or without rem lengths that rem at each end of rows. Trim ends to desired length. ✂

Sea Breeze Poncho

Design by Katherine Eng

Stitched in beautiful sea green yarns with a variety of tempting textures, our pretty poncho is perfect for a cool summer evening when only gentle warmth is needed.

Gauge

Rnds 1 and 2 = 1½ inches; (sc, ch 2, sc) = 1½ inches
Check gauge to save time.

Pattern Notes

Weave in loose ends as work progresses. Join rounds with a slip stitch unless otherwise stated.

Special Stitch

Shell: (3 dc, ch 2, 3 dc) in indicated st.

Poncho

Rnd 1 (RS): With A, ch 62, join in first ch to form a ring, ch 1, sc in same st as beg ch-1, ch 1, sk 1 ch, [sc in next ch, ch 1, sk next ch] around, join in beg sc, sl st into ch-1 sp. *(31 sc)*

Rnd 2: Ch 1, sc in same ch-1 sp, ch 2, [sc in next ch-1 sp, ch 2] around, join in beg sc, sl st into next ch sp.

Rnd 3: Ch 1, sc in same sp, ch 2, [sc in next ch-2 sp, ch 2] around, join in beg sc, fasten off.

Rnd 4: Attach citrus in ch-2 sp, ch 1, sc in same ch-2 sp, ch 3, [sc in next ch-2 sp, ch 3] around, join in beg sc, fasten off.

Rnd 5: Attach B in ch-3 sp, ch 1, (sc, ch 2, sc) in same ch-3 sp, ch 2, *(sc, ch 2, sc) in next ch-3 sp, ch 2, rep from * around, join in beg sc, sl st into ch sp. *(62 sc)*

Rnds 6 & 7: Rep rnd 3. At the end of rnd 7, fasten off.

Rnd 8: Attach peacock, rep rnd 4.

Rnd 9: Attach B in ch-3 sp, ch 1, sc in same ch-3 sp, ch 2, [sc in next ch-3 sp, ch 2] around, join in beg sc, sl st into next ch sp.

Rnds 10 & 11: Rep rnd 3. At the end of rnd 11, fasten off.

Rnd 12: With tropical, rep rnd 4.

Rnd 13: Attach A in ch-3 sp, ch 1, sc in same ch-3 sp, [ch 1, sc in next ch-3 sp] around, ending with ch 1, join in **back lp** *(see Stitch Guide)* of first sc.

Rnd 14: Ch 1, sc in back lp of same sc, [ch 1, sc in back lp of next sc] around, ending with ch 1, join in back lp of first sc.

Rnd 15: Rep rnd 14, join in back lp of first sc, fasten off.

Rnd 16: Attach citrus in ch sp, ch 1, sc in same ch sp, ch 3, [sc in next ch-1 sp, ch 3] around, join in beg sc, fasten off.

Rnd 17: Attach B in ch sp, ch 1, (sc, ch 2, sc) in same ch sp, [ch 2, sc in next ch sp] 30 times, (sc, ch 2, sc) in next ch sp, [ch 2, sc in next ch sp] 30 times, join in beg sc, sl st in next ch sp. *(64 sc)*

Rnd 18: Ch 1, (sc, ch 2, sc) in same ch sp, *[ch 2, sc in next ch-2 sp] 7 times, ch 2**, (sc, ch 2, sc) in next ch-2 sp, rep from * around, ending last rep at **, join in beg sc. *(72 sc)*

Rnd 19: Rep rnd 3.

Rnd 20: Attach peacock, rep rnd 4.

Rnd 21: Attach B, ch 1, sc in same ch sp, [ch 2, sc in next ch sp] around, working [sc, ch 2, sc] 4 times evenly sp around, join in beg sc. *(76 sc)*

Rnds 22 & 23: Rep rnd 3. At the end of rnd 23, fasten off.

Rnd 24: With tropical, rep rnd 4.

Rnds 25–27: Rep rnds 13–15.

Rnd 28: Attach citrus, rep rnd 16.

Rnd 29: Rep rnd 9.

Rnd 30: Rep rnd 3, do not fasten off.

Rnd 31: Sl st into next ch sp, ch 1, sc in same ch sp, *shell *(see Special Stitch)* in next ch-2 sp**, sc in next ch-2 sp, rep from * around, ending last rep at **, join in beg sc. *(38 shells; 38 sc)*

Rnd 32: Ch 1, sc in same sc as beg ch-1, *ch 1, sk 1 dc, sc in next dc, ch 1, sk 1 dc, (sc, ch 2, sc) in ch-2 sp, ch 1, sk 1 dc, sc in next dc, ch 1, sk 1 dc**, sc in next sc, rep from * around, ending last rep at **, join in beg sc, fasten off.

Neckline Trim

Rnd 1: Working in opposite side of foundation ch, draw up a lp of tropical in any ch-1 sp on either side of joining, ch 1, sc in same ch-1 sp, ch 3, [sc in next ch-1 sp, ch 3] around, join in beg sc, fasten off.

Rnd 2: Draw up a lp of B in first ch-3 sp of previous rnd, ch 1, (sc, ch 2, sc) in each ch-3 sp around, join in beg sc, fasten off.

Bow

Holding 1 strand each A and tropical tog, leaving a 3-inch length at beg, ch 60, leaving a 3-inch length, fasten off.

Draw 3 strands each 6 inches long of tropical through each end of ch, fold in half and tie in an overhand knot with rem tails. Trim ends as desired. Tie ch in a bow over sc of rnd 4 to the left or right of center front. ✂

INTERMEDIATE

Finished Size

Adult: 13 inches long

Materials

- Lion Brand Chenille Thick & Quick super bulky (super chunky) weight yarn (100 yds/90m per skein): 1 skein #123 seaspray *(A)*
- Lion Brand Wool-Ease medium (worsted) weight yarn (3 oz/197 yds/ 85g per skein): 1 skein #123 seaspray *(B)*
- Lion Brand Fun Fur bulky (chunky) weight eyelash yarn (1¾ oz/60 yds/50g per skein): 1 skein each #207 citrus, #170 peacock and #208 tropical
- Size H/8/5mm crochet hook or size needed to obtain gauge
- Tapestry needle

Design by Katherine Eng

Colors of Fall Capelet

Combine plush, bulky yarns in warm autumn colors for a great-looking wrap that features an eye-catching button closure in front and a deep triangle in back.

Gauge
Size H hook: Rows 1 and 2 = 1½ inches; 3 sc = 1 inch
Check gauge to save time.

Pattern Notes
Weave in loose ends as work progresses. Join rounds with a slip stitch unless otherwise stated.

Special Stitch
Shell: (2 dc, ch 2, 2 dc) in indicated st.

Capelet
Row 1 (WS): With size H hook and spice, ch 110, sc in 2nd ch from hook, sc in each rem ch across, turn. *(109 sc)*
Row 2: Ch 1, sc in first sc, [sk 2 sc, **shell** *(see Special Stitch)* in next sc, sk next 2 sc, sc in next sc] 18 times, turn, sl st into next ch-2 sp of shell. *(18 shells; 19 sc)*
Row 3: Ch 1, sc in same ch-2 sp of shell, [ch 2, dc in next sc, ch 2, sc in next ch-2 sp of shell] across, turn. *(18 sc; 17 dc)*
Row 4: Ch 1, sc in first sc, [shell in next dc, sc in next sc] across, fasten off. *(17 shells; 18 sc)*
Row 5: Draw up a lp of olive in first ch-2 sp, ch 1, sc in same ch-2 sp of shell, [ch 2, dc in next sc, ch 2, sc in next ch-2 sp] across, turn. *(16 dc; 17 sc)*
Row 6: Rep row 4, turn, sl st into next ch-2 sp. *(16 shells; 17 sc)*
Row 7: Rep row 5. *(16 sc; 15 dc)*
Row 8: Rep row 4. *(15 shells; 16 sc)*
Rows 9–36: Rep rows 5–8 in mocha, eggplant, rose, teal, fuchsia, coffee and spice. *(1 shell; 2 sc)*

Border
Rnd 1 (RS): With size H hook, draw up a lp of eggplant in bottom ch-2 sp of shell of row 36, ch 1, (sc, ch 2, sc) in same ch-2 sp, [ch 2, sk next sc *(at end of row)*, sc in next sc, ch 2, sc in next ch-2 sp] across edge *(35 sc across)* ending with ch 2, sk next sc *(at end of row 1)*, (sc, ch 2, sc) in end ch, working across opposite side of foundation ch, [ch 2, sk next 2 chs, sc in next ch] 35 times, ending with ch 2, sk next 2 chs, (sc, ch 2, sc) in last ch, working across left edge, ch 2, sk next sc *(at end of row 1)* sc in next sc, [ch 2, sc in next ch-2 sp, ch 2, sk next sc *(at end of row)*, sc in next sc] across edge *(35 sc across)*, ending with ch 2, join in beg sc, fasten off.

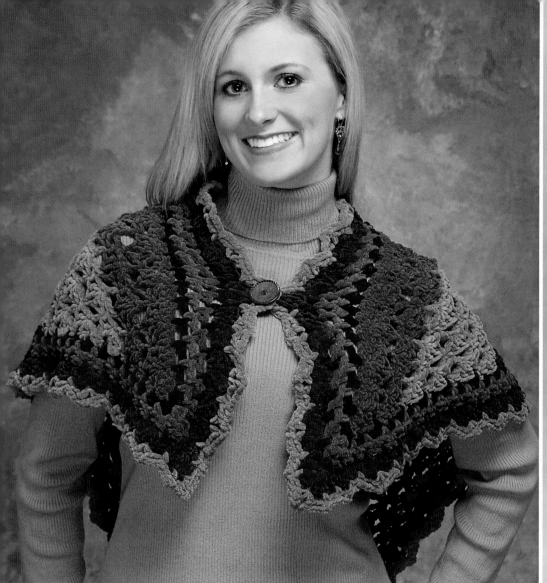

INTERMEDIATE

Finished Size

Adult

Materials

- Lion Brand Lion
  Suede bulky
  (chunky) weight
  yarn (3 oz/122 yds/
  85g per skein):
  1 skein each #210-
    133 spice, #210-
    132 olive, #210-
    140 rose, #210-146
    fuchsia, #210-147
    eggplant, #210-
    178 teal, #210-126
    coffee and #210-
    125 mocha
- Sizes G/6/4mm and
  H/8/5mm crochet
  hooks or size needed
  to obtain gauge
- Tapestry needle
- 1⅜-inch brown
  button

Rnd 2: Draw up a lp of rose in ch-2 sp near center of either side, ch 1, sc in same ch sp, [ch 2, sc in next ch-2 sp] around, working at each of 3 corners, ch 2, (sc, ch 2, sc) in corner ch-2 sp, join last ch 2 to beg sc, fasten off.

Rnd 3: With teal, rep rnd 2.

Rnd 4: With fuchsia, rep rnd 2.

Rnd 5: Draw up a lp of coffee in 3rd ch-2 sp to the left of any corner ch-2 sp, ch 1, sc in same sp, [shell in next ch-2 sp, sc in next ch-2 sp] around, working at each corner (3 dc, ch 3, 3 dc) in corner ch-2 sp, sc in next ch-2 sp, join in beg sc, fasten off.

Rnd 6: Draw up a lp of olive in a sc near center of either side, ch 1, sc in same sc, *ch 2, (sc, ch 2, sc) in next ch-2 sp, ch 2, sc in next sc, rep from * around, working at each corner, ch 2, sk 1 dc, sc in next dc, ch 2, sk next dc, (sc, ch 3, sc) in corner ch-3 sp, ch 2, sk 1 dc, sc in next dc, ch 2, sk next dc, sc in next sc, join in beg sc, fasten off.

Rnd 7: Draw up a lp of mocha in sc between 2 shells near center of either side, *ch 3, (sl st, ch 2, sl st) in next ch-2 sp, ch 3, sl st in next sc at center between 2 shells, rep from * around, working at each corner ch 2, (sl st, ch 2, sl st) in next ch-2 sp, ch 2, sl st in next sc, ch 3, (sl st, ch 3, sl st) in corner ch-3 sp, ch 3, sk next sc, (sl st, ch 2, sl st) in next sc, ch 2, sl st in next sc, join in beg st, fasten off.

Sew button to 4th shell from left corner shell on top edge. Use ch-2 sp of 4th shell on opposite edge for buttonhole. ✄

From Scraps to Sensational

Sassy Stripes Tank Top

Design by Katherine Eng

Wear this versatile top to the office or for a romantic evening out on the town. A deep midnight black background is the perfect complement to the neon bright stripes.

Gauge
Size H hook: Rows 1 and 2 = ¾ inch; 5 sts (3 sc and 2 ch-1 sps) = 1½ inches
Check gauge to save time.

Pattern Notes
Weave in loose ends as work progresses.
Join rounds with a slip stitch unless otherwise stated.
Top is crocheted from under bust upwards and from under bust downward.
On top section, unless otherwise indicated, work in **front loops** *(see Stitch Guide)* of stitches.
Use size G hook for front opening edge and final border rounds only.

Special Stitch
Shell: 3 dc in indicated st.

Top Section
Row 1 (RS): With size H hook and black, ch 106 [114, 122], sc in 2nd ch from hook, [ch 1, sk next ch, sc in next ch] across, turn. *(53 sc, 52 ch-1 sps [57 sc, 56 ch-1 sps; 61 sc; 60 ch-1 sps])*
Row 2: Ch 1, sc in first sc, [ch 1, sk next ch-1 sp, sc in next sc] across, fasten off, turn.
Row 3: Draw up a lp of lilac in first sc, ch 1, sc in first sc, [ch 1, sk next ch-1 sp, sc in next sc] across, fasten off, turn.
Row 4: Draw up a lp of black in first sc, ch 1, sc in same sc, [ch 1, sk next ch-1 sp, sc in next sc] across, turn.
Row 5: Rep row 2.
Row 6: Draw up a lp of coral in first sc, ch 1, sc in first sc, [ch 3, sk next ch-1 sp, next sc and next ch-1 sp, sc in next sc] across, fasten off.
Row 7: Draw up a lp of black in first sc, ch 1, sc in first sc, [ch 1, sc over ch-3 sp in **back lp** *(see Stitch Guide)* of sc of row 5, ch 1, sc in next sc] across, turn.
Row 8: Rep row 2.
Row 9: Draw up a lp of lime in first sc, rep row 2.
Note: *Divide number of sc in half for back and two quarters for each side of front adding 1 extra st to back. Mark ch-1 sp at*

each side with a st marker.

Row 10: For beg neck edge dec, draw up a lp of black in 2nd sc from edge, rep row 2 leaving 1 sc open on opposite end of row, turn, sl st to next sc.

Row 11: Rep row 2 across leaving 1 sc open on opposite end of row, turn, sl st to next sc.

Note: Move side markers up 2 rows to mark underarms.

Right front

Row 12: Rep row 2 across to 3rd sc from marker, turn, sl st in next sc. *(7 sc)*

Row 13: Rep row 2, leaving last sc unworked on end, turn. *(5 sc)*

Row 14: Rep row 13, turn, sl st in next sc. *(4 sc)*

Note: On sizes medium and large, continue working dec pattern until 4 sc rem then work rows 15–28.

Row 15: Ch 1, sc in same sc, ch 1, sk next ch-1 sp, sc in next sc, turn.

Row 16: Ch 1, sc in first sc, sk next ch-1 sp, sc in next sc, turn.

Row 17 (RS): Ch 1, **sc dec** *(see Stitch Guide),* in next 2 sc, turn. *(1 sc)*

Rows 18–28: Working through both lps of sc sts, [ch 1, sc in next sc, turn] 11 times. At the end of row 28, fasten off.

Left Front

Row 12 (WS): Rep on opposite side beg with WS facing at armhole marker and working pat in reverse beg with draw up a lp of black in 3rd sc from marker, rep row 2. *(7 sc)*

Rows 13–28: Rep rows 13–28 of Right Front.

Back

Row 12 (WS): Draw up a lp of black in 3rd sc to the left of marker, rep row 2 across leaving 2 sc unworked on opposite end of row, turn, sl st in next sc. *(23 sc)*

Row 13: Rep row 2 across leaving last sc unworked, turn, sl st in next sc. *(21 sc)*

Row 14: Rep row 2, leaving last sc unworked, turn. *(19 sc)*

Rows 15 & 17: Rep row 2.

Note: On sizes medium and large, continue to rep row 2 [2, 4] times, continue working rows 18–28.

Rows 18–28: Rep rows 18–28 of Right Front on each outer edge of back for straps.

With a length of black, sew front straps to back straps.

Bottom Section

Row 1 (RS): Working on opposite side of foundation ch, with size H hook, draw up a lp of black in first ch, ch 1, sc in same ch as beg ch-1, [ch 1, sk next ch, sc in next ch] across, turn. *(53 sc, 52 ch-1 sps [57 sc, 56 ch-1 sps; 61 sc, 60 ch-1 sps])*

Row 2: Ch 1, sc in first sc, [ch 1, sk next ch-1 sp, sc in next sc] across, turn.

Row 3 (RS): Sk over ch-1 sps and working in sc sts only, ch 1, sc in first sc, [**shell** *(see Special Stitch)* in next sc, sc in next sc] across, turn. *(26 [28, 30] shells)*

Row 4 (WS): Ch 3 *(counts as first dc)*, dc in

INTERMEDIATE

Finished Size

Small [medium, large] Pattern is written for smallest size with changes for larger sizes in brackets.

Materials

- Lion Brand Wool-Ease medium (worsted) weight yarn (3 oz/197 yds/ 85g per skein): 3 skeins #153 black
- Lion brand Micro-Spun light (sport) weight yarn: ¾ oz/75 yds/21.26g each #103 coral, #194 lime and #144 lilac
- Sizes G/6/4mm and H/8/5mm crochet hooks or size needed to obtain gauge
- Tapestry needle
- ¾-inch buttons: 6
- 2 stitch markers

first sc, sc in center dc of next shell, [ch 1, dc in next sc, ch 1, sc in center dc of next shell] across to last sc, 2 dc in last sc, turn.

Row 5 (RS): Ch 1, sc in first dc, [shell in next sc, sc in next dc] across, ending with sk next to last dc, sc in top of ch-3, turn.

Rows 6–17: Rep rows 4 and 5.

Row 18: Rep row 4, fasten off.

Row 19: Draw up a lp of coral, ch 1, rep row 5, fasten off.

Row 20: Draw up a lp of black in first sc, rep row 4.

Row 21: Rep row 5.

Row 22: Rep row 4.

Row 23: With lime, rep row 19.

Rows 23–27: Rep rows 4 and 5. At the end of last rep, do not fasten off.

Right Front Opening

Row 1 (RS): With size G hook, ch 1, sc in end of each sc row, 2 sc in end of each dc row *(over **post**—see Stitch Guide—of and in top of dc)*, continue to top, stopping at beg of neck dec, turn. *(49 sc)*

Row 2: Ch 1, sc in each sc across, turn.

Row 3: Ch 1, sc in each of next 6 sc, [ch 2, sk next 2 sc *(buttonhole)*, sc in each of next 6 sc] 5 times, ch 2, sk next 2 sc, sc in last sc, turn. *(6 buttonholes)*

Row 4: Ch 1, sc in each sc across and 2 sc in each ch-2 sp across, fasten off.

Left Front Opening

Row 1 (RS): With size G hook, draw up a lp of black at beg of neck dec, ch 1, sc in end of each sc row, 2 sc in each dc row *(over post of dc and in top of dc)*, continue to bottom edge, turn. *(49 sc)*

Rows 2–4: Ch 1, sc in each sc across, turn. At the end of rnd 4, do not fasten off, turn.

Border

Rnd 1 (RS): Ch 1, (sc, ch 2, sc) in first sc, sc in each sc to last sc, (sc, ch 2, sc) in bottom corner sc, working across bottom edge, sc in end of next 3 rows, sc in next sc, sc in each rem st across bottom, working (sc, ch 2, sc) in each center dc of each shell, sc in end of next 3 rows, (sc, ch 2, sc) in next corner sc, sc in each sc up front to last sc, (sc, ch 2, sc) in top corner sc, sc evenly sp across neck to strap, sc in each sc of strap, sc in each ch-1 sp and each sc across back, sc in each sc of strap, sc evenly sp across neck edge, join in beg sc, fasten off.

Rnd 2: Draw up a lp of lilac in first ch-2 sp of left front bottom, ch 1, (sc, ch 2, sc) in same ch-2 sp, sk next 2 sc, sc in next sc, [sk next 2 sc, (sc, ch 2, sc) in next ch-2 sp across, sk next 2 sc, sc in next sc] across bottom edge, ending with sk 2 sc, (sc, ch 2, sc) in next sc on bottom edge of Right Front Opening, (sc, ch 2, sc) in corner ch-2 sp, ch 1, sk next 2 sts, *(sc, ch 2, sc) in next st, ch 1, sk next 2 sts, rep from * around adjusting as necessary to keep Border flat, working (sc, ch 2, sc) in each corner ch-2 sp, ending with (sc, ch 2, sc) in center sc bottom edge of Left Front Opening, sk 2 sts, sc in next st, join in beg sc, fasten off.

Armhole Border
Make 2.

Rnd 1 (RS): Draw up a lp of black at underarm, ch 1, sc evenly sp around armhole opening ending with an even number of sc sts, join in beg sc, fasten off.

Rnd 2: Draw up a lp of lilac in a sc opposite a (sc, ch 2, sc) of rnd 2 of Border, ch 1, (sc, ch 2, sc) in same sc as beg ch-1, adjusting as necessary work a (sc, ch 2, sc) in each sc opposite that of rnd 2 of border to balance Armhole Border with previous border, join in beg sc, fasten off.

Sew buttons opposite buttonholes. With WS facing block lightly. ✄

Design by Katherine Eng

Wild Lime Cloche

Make this sassy cloche in double strands of bright lime green yarn to add a vivid splash of color to your cool-weather wardrobe. A pretty flower adds a fun touch.

Gauge
Rnds 1 and 2 = 2 inches in diameter; [sc, ch 2] twice = 1½ inches
Check gauge to save time.

Pattern Notes
Weave in loose ends as work progresses.
Join rounds with a slip stitch unless otherwise stated.

Special Stitch
Shell: 5 dc in indicated st.

Cloche
Rnd 1 (RS): With 1 strand each A and B held tog, ch 3, join in first ch to form a ring, ch 1, 8 sc in ring, join in beg sc. *(8 sc)*
Rnd 2: Ch 1, sc in first sc, ch 1, [sc in next sc, ch 1] around, join in beg sc. *(8 sc; 8 ch-1 sps)*
Rnd 3: Ch 1, sc in same sc as beg ch-1, sc in next ch sp, [sc in next sc, sc in next ch sp] around, join in beg sc. *(16 sc)*
Rnd 4: Rep rnd 2. *(16 sc; 16 ch-1 sps)*
Rnd 5: Rep rnd 3. *(32 sc)*
Rnd 6: Rep rnd 2. *(32 sc; 32 ch-1 sps)*
Rnd 7: Ch 1, sc in same sc as beg

Continued on page 142

Finished Size
Adult

Materials
- Red Heart Hokey Pokey medium (worsted) weight yarn:
  1½ oz/75 yds/42.53g each #7114 lime *(A)* and #7110 spearmint *(B)*
- Red Heart Kids medium (worsted) weight yarn:
  1 oz/50 yds/28.35g #2652 lime *(C)*
- Size H/8/5mm crochet hook or size needed to obtain gauge
- Yarn needle
- ⅜-inch wooden beads: 2

Black Magic Cardigan

Design by Lori Zeller

Create a beautiful cardigan in a double-ended technique from leftover fashion yarns in coordinating colors. Vertical stripes give it an elegant, sophisticated look.

Gauge

Size K double-ended hook: 11 rows = 4½ inches; 13 sts = 4½ inches
Check gauge to save time.

Pattern Notes

Weave in loose ends as work progresses. Join rounds with a slip stitch unless otherwise stated.

Special Stitches

Double crochet knit (dck): Yo, insert hook between front and back vertical bars and under horizontal bar of next st, yo, draw lp through, yo, draw through 2 lps on hook.

Single crochet knit (sck): Insert hook between front and back vertical bars and under horizontal bar of next st, yo, draw lp through, yo, draw through 1 lp on hook.

First Body Side

With size K double-ended hook and A, ch 28 [30, 32, 34, 36], fasten off, set aside.

Row 1: Beg at center back, with size K hook and A, ch 64 [68, 72, 76, 80], yo, insert hook in 3rd ch from hook, yo, draw lp through, yo, draw through 2 lps on hook, *yo, insert hook in next ch, yo, draw lp through, yo, draw through 2 lps on hook, retaining lps on hook, rep from * across, turn.

Row 2: With A, yo, draw through first lp on hook, *yo, draw through 2 lps on hook, rep from * across until 1 lp remains on hook, do not turn.

Row 3: Ch 1, sk first vertical bar, **dck** *(see Special Stitches)* across row, turn.

Row 4: With A, rep row 2.

Row 5: Rep row 3.

Row 6: With B, rep row 2.

Row 7: Rep row 3.

Rows 8 & 9: Rep rows 4 and 5.

Row 10: With C, rep row 2.

Row 11: Rep row 3.

Rows 12 & 13: Rep rows 4 and 5.

Row 14: With D, rep row 2.

Row 15: Rep row 3.

Rows 16 & 17: Rep rows 4 and 5.

Rows 18–24 [18–26, 18–28, 18–30, 18–32]: Rep rows 2–8 [2–10, 2–12, 2–14, 2–16].

Row 25 [27, 29, 31, 33]: Ch 1, sk first vertical bar, dck 34 times, pick up ch length made at beg and set aside, yo, insert hook in first ch, yo, draw lp through, yo, draw through 2 lps on hook, *yo, insert hook in next ch, yo, draw lp through, yo, draw through 2 lps on hook, rep from * across, do not turn.

INTERMEDIATE

Finished Size

Small [medium, large,
    X-large and 2X-large]
Pattern is written for small-
    est size with changes for
    larger sizes in brackets.

Materials

- Red Heart Super Saver
    medium (worsted)
    weight yarn:
    16 [18, 20, 22, 24] oz/800
        [900, 1000, 1100, 1200]
        yds/454 [510, 567, 624,
        680]g #312 black (A)
- Lion Brand Color Waves
    bulky (chunky) weight
    yarn:
    3 [4,4,4,5] oz/105 [140, 140,
        140, 175] yds/85.05 [113,
        113, 113, 142]g #4353
        lava (B)
- Sensations Angel
    Hair bulky (chunky)
    weight yarn:
    3 [4, 5, 5, 6] oz/105 [140,
        175, 175, 210] yds/85
        [113, 142, 142, 170]g
        black/gray (C)
- Bernat Boa bulky
    (chunky) weight yarn:
    1 [1 1/2, 2, 2, 2½] oz/35
        [53, 70, 70, 88]
        yds/28.35 [42.53, 57, 57,
        71]g #81042 ostrich (D)
- Size J/10/6mm
    crochet hook
- Size K/10/6.5mm
    double-ended crochet
    hook or size needed to
    obtain gauge
- Tapestry needle
- Sewing needle
- Black sewing thread
- 20mm charcoal buttons: 6

Rows 26–35 [28–39, 30–43, 32–47, 34–51]: Rep rows 10–19 [4–15, 14 and 3–15, 4–19, 6–23].

Row 36 [40, 44, 48, 52]: With A, yo, draw through 2 lps on hook, yo, draw through 3 lps on hook, work rem lps off hook as usual, do not turn.

Row 37 [41, 45, 49, 53]: Ch 1, sk first vertical bar, dck 55 times, (sk next vertical bar, dck in next vertical bar) twice, turn.

Row 38 [42, 46, 50, 54]: With B [C, D, A, B] work lps off hook until there are 4 lps rem, [yo, draw through 3 lps on hook] twice, do not turn.

Row 39 [43, 47, 51, 55]: Ch 1, sk first 2 vertical bars, dck across, turn.

Row 40 [44, 48, 52, 56]: Rep row 36 [40, 44, 48, 52].

Row 41 [45, 49, 53, 57]: Ch 1, sk first vertical bar, dck 50 times, turn.

Row 42 [46, 50, 54, 58]: With C [D, A, B, C] work lps off until there are 4 lps rem, [yo, draw through 3 lps on hook] twice, do not turn.

Row 43 [47, 51, 55, 59]: Rep row 39 [43, 47, 51, 55].

Rows 44 & 45 [48 & 49, 52 & 53, 56 & 57, 60 & 61]: Rep rows 4 and 5.

Row 46 [50, 54, 58, 62]: With A [B, C, D, A] work lps off hook, do not turn.

Row 47 [51, 55, 59, 63]: Ch 1, sk first vertical bar, dck across, turn.

Row 48 [52, 56, 60, 64]: With A, work lps off hook, fasten off.

2nd Body Side

Row 1: Beg at neck edge with A and working in opposite side of foundation ch, place sl knot on hook, yo, insert hook in first ch, yo, draw lp through, yo, draw through 2 lps on hook, *yo, insert hook in next ch, yo, draw lp through, yo, draw through 2 lps on hook, rep from * across, turn.

Rows 2–24 [2–26, 2–28, 2–30, 2–32]: Rep rows 2–24 [2–26, 2–28, 2–30, 2–32] of First Body Side. At the end of last rep, fasten off.

Row 25 [27, 29, 31, 33]: Attach A in 35th [37th, 39th, 41st, 43rd] horizontal bar from bottom of cardigan, ch 30 [32, 34, 36, 38] yo, insert hook in 3rd ch from hook, yo, draw lp through, yo, draw through 2 lps on hook, yo, insert hook in next ch, yo, draw lp through, yo, draw through 2 lps on hook, rep from * across ch, dck in each rem st across row 24, turn.

Rows 26–35 [28–39, 30–43, 32–47, 34–51]: Rep rows 10–19 [4–15, 14 and 3–15, 4–19, 6–23] of First Body Side.

Row 36 [40, 44, 48, 52]: With A, work lps off hook until there are 4 lps rem, [yo, draw through 3 lps on hook] twice, do not turn.

Row 37 [41, 45, 49, 53]: Ch 1, sk first 2 vertical bars, dck across, turn.

Row 38 [42, 46, 50, 54]: With B, yo, draw through 2 lps on hook, yo, draw through 3 lps on hook, work rem lps off hook as

usual, do not turn.

Row 39 [43, 47, 51, 55]: Ch 1, sk first vertical bar, dck 54 times, turn.

Row 40 [44, 48, 52, 56]: With A, work lps off hook until there are 4 lps rem, [yo, draw through 3 lps on hook] twice, do not turn.

Row 41 [45, 49, 53, 57]: Ch 1, sk first 2 vertical bars, dck across, turn.

Row 42 [46, 50, 54, 58]: With C, yo, draw through 2 lps on hook, yo, draw through 3 lps on hook, work rem lps off hook as usual, do not turn.

Row 43 [47, 51, 55, 59]: Ch 1, sk first vertical bar, dck 48 times, turn.

Row 44 [48, 52, 56, 60]: With A, work lps off hook until there are 4 lps rem, [yo, draw through 3 lps on hook] twice, do not turn.

Row 45 [49, 53, 57, 61]: Rep row 5.

Row 46 [50, 54, 58, 62]: With A, work lps off hook, do not turn.

Row 47 [51, 55, 59, 63]: Ch 1, sk first vertical bar, dck across, turn.

Row 48 [52, 56, 60, 64]: With A, work lps off hook, fasten off.

Edging

With size J hook and A, working around entire outer edge, sc in each vertical bar down sweater front, 3 sc in last vertical bar, sc evenly across cardigan bottom, 3 sc in next vertical bar at bottom front on other side of cardigan, sc in each vertical bar up front, sc around top edges, join in first sc, fasten off.

Sleeve
Make 2.
First side
Row 1: With size K double-ended hook, beg at center arm with A, ch 50 [52, 64, 56, 58], yo, insert hook in 3rd ch from hook, yo, draw lp through, yo, draw through 2 lps on hook, *yo, insert hook in next ch, yo, draw lp through, yo, draw through 2 lps on

hook, rep from * across, turn.

Row 2: With A, work lps off hook, do not turn.

Row 3: Ch 1, sk first vertical bar, dck across, turn.

Row 4: With A, work lps off hook, do not turn.

Row 5: Ch 1 sk first vertical bar, dck across, turn.

Row 6: With B, work lps off hook, do not turn.

Row 7: Ch 1, sk first vertical bar, dck across, turn.

Rows 8 & 9: Rep rows 4 and 5.

Row 10: With C, work lps off hook, do not turn.

Row 11: Ch 1, sk first vertical bar, dck across, turn.

Rows 12 & 13: Rep rows 4 and 5.

Row 14: With D, work lps off hook, do not turn.

Row 15: Ch 1, sk first vertical bar, dck in next 36 [36, 38, 38, 40] sts, **sck** *(see Special Stitches)* in last 12 [14, 14, 16, 16] sts, turn.

Row 16: With A, work lps off hook, do not turn.

Row 17: Ch 1, sk first vertical bar, sck in next 12 [14, 14, 16, 16] sts, dck across, turn.

Row 18: With B, work lps off hook, do not turn.

Row 19: Ch 1, sk first vertical bar, dck in next 36 [36, 38, 38, 40] sts, sck across, turn.

Rows 20 & 21 [20–23, 20–25, 20–27, 20–29]: Rep rows 16 and 17.

Row 22 [24, 26, 28, 30]: Rep row 10.

Row 23 [25, 27, 29, 31]: Ch 1, sk first vertical bar, dck 36 [36, 38, 38, 40] times, sck 6 [8, 8, 10, 10] times, leaving rem sts unworked, turn.

Row 24 [26, 28, 30, 32]: Rep row 4, fasten off A.

Row 25 [27, 29, 31, 33]: Attach A in 7th vertical bar from end, ch 1, sck 6 [8, 8, 10, 10] times, dck across, turn.

Row 26 [28, 30, 32, 34]: Rep row 2.

Row 27 [29, 31, 33, 35]: Ch 1, sk first vertical bar, dck 24 [24, 26, 26, 28] times, sck 6 [8, 8, 10, 10] times, leaving rem sts unworked.

Row 28 [30, 32, 34, 36]: With A, work lps off

hook, fasten off.

2nd side

Row 1: Beg at shoulder edge and working in opposite side of foundation ch, place sl knot on hook, yo, insert hook in first ch, yo, draw lp through, yo, draw through 2 lps on hook, *yo, insert hook in next ch, yo, draw lp through, yo, draw through 2 lps on hook, rep from * across, turn.

Rows 2–14: Rep rows 2–14 of First Side of Sleeve.

Row 15: Ch 1, sk first vertical bar, sck in next 12 [14, 14, 16, 16] sts, dck in last 36 [36, 38, 38, 40] sts, turn.

Row 16: With A, work lps off hook, do not turn.

Row 17: Ch 1, sk first vertical bar, dck in next 36 [36, 38, 38, 40] sts, sck across, turn.

Row 18: With B, work lps off hook, do not turn.

Row 19: Ch 1, sk first vertical bar, sck in next 12 [14, 14, 16, 16] sts, dck across, turn.

Rows 20 & 21 [20–23, 20–25, 20–27, 20–29]: Rep rows 16 and 17. After last row, do not turn, continuing with A, work first 6 lps off hook, turn.

Row 22 [24, 26, 28, 30]: With C, work lps off hook, do not turn.

Row 23 [25, 27, 29, 31]: Ch 1, sk first vertical bar, sck 6 [8, 8, 10, 10] times, dck 36 [36, 38, 38, 40] times, turn.

Row 24 [26, 28, 30, 32]: Rep row 4.

Row 25 [27, 29, 31, 33]: Ch 1, sk first vertical bar, dck 36 [36, 38, 38, 40] times, sck 6 [8, 8, 10, 10] times, turn.

Row 26 [28, 30, 32, 34]: Rep row 2.

Row 27 [29, 31, 33, 35]: Ch 1, sk first vertical bar, sck 6 [8, 8, 10, 10] times, dck 24 [24, 26, 26, 28] times, leaving rem sts unworked.

Row 28 [30, 32, 34, 36]: With A, work lps

Continued on page 144

From Scraps to Sensational

Design by Becky Symons for Mary Maxim

Americana Cardigan

Blocks of Americana-inspired colors worked in a variety of interesting stitch patterns come together in this striking, light-weight cardigan with patriotic appeal.

Gauge
7 dc = 1½ inches; 6 dc rows = 2½ inches; square = 4 x 4 inches
Check gauge to save time.

Pattern Notes
Weave in loose ends as work progresses.
Join rounds with a slip stitch unless otherwise stated.
Squares are crocheted separately and then crocheted together.

Special Stitches
Long double crochet (ldc): Yo, insert hook in indicated st, yo, draw up a lp level with working rnd, [yo, draw through 2 lps on hook] twice.
4-double crochet cluster (4-dc cl): [Yo hook, insert hook in indicated st, yo, draw up a lp, yo, draw through 2 lps on hook] 4 times, yo, draw through all 5 lps on hook.

Square No. 1
Make 1 [2, 2] each with MC and CC.
Make 2 [2, 3] with CC3.
Make 3 [4, 4] with CC2.
Rnd 1 (RS): Ch 4, sl st to join in first ch to form a ring, ch 5 *(counts as first dc, ch 2 throughout)*, [3 dc in ring, ch 2] 3 times, 2 dc in ring, sl st to join in 3rd ch of beg ch-5. *(12 dc)*
Rnd 2: Sl st into ch-2 sp, ch 3 *(counts as first dc throughout)*, (2 dc, ch 2, 3 dc) in same ch-2 sp, ch 1, *(3 dc, ch 2, 3 dc) in next ch-2 sp, ch 1, rep from * around, join in 3rd ch of beg ch-3. *(24 dc)*
Rnd 3: Sl st into ch-2 sp, ch 3, (2 dc, ch 2, 3 dc) in same ch-2 sp, ch 1, 3 dc in next ch-1 sp, ch 1, *(3 dc, ch 2, 3 dc) in next ch-2 sp, ch 1, 3 dc in next ch-1 sp, ch 1, rep from * around, join in 3rd ch of beg ch-3. *(36 dc)*
Rnd 4: Sl st into ch-2 sp, ch 3, (2 dc, ch 2, 3 dc) in same ch-2 sp, [ch 1, 3 dc in next ch-1 sp] twice, ch 1, *(3 dc, ch 2, 3 dc) in next ch-2 sp, [ch 1, 3 dc in next ch-1 sp] twice, ch 1, rep from * around, join in 3rd ch of beg ch-3, fasten off. *(48 dc)*

Square No. 2
Make 0 [1, 1] with CC2.
Make 1 [1, 1] with CC3.
Make 2 [2, 2] with CC1. Make 3 [4, 5] with MC.
Row 1: Ch 19, dc in 4th ch from hook, ch 2, sk each of next 2 chs, sc in next ch, ch 2, sk each of next 2 chs, dc in each of next 3

chs, ch 2, sk each of next 2 chs, sc in next ch, ch 2, sk each of next 2 chs, dc in each of next 2 chs, turn. *(7 dc; 2 sc; 4 ch-2 sps)*

Row 2: Ch 3, dc in next dc, ch 2, sc in next ch-2 sp, ch 3, sc in next ch-2 sp, ch 2, dc in each of next 3 dc, ch 2, sc in each of next ch-2 sp, ch 3, sc in next ch-2 sp, ch 2, dc in each of last 2 dc, turn. *(7 dc; 4 sc; 4 ch-2 sps; 2 ch-3 sps)*

Row 3: Ch 3, dc in next dc, 4 dc in next ch-3 sp, dc in each of next 3 dc, 4 dc in next ch-3 sp, dc in each of next 2 dc, turn. *(15 dc)*

Row 4: Ch 3, dc in next dc, ch 2, sc in sp between 2nd and 3rd dc of 4-dc group, sk last 2 dc of 4-dc group, ch 2, dc in each of next 3 dc, ch 2, sc in sp between 2nd and 3rd dc of 4-dc group, sk last 2 dc of 4-dc group, ch 2, dc in each of last 2 dc, turn. *(7 dc; 2 sc; 4 ch-2 sps)*

Rows 5–7: Rep rows 2–4.

Rows 8 & 9: Rep rows 2 and 3. At the end of row 9, do not turn.

Rnd 10: Now working in rnds, ch 1, work 14 sc down side edge of square, 3 sc in corner, 13 sc across bottom edge, 3 sc in corner, 14 sc along other side to corner, fasten off.

Square No. 3
Make 2 [5, 5] with CC1.
Make 2 [2, 3] with CC2.
Make 0 [1, 1] with MC.

Rnd 1: Ch 4, sl st to join in first ch to form a ring, ch 5, [dc in ring, ch 2]7 times, sl st to join in 3rd ch of beg ch-5. *(8 dc)*

Rnd 2: Ch 1, sc in same st as beg ch-1, 2 sc in next ch-2 sp, [sc in next dc, 2 sc in next ch-2 sp] around, join in beg sc. *(24 sc)*

Rnd 3: Ch 1, sc in same st, [ch 3, sk each of next 2 sc, sc in next sc] around, join in beg sc. *(8 sc; 8 ch-3 sps)*

Rnd 4: Sl st into next ch-3 sp, ch 1, sc in same ch-3 sp, ch 3, **ldc** *(see Special Stitches)* in next dc of rnd 1 directly below, ch 3, *sc in next ch-3 sp, ch 3, ldc in next dc of rnd 1 directly below, ch 3, rep from * around, join in beg sc. *(8 ldc; 16 ch-3 sps)*

Rnd 5: Sl st into next ldc, ch 3, (2 dc, ch 2, 3 dc) in same ldc, *ch 2, sk next ch-3 sp, [sc in next ch-3 sp, ch 2] twice, sk next ch-3 sp **, (3 dc, ch 2, 3 dc) in next ldc for shell, rep from * around, ending last rep at **, join in 3rd ch of beg ch-3. *(4 shells)*

Rnd 6: Ch 1, sc in each dc, 3 sc in each corner ch sp of each shell and 2 sc in each ch-2 sp across each side edge, join in beg sc, fasten off. (60 sc)

Square No. 4
Make 5 [8, 9].

Row 1: With CC3, ch 19, 3 dc in 5th ch from hook, [sk each of next 2 chs, 3 dc in next ch] across to last 2 chs, sk next ch, dc in last ch, turn. *(17 dc)*

Row 2: Ch 1, sc in first st, [ch 3, sc between

Size

Small [medium, large]

Finished bust: 37 [44, 53] inches

Back length: 22 inches

Sleeve length: 20 inches

Pattern is written for smallest size with changes for larger sizes in brackets.

Materials

- Light (DK) weight yarn (1¾/170 yds/ 50g per ball): 8 [8, 9] balls white *(MC)* 2 [2, 3] balls each red *(CC1)*, navy *(CC2)* and denim blue *(CC3)*
- Size G/6/4mm crochet hook or size needed to obtain gauge
- Tapestry needle
- 20mm red buttons: 7
- Straight pins

next 3-dc groups] 4 times, ch 3, sc in last st, change to CC2.

Row 3: With CC2, ch 3, [3 dc in next ch-3 sp] 5 times, ending with dc in rem sc, turn. *(17 dc)*

Row 4: With CC2, rep row 2.

Rows 5 & 6: With MC, rep rows 3 and 4.

Rows 7 & 8: With CC1, rep rows 3 and 4.

Row 9: With CC3, rep row 3.

Rnd 10: Now working in rnds, ch 1, work 14 sc down side edge, 2 sc in same corner as last st, 13 sc across bottom edge, 2 sc in same st as last sc, rep from * once, join in beg sc, fasten off.

Square No. 5

Make 2 [4, 4] with CC2.
Make 2 [2, 3] with CC1.
Make 2 [2, 2] with MC.
Make 0 [1, 1] with CC3.

Row 1: Ch 18, **4-dc cl** *(see Special Stitches)* in 6th ch from hook, ch 1, *sk next ch, dc in each of next 2 chs, ch 1, sk next ch, 4-dc cl in next ch, ch 1, rep from * across, ending with dc in last ch, turn. *(3 dc cls; 6 dc)*

Row 2: Ch 1, sc in first st, ch 3, *sc in each of next 2 dc, ch 3, rep from * across, ending with sk 1 ch, sc in next ch, turn. *(6 sc; 3 ch-3 sps)*

Row 3: Ch 4 *(counts as first dc and ch-1 throughout)*, [4-dc cl in next ch-3 sp, ch 1, dc in each of next 2 sc, ch 1] twice, 4-dc cl in next ch-3 sp, ch 1, dc in last st, turn. *(3 dc cls; 6 dc)*

Rows 4–9: Rep rows 2 and 3.

Rnd 10: Now working in rnds, ch 1, work 3 sc in each corner and 13 sc across each side of square, join in beg sc, fasten off.

Back Assembly

Using diagram as a guide for placement of squares, with RS facing and working in **back lps** *(see Stitch Guide)* only, attach MC in bottom right corner of square 5 [5, 2], ch 1, sc in same st, ch 2, sc in left corner of square 4 [4, 5], ch 2, then sk next st on square 5 [5, 2], sc in next st, ch 2, sk next st on square 4 [4, 5], sc in next st, continue working along each side edge until 9 sc have been worked along each square, ending with sc in corner of each square and last sc should be worked in square 4 [4, 5], ch 2, sc in right corner of square 1 [1, 3], ch 3, sc in left corner of square 2 [2, 1] and then continue as before. Rep this process until 4 [6, 5] strips of 5 squares each has been completed. Now join the strips in the same manner, but working from side to side.

Back Border

With RS facing, attach MC in any st, ch 1, sc evenly sp around outer edge, working 3 sc in each center corner st, join in beg sc, fasten off.

Half Squares for Front & Side Edges
Single crochet half square
Make 4 [2, 4] with CC1.
Make 3 [2, 3] CC2.
Make 1 [0, 1] with MC.

Row 1: Ch 8, sc in 2nd ch from hook, sc in each rem ch across, turn. *(7 sc)*

Row 2: Ch 1, sc in each sc across, turn.

Rows 3–14: Rep row 2. At the end of Row 14, do not turn.

Rnd 15: Now working in rnds, ch 1, [work 13 sc across side edge of rows, 3 sc in corner, 5 sc across short edge, 3 sc in corner] twice, join in beg sc, fasten off.

Double crochet half square
Make 3 [2, 3] with CC3.
Make 3 [2, 3] with MC.

Crochet With Bits & Pieces

Make 3 [0, 3] with CC2.
Make 1 [0, 1] with CC1.
Row 1: Ch 9, dc in 4th ch from hook, dc in each rem ch across, turn. *(7 dc)*
Row 2: Ch 3, dc in each of next 6 dc, turn.
Rows 3–7: Rep row 2. At the end of row 7, do not turn.
Rnd 8: Now working in rnds, ch 1, [work 13 sc across side edge of rows, 3 sc in corner, 5 sc across short edge, 3 sc in corner] twice, join in beg sc, fasten off.

Small half square
Make 2 [2, 2] with CC1.
Row 1: Ch 9, dc in 4th ch from hook, dc in each rem ch across, turn. *(7 dc)*
Row 2: Ch 3, dc in each of next 6 dc, turn.
Row 3: Ch 3, dc in each of next 6 dc, do not turn.
Rnd 4: Now working in rnds, ch 1, work 5 sc evenly sp across each side edge, working 3 sc in each corner, join in beg sc, fasten off.

Right Front Neck Square No. 2
Make 1 [1, 1] with CC3.
Rows 1–4: Rep rows 1–4 of Square No. 2. *(7 dc; 2 sc; 4 ch-2 sps)*
Row 5: Rep row 2 of Square No. 2.
Row 6: Ch 3, dc in next dc, 4 dc in next ch-3 sp, dc in each of next 3 dc, 4 dc in next ch-3 sp, turn leaving rem sts unworked. *(13 dc)*
Row 7: Sl st over next 2 sts, ch 1, sc between 2nd and 3rd dc of 4-dc group, ch 2, sk rem dc sts of 4-dc group, dc in each of next 3 dc, ch 2, sc between 2nd and 3rd dc of next 4-dc group, ch 2, sk rem dc sts of 4-dc group, dc in each of last 2 dc, turn. *(5 dc; 2 sc; 3 ch-2 sps)*
Row 8: Ch 3, dc in next dc, ch 2, sc in next ch-2 sp, ch 3, sc in next ch-2 sp, ch 2, dc in each of next 3 dc, turn. *(5 dc; 2 ch-2 sps; 1 ch-3 sps)*
Row 9: Ch 3, dc in each of next 2 dc, 5 dc in next ch-3 sp, dc in each of next 2 dc, do not turn. *(9 dc)*
Rnd 10: Now working in rnds, ch 1, work 14 sc down side edge, 3 sc in corner st, 13 sc across bottom edge, 3 sc in corner, 9 sc evenly along short side, 8 sc evenly along shaping edge and 8 sc across top edge, 3 sc in corner, join in beg sc, fasten off.

Left Front Neck Square No. 4
Make 1.
Rows 1–6: Rep rows 1–6 of Square No. 4.
Row 7: With CC1, ch 3, [3 dc in next ch-3 sp] 4 times, turn. *(13 dc)*
Row 8: Sl st over next 3 sts, ch 1, sc in same st, [ch 3, sc between next 2 groups of 3-dc] twice, sc in last st, change to CC3, turn.
Row 9: Ch 3, [3 dc in next ch-3 sp] 3 times, do not turn. *(10 dc)*
Rnd 10: Ch 1, work 8 sc evenly along shaped edge, 9 sc along short edge, 3 sc in corner, 13 sc across bottom edge, 3 sc in corner, 14 sc across long edge, 3 sc in corner, 9 sc across top, join in beg sc, fasten off.

Right Front Assembly
Using diagram as a guide for placement of squares, with RS facing and working in back lps only, lay out squares as indicated, taking care to have Right Front Neck Square No. 2 properly placed. With MC, working in back lps only, crochet squares tog the same as for back assembly.

Right Front Border
With RS facing, attach MC, ch 1, work sc around entire front, working 3 sc in each corner, including corner of neck shaping, join in beg sc, fasten off.

Left Front Assembly
Using diagram as a guide for placement of squares, with RS facing and working in

---

back lps only, lay out squares as indicated, taking care to have Left Front Neck Square No. 4 properly placed. With MC, working in back lps only, crochet squares tog the same as for back.

Left Front Border

Work the same as Right Front Border.

Sleeve

Make 2.

Foundation row: With MC, ch 50, dc in 4th ch from hook, dc in each rem ch across, turn. *(48 dc)*

Row 1: Ch 3 *(counts as first dc throughout)*, dc in each dc across, turn.

Continued on page 145

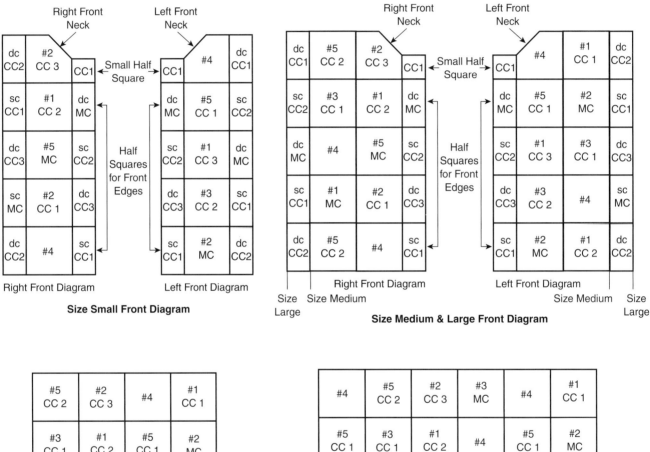

Size Small Front Diagram

Right Front Diagram

dc CC2	#2 CC3	CC1
sc CC1	#1 CC2	dc MC
dc CC3	#5 MC	sc CC2
sc MC	#2 CC1	dc CC3
dc CC2	#4	sc CC1

Left Front Diagram

CC1	#4	dc CC1
dc MC	#5 CC1	sc CC2
sc CC2	#1 CC3	dc MC
dc CC3	#3 CC2	sc CC1
sc CC1	#2 MC	dc CC2

Small Half Square. Half Squares for Front Edges.

Size Medium & Large Front Diagram

Right Front Diagram

dc CC1	#5 CC2	#2 CC3	CC1
sc CC2	#3 CC1	#1 CC2	dc MC
dc MC	#4	#5 MC	sc CC2
sc CC1	#1 MC	#2 CC1	dc CC3
dc CC2	#5 CC2	#4	sc CC1

Left Front Diagram

CC1	#4	#1 CC1	dc CC2
dc MC	#5 CC1	#2 MC	sc CC1
sc CC2	#1 CC3	#3 CC1	dc CC3
dc CC3	#3 CC2	#4	sc MC
sc CC1	#2 MC	#1 CC2	dc CC2

Small Half Square. Half Squares for Front Edges. Size Large | Size Medium.

Size Small Back Diagram

#5 CC2	#2 CC3	#4	#1 CC1
#3 CC1	#1 CC2	#5 CC1	#2 MC
#4	#5 MC	#1 CC3	#3 CC1
#1 MC	#2 CC1	#3 CC2	#4
#5 CC2	#4	#2 MC	#1 CC2

Size Medium & Large Back Diagram

#4	#5 CC2	#2 CC3	#3 MC	#4	#1 CC1
#5 CC1	#3 CC1	#1 CC2	#4	#5 CC1	#2 MC
#1 CC3	#4	#5 MC	#2 CC2	#1 CC3	#3 CC1
#3 CC2	#1 MC	#2 CC1	#5 CC3	#3 CC2	#4
#2 MC	#5 CC2	#4	#3 CC1	#2 MC	#1 CC2

Size Large | Size Medium

Designs by Cindy Carlson

Denim Fur Hat & Scarf

Whether your look is casual or dressy, you'll be warm and stylish in this trendy set worked in luxuriously soft cotton-blend and eyelash yarns.

Gauge
5 hat rnds = 2¼ inches; 6 hdc = 2 inches
Check gauge to save time.

Pattern Notes
Weave in loose ends as work progresses. Do not join rounds unless otherwise stated, use a stitch marker to mark each round.

Hat
Rnd 1 (RS): With dark blue, ch 2, 6 hdc in first ch of beg ch-2, place st marker. *(6 hdc)*

Rnd 2: Ch 2 *(counts as first hdc throughout)*, hdc in same st as beg ch-2, 2 hdc in each hdc around. *(12 hdc)*

Rnd 3: Ch 2, hdc in same st as beg ch-2, hdc in next hdc, [2 hdc in next hdc, hdc in next hdc] around. *(18 hdc)*

Rnds 4 & 5: Rep rnd 3. *(27, 41 hdc)*

Rnd 6: Ch 2, hdc in same hdc as beg ch-2, [hdc in each of next 2 hdc, 2 hdc in next hdc] 13 times, hdc in last st. *(55 hdc)*

Rnd 7: Ch 2, hdc in each hdc around.

Rnd 8: Rep rnd 7.

Rnd 9: Ch 2, hdc in same st as beg ch-2, hdc in each of next 4 hdc, [2 hdc in next hdc, hdc in each of next 4 hdc] around. *(66 hdc)*

Continued on page 145

Designs by Sandy Abbate

Neon Bright Winter Warmers

Bold neon colors highlight this light-hearted set worked with simple stitches and medium weight yarn. Repeating triangles and tassels complete the look.

Gauge

Square = 3 inches; 7 dc = 2 inches; 10 pattern rows = 4 inches
Check gauge to save time.

Pattern Notes

Weave in loose ends as work progresses.
Join rounds with a slip stitch unless otherwise stated.
When changing yarn color, drop old color yarn to wrong side of square.

Hat

Square
Make 6.
Note: Make 1 square each with color combinations of A/B, C/D, A/D, C/A, A/C and D/A.
Row 1 (RS): With color 1, ch 11, **change color** *(see Stitch Guide)* to color 2, ch 1, with color 2, sc in 2nd ch from hook, with color 1, sc in each of next 10 chs, turn. *(11 sc)*
Row 2: With color 1, ch 1, sc in each of next 9 sc, with color 2, sc in next 2 sc, turn.
Row 3: With color 2, ch 1, sc in each of next 3 sc, with color 1, sc in next 8 sc, turn.
Row 4: With color 1, ch 1, sc in each of next 7 sc, with color 2, sc in next 4 sc, turn.
Row 5: With color 2, ch 1, sc in each of next 5 sc, with color 1, sc in each of next 6 sc, turn.
Row 6: With color 1, ch 1, sc in each of next 5 sc, with color 2, sc in next 6 sc, turn.
Row 7: With color 2, ch 1, sc in each of next 7 sc, with color 1, sc in each of next 4 sc, turn.
Row 8: With color 1, ch 1, sc in each of next 3 sc, with color 2, sc in each of next 8 sc, turn.
Row 9: With color 2, ch 1, sc in each of next 9 sc, with color 1, sc in each of next 2 sc, turn.
Row 10: With color 1, ch 1, sc in next sc, with color 2, sc in each of next 10 sc, turn.
Row 11: With color 2, sc in each of next 11 sc, fasten off both colors.
Sew 6 Squares tog in a strip. Sew last Square to first Square to form a ring.

Body

Rnd 1 (RS): With WS of Squares facing, attach A in first st of any Square, ch 1, sc in same st as beg ch-1, work 9 sc across same

next 2 sts, sc in each of next 7 sts] 6 times, join in beg sc. *(48 sc)*

Rnd 17: Ch 2, dc in each of next 3 sc, [dc dec in next 2 sts, dc in each of next 2 sts] 11 times, sk beg ch-2, join in first dc of rnd. *(36 dc)*

Rnd 18: Ch 1, sc in same st as beg ch-1, sc dec in next 2 sts, [sc in next st, sc dec in next 2 sts] 11 times, join in beg sc. *(24 sc)*

Rnd 19: Ch 2, dc in next st, [dc dec in next 2 sts] 11 times, sk beg ch-2, join in first dc of rnd. *(12 dc)*

Rnd 20: Ch 1, [sc dec in next 2 sts] 6 times, join in beg sc, leaving a length of yarn, fasten off. *(6 sc)*

Tassel

Cut 6 20-inch strands of each of the 4 colors. *Holding 1 strand of each color tog, fold strands in half, insert hook from front to back in sc of rnd 20, draw strands through at fold to form a lp on hook, draw cut ends through lp on hook, pull tightly to secure, rep from * 5 times.

Thread yarn needle with rem length of yarn from rnd 20, from WS, weave through sts, pull to close opening, knot to secure, fasten off.

Cut a length of A 22 inches long. Holding all strands tog, wrap the strand of A around the Tassel ¾ inch down from top. Knot around Tassel to secure, trim Tassel ends even.

Fold band of Squares upward to RS of Hat.

Scarf

Square

Make 8.

Make Squares the same as for Hat Squares, [sew 4 tog 2 x 2] twice to form 2 Squares.

Square, work 10 sc across side edge of each of next 5 Squares, join in beg sc. *(60 sc)*

Rnd 2: Ch 1, sc in same st as beg ch-1, sc in each rem sc around, join in beg sc.

Rnd 3: Ch 3 *(counts as first dc throughout)*, dc in each sc around, join in 3rd ch of beg ch-3.

Rnd 4: Ch 1, sc in same st as beg ch-1, sc in each rem dc around, join in beg sc.

Rnds 5–14: Rep rnds 3 and 4.

Rnd 15: Ch 2, dc in each of next 9 sts, [**dc dec** *(see Stitch Guide)* in next 2 sts, dc in each of next 8 sts] 6 times, sk beg ch-2, join in first dc of rnd. *(54 dc)*

Rnd 16: Ch 1, [**sc dec** *(see Stitch Guide)* in

INTERMEDIATE

Finished Sizes

Hat: 19 inches in diameter

Scarf: 53 inches, excluding tassels

Mittens: Child's small [medium, large]

Pattern is written for smallest size with changes for larger sizes in brackets.

Materials

- Red Heart Super Saver medium (worsted) weight yarn (3 oz/160 yds/ 85g per skein): 2 skeins #655 lime (A)
- Red Heart Classic medium (worsted) weight yarn (3½ oz/190 yds/99g per skein): 1 skein each #513 parakeet (B), #254 pumpkin (C) and #584 lavender (D)
- Size I/9/5.5mm crochet hook or size needed to obtain gauge
- Yarn needle

Body

Row 1: With RS of first block of Squares facing, attach A with sc in corner of First Square, work 9 more sc evenly sp across Square, work 10 sc across 2nd Square, turn. *(20 sc)*

Row 2: Ch 3, dc in each sc across, turn.

Row 3: Ch 1, sc in each dc across, turn.

Rows 4–81: Rep rows 2 and 3. At the end of row 81, leaving a length of yarn, fasten off. Sew 2nd block of Squares to row 81 of Scarf.

End shaping

Row 1: Attach A with a sc to lower edge of first block of Squares, work 9 sc evenly sp across First Square, work 10 sc across 2nd Square, turn. *(20 sc)*

Row 2: Ch 3, dc in each sc across, turn.

Row 3: Ch 1, sc in first st, sc dec in next 2 sts, sc in each st across to last 3 sts, sc dec in next 2 sts, sc in last st, turn. *(18 sc)*

Row 4: Ch 3, dc dec in next 2 sts, dc in each st across to last 3 sts, dc dec in next 2 sts, dc in last st, turn. *(16 dc)*

Rows 5–10: Rep rows 3 and 4.

Row 11: Ch 1, sc dec in next 2 sts, ch 1, sc dec in next 2 sts, fasten off.

Attach A with sc to lower edge of 2nd block of Squares, rep rows 1–11 on End Shaping.

Tassel
Make 2.

Cut 6 strands of each of the 4 colors each 20 inches long. Cut a 12-inch length of A and tie securely around center of bundle. Cut a 22-inch length of A, wrap around Tassel ¾ inch down from top of Tassel, knot ends to secure, trim ends. Attach Tassel in ch-1 sp of row 11 of End Shaping.

Mitten
Make 2.
Ribbing

Row 1: With C, ch 11, sc in 2nd ch from hook, sc in each rem ch across, turn. *(10 sc)*

Row 2: Ch 1, working in **back lps** *(see Stitch Guide)* only, sc in each st across, fasten off, turn.

Row 3: Working in back lps only, attach B, ch 1, sc in each st across, turn.

Row 4: Rep row 2.

Row 5: Working in back lps only, attach D, ch 1, sc in each st across, turn.

Row 6: Rep row 2.

Row 7: Working in back lps only, attach C, ch 1, sc in each st across, turn.

Row 8: Rep row 2.

Rows 9–20: Rep rows 3–8.

Rows 21–24: Rep rows 3–6. At the end of row 24, leaving a length of yarn, fasten off. With WS of cuff tog and rem length of yarn, sew row 24 to opposite side of foundation ch.

Hand

Rnd 1: Attach A in side edge of Ribbing, ch 1, sc in same st as beg ch-1, sc in each Ribbing row around, join in beg sc. *(24 sc)*

Rnd 2: Ch 3, dc in each sc around, join in 3rd ch of beg ch-3.

Rnd 3: Ch 1, sc in each dc around, join in beg sc.

Rnds 4 & 5: Rep rnds 2 and 3.

Rnd 6: Ch 3, dc in each of next 9 sc, [3 dc in next sc] 4 times, dc in each of next 10 sc, join in 3rd ch of beg ch-3. *(32 dc)*

Rnd 7: Ch 1, sc in same dc as beg ch-1, sc in each of next 11 dc, sk next 8 dc *(Thumb)*, sc in each of next 12 dc, join in beg sc. *(24 sc)*

Rnds 8–11 [8–13, 8–15]: Rep rnds 2 and 3.

Rnd 12 [14, 16]: Ch 2, dc in next sc, [dc dec in next 2 sc] 11 times, sk beg ch-2 sp, join in next dc. *(12 dc)*

Rnd 13 [15, 17]: Ch 1, [sc dec in next 2 dc] 6 times, join in beg sc, leaving a length of yarn, fasten off. *(6 sc)*

Thread yarn needle with rem length, weave through sts of rnd 13 [15, 17], pull to close opening, knot to secure, fasten off.

Continued on page 143

Design by Terrie Mays
for Caron International

Diagonal Stripes Hat

Festive rows of brightly colored diagonal stripes worked in an unusual spiral pattern adorn this whimsical hat that features optional curly corkscrew hair!

INTERMEDIATE

Finished Size

21 inches in diameter x
  7 inches long,
  excluding hair

Materials

- Caron Simply Soft
  Brites medium
  (worsted) weight
  yarn (6 oz/300 yds/
  170g per skein):
  1 skein each #9607
    limelight *(A)*,
    #9603 papaya *(B)*,
    #9606 lemonade
    (C), #9610 grape
    (D), #9601 coconut
    (E) and #9727
    black *(F)*
- Sizes H/8/5mm
  and J/10/6mm
  crochet hooks or
  sizes needed to
  obtain gauge
- Tapestry needle
- 3 x 10-inch piece
  cardboard

Gauge

Size H hook: hair curl = 4 inches long
Size J hook: rnds 1–3 = 1½ inches;
[ch 3, tr, sc] 4 times = 4 inches
Check gauge to save time.

Pattern Notes

Weave in loose ends as work progresses.
Join rounds with a slip stitch unless otherwise stated.
Work with 2 strands of yarn held together throughout unless otherwise stated.

Hat

Rnd 1 (RS): With size J hook and 2 strands of A, ch 63, join in first ch to form a ring, ch 3, tr in same ch as sl st, *sk next 2 chs, (sc, ch 3, tr) in next ch, rep from * 19 times, ending with sc in same st as beg sl st, **change color** *(see Stitch Guide)* to B. *(21 tr)*

Rnd 2: (Ch 3, tr) in same st as sc, *(sc, ch 3, tr) in next sc, rep from * 19 times, ending with sc in same st as beg ch-3, change color to C. *(21 tr)*

Rnd 3: Rep rnd 2, change color to D.
Rnd 4: Rep rnd 2, change color to E.
Rnd 5: Rep rnd 2, change color to A.
Rnd 6: Rep rnd 2, change color to B.
Rnd 7: (Ch 3, tr) in same st, *[(sc, ch 3, tr) in next sc] 4 times, insert hook in next sc, yo, draw up a lp, insert hook in next sc, yo, draw up a lp, yo, draw through all 3 lps on hook, ch 3, tr in same sc as ch-3, rep from * twice,

Continued on page 144

Jingle Bells Necklace

Design by Katherine Eng

Celebrate Christmas all year long with this whimsical necklace made from scraps of lush eyelash yarn and trimmed with tiny gold jingle bells.

EASY

Finished Size

Fits adult 24–25 inches

Materials

- Lion Brand Fun Fur bulky (chunky) weight eyelash yarn: 25 yds #124 champagne
- Size 10 crochet cotton: 25 yds white
- Size C/2/2.75mm crochet hook or size needed to obtain gauge
- Tapestry needle
- 8mm gold jingle bells: 48

Gauge

Rows 1–4 = 1 inch; 2 sc = ½ inch
Check gauge to save time.

Pattern Notes

Weave in loose ends as work progresses.

Necklace

Row 1 (RS): To begin, thread jingle bells onto crochet cotton. With 1 strand each white and champagne held tog throughout, ch 3, sc in 2nd ch from hook, sc in next ch, turn. *(2 sc)*

Row 2 (WS): Ch 1, sc in first sc, push 1 jingle bell up next to lp on hook, sc in next sc, turn.

Row 3 (RS): Ch 1, sc in each of next 2 sc, turn.

Rows 4–96: Rep rows 2 and 3.

Rows 97–106: Rep row 3. At the end of row 106, leaving a 4-inch length, fasten off.

Sew row 106 of Necklace to opposite side of foundation ch. ✂

Royal Print Tote

Design by Katherine Eng

Double strands of yarn held together throughout lend strength and durability to this striking tote bag. Make one in each of your favorite colors to accent your wardrobe!

Gauge

Size G hook: Rnds 1–3 = 2 inches width; Rnds 1–3 = 3¾ inches long

Pattern Notes

Weave in loose ends as work progresses.
Join rounds with a slip stitch unless otherwise stated.
Work with 2 strands held together throughout.

Special Stitch

Shell: 5 dc in indicated st.

Tote

Bottom

Rnd 1 (RS): With size G hook and 2 strands of royal, ch 8, sc in 2nd ch from hook, sc in each of next 5 chs, 3 sc in next ch, working on opposite side of foundation ch, sc in each of next 5 chs, 2 sc in same ch as beg sc, join in beg sc. *(16 sc)*

Rnd 2: Ch 1, 2 sc in same sc as beg ch-1, sc in each of next 5 sc, 2 sc in each of next 3 sc, sc in each of next 5 sc, 2 sc in each of next 2 sc, join in beg sc, join in beg sc. *(22 sc)*

Rnd 3: Ch 1, 2 sc in same sc as beg ch-1, sc in each of next 8 sc, 2 sc in each of next 3 sc, sc in each of next 8 sc, 2 sc in each of next 2 sc, join in beg sc. *(28 sc)*

Rnd 4: Ch 1, sc in each of next 12 sc, 2 sc in each of next 2 sc, sc in each of next 12 sc, 2 sc in each of next 2 sc, join in beg sc. *(32 sc)*

Rnd 5: Ch 1, sc in same sc as beg ch-1, 2 sc in next sc, [sc in next sc, 2 sc in next sc] 15 times, join in beg sc. *(48 sc)*

Rnd 6: Ch 1, sc in each sc around, join in beg sc.

Rnd 7: Ch 1, [sc in each of next 18 sc, 2 sc in each of next 6 sc] twice, join in beg sc. *(60 sc)*

Rnd 8: Rep rnd 6, fasten off.

Note: *From stiff felt, using Tote Bottom as a pattern, cut Tote Bottom insert. Set aside.*

Sides

Rnd 1 (RS): With size G hook, draw up 1 strand each royal and artist

Continued on page 143

Finished Size

10 x 10 inches tapered

Materials

- Red Heart Super Saver medium (worsted) weight yarn:
  6 oz/300 yds/170g #385 royal
  2 oz/100 yds/57g #315 artist print
- Sizes G/6/4mm and H/8/5mm crochet hooks or size needed to obtain gauge
- Tapestry needle
- ⅞-inch royal button
- 6 x 8-inch piece blue stiff felt
- Stitch markers

Designs by Svetlana Avrakh for Patons

Patchwork Blanket & Pillows

Surprise someone special with this bold, beautiful geometric blanket and pillow set worked in bright citrus colors of super bulky yarn with a large hook.

Gauge
7 sc = 4 inches; 7 rows = 4 inches
Check gauge to save time.

Pattern Notes
Weave in loose ends as work progresses. Join rounds with a slip stitch unless otherwise stated.

Graph-reading knowledge is necessary. Read right-side rows right to left and wrong-side rows left to right.

Each strip has 6 blocks consisting of 16 rows each and a total of 96 rows for each strip. Work each strip from the bottom upward as indicated by afghan diagram.

Blanket
Strip 1
Row 1 (RS): With MC, ch 17, sc in 2nd ch from hook, sc in each rem ch across, turn. *(16 sc)*
Row 2: Ch 1, sc in each sc across, turn.
Rows 3–16: Rep row 2. At the end of last rep **change color** *(see Stitch Guide)* to A, turn.

Row 17: With A, rep row 2. *(16 sc)*
Rows 18–32: Rep row 2, changing color as indicated by Chart 1 *(see page 147)*. At the end of last rep change color to MC, turn.
Row 33: With MC, rep row 2. *(16 sc)*
Rows 34–48: Rep row 2. At the end of last rep change color to A, turn.
Row 49: With A, rep row 2. *(16 sc)*
Rows 50–64: Ch 1, sc in each sc across, changing color as indicated by Chart 1 *(see page 147)*. At the end of last rep, change color to MC.
Row 65: With MC, rep row 2.
Rows 66–80: Rep row 2. At the end of last rep, change color to B.
Row 81: With B, rep row 2.
Rows 82–98: Rep row 2, changing color as indicated on Chart 2 *(see page 147)*. At the end of row 98, fasten off.

Strip 2

Row 1 (RS): With B, ch 17, sc in 2nd ch from hook, sc in each rem ch across, turn. *(16 sc)*
Rows 2–16: Ch 1, sc in each sc across, changing color as indicated by Chart 3 *(see page 147)*. At the end of last rep, change color to B.
Rows 17–32: With B, rep row 2 of Strip 1. At the end of last rep, change color to C.
Row 33: With C, rep row 2 of Strip 1
Rows 34–48: Ch 1, sc in each sc across, changing color as indicated by Chart 4 *(see page 147)*. At the end of last rep, change color to B.
Row 49–64: With B, rep row 2 of Strip 1. At the end of last rep, change color to MC.
Row 65: With MC, rep row 2 of Strip 1.
Rows 66–80: Ch 1, sc in each sc across, changing color as indicated by Chart 5 *(see page 147)*. At the end of last rep, change color to MC.
Rows 81–96: With MC, rep row 2 of Strip 1. At the end of last rep, fasten off.

Strip 3

Row 1 (RS): With A, ch 17, sc in 2nd ch from hook, sc in each rem ch across, turn. *(16 sc)*
Rows 2–16: Rep row 2 of Strip 1. At the end of last rep, change color to C.
Row 17: With C, rep row 2 of Strip 1.
Rows 18–32: Ch 1, sc in each sc across, changing color as indicated by Chart 4. At the end of last rep, change to MC.
Rows 33–48: With MC, rep row 2 of Strip 1. At the end of last rep, change color to B.
Row 49: With B, rep row 2 of Strip 1.
Rows 50–64: Ch 1, sc in each sc across, changing color as indicated by Chart 3. At the end of last rep, change color to A.
Rows 65–80: With A, rep row 2 of Strip 1. At the end of last rep, change color to C.
Row 81: With C, rep row 2 of Strip 1.
Rows 82–96: With C, rep rows 17–32.

Strip 4

Row 1 (RS): With B, ch 17, sc in 2nd ch from hook, sc in each rem ch across, turn. *(16 sc)*
Rows 2–16: Ch 1, sc in each sc across, changing color as indicated by Chart 2. At the end of last rep, change color to MC.
Rows 17–32: With MC, rep row 2 of Strip 1. At the end of last rep, change color to A,
Row 33: With A, rep row 2 of Strip 1.
Rows 34–48: Ch 1, sc in each sc across, changing color as indicated by Chart 1. At the end of last rep, change color to MC.
Rows 49–64: With MC, rep row 2 of Strip 1.

Continued on page 146

INTERMEDIATE

Finished Size

Blanket: 46 x 55 inches
Pillows: 14 x 14 inches

Materials

- Patons Melody super bulky (super chunky) weight yarn (3½ oz/85 yds/100g per ball):
  7 balls #09742 peacock *(MC)*
  5 balls #09622 sunny yellow *(B)*
  4 balls #09714 mango *(C)*
  3 balls #09712 apple green *(A)*
- Size N/15/10mm crochet hook or size needed to obtain gauge
- Yarn needle
- 14 x 14-inch pillow forms: 2

Maple Leaves Afghan

Design by Katherine Eng

Creatively arranged motifs worked in a pleasing palette of rich, fall colors suggest gently falling leaves on a crisp autumn day.

Gauge
Size G hook: Maple Leaf = 3 x 3½ inches;
Size H hook: Square = 4½ inches square

Pattern Notes
Weave in loose ends as work progresses.
Join rounds with a slip stitch unless otherwise stated.
Make 96 squares.

Special Stitch
Shell: 5 dc in indicated st.

Maple Leaf
Make 24 each gold, cranberry, chestnut heather and loden.
Rnd 1 (RS): With size G hook, ch 4, join in first ch to form a ring, ch 1, (sc, ch 3) 4 times in ring, sc in ring, hdc in beg sc to form last ch sp. *(5 sc; 5 ch sps)*
Rnd 2: Ch 1, sc in same sp as beg ch-1, ch 5, sc in next ch-3 sp, ch 6, sc in next ch-3 sp, ch 7, sc in next ch-3 sp, ch 6, sc in next ch-3 sp, ch 5, join in beg sc. *(5 sc; 5 ch sps)*
Rnd 3: Ch 1, (sc, ch 3, sc, ch 5, sc, ch 3, sc) in ch-5 sp, ({sc, ch 3} twice, sc, ch 5, sc, ch 3, sc) in ch-6 sp, (sc, ch 3, sc, ch 4, sc, ch 6, sc, ch 4, sc, ch 3, sc) in ch-7 sp, (sc, ch 3, sc, ch

5, {sc, ch 3} twice, sc) in ch-6 sp, (sc, ch 3, sc, ch 5, sc, ch 3, sc) in ch-5 sp, join in beg sc, ch 7, leaving a length of yarn, fasten off.

Note: *On rem rnds of Square, use deco on loden and gold leaves; on cranberry and chestnut heather leaves use rococo.*

On rnd 4, pick up 2 lps at back of sc sts, not top back lps of sc.

Rnd 4: Draw up a lp of deco (rococo) in back lps of first sc of rnd 2, [ch 5, sl st in **back lps** (see Stitch Guide) of next sc] 4 times, ch 5, sl st in beg sl st.

Rnd 5: Ch 1, work 6 sc in first ch sp, 7 sc in 2nd ch sp, 6 sc in 3rd ch sp, 7 sc in 4th ch sp, 6 sc in 5th ch sp, join in beg sc. *(32 sc)*

Rnd 6: Ch 3 (counts as first dc), (dc, ch 3, 2 dc) in same sc, *ch 1, sk next 2 sc, sc in next sc, ch 1, sk next sc, sc in next sc, ch 1, sk next 2 sc**, (2 dc, ch 3, 2 dc) in next sc, rep from * around, ending last rep at **, join in 3rd ch of beg ch-3, fasten off. *(4 corner ch-3 sps)*

Placement of Squares

With matching heavy thread, tack down 5 Leaf points.

Arrange Squares from top to bottom, left to right in 8 rows of 12 Squares. Row 1 is [gold, cranberry, loden and chestnut heather] 3 times. Row 2 is [cranberry, loden, chestnut heather and gold] 3 times. Leaves point down and direction of bottom center point alternates right and left with each Square. Alternate rows 1 and 2 for Square placement.

Note: *On rnd 7, use wheat on deco Squares and mushroom on rococo Squares. Start on designated bottom edge, draw up a lp in first ch-1 sp to the left of corner, ch 1, work all around first Square, then join while working rnd 7 on rem. Join on 1 or 2 sides as necessary. To join ch-2 sps, continuing in pattern st, ch 1, drop lp, draw lp under to over through opposite ch-2 sps, ch 1 and continue. To join corner ch-4 sps, ch 2, drop lp, draw lp under to over through opposite ch-4 sp, ch 2 and continue. Where 4 corners meet, ch 2, drop lp, draw lp under to over through opposite ch-4 sp, ch 1, drop lp, sk next ch-4 sp, draw lp under to over through next ch-4 sp, ch 2 and continue.*

Rnd 7: *(Sc, ch 2, sc) in each ch-1 sp across side, sk next dc, (sc, ch 2, sc) in next dc, ch 1, (sc, ch 4, sc) in next ch-3 sp, ch 1, (sc, ch 2, sc) in next dc, rep from * around, join in beg sc, fasten off.

When all Squares are joined, work Border.

Border

Rnd 1 (RS): Draw up a lp of mushroom in any ch-2 sp on either long side edge, ch 1, (sc, ch 2, sc) in each ch-2 sp and in each ch-4 sp on each side of joining seams, working ({sc, ch 3} 3 times, sc) in each of 4 corner ch-4 sps, join last sc to beg sc, fasten off, turn.

Rnd 2: Draw up a lp of rococo in any ch-2 sp on side edge, ch 1, (sc, ch 2, sc) in each ch sp around, join in beg sc, fasten off, turn.

Rnd 3 (RS): Draw up a lp of mushroom in any ch-2 sp on side edge, ch 1, (sc, ch 2, sc) in each ch-2 sp around, working (sc, ch 4, sc) in each center corner ch-2 sp, join in beg sc, fasten off.

Rnd 4: Draw up a lp of loden in 3rd ch-2 sp to the left of any corner ch-4 sp, ch 1, sc in same ch-2 sp, [**shell** (see Special Stitch) in next ch-2 sp, sc in next ch-2 sp] around, working at each corner, shell in next ch-2 sp, (sc, 7 dc) in corner ch-4 sp, sc in next ch-2 sp, join in beg sc.

Finished Size

41½ x 62 inches

Materials

- Lion Brand Wool-Ease medium (worsted) weight yarn:
  6 oz/300 yds/170g #403 mushroom
  4 oz/200 yds/113g #177 loden
  3 oz/150 yds/85g each #179 chestnut heather and #402 wheat
  2 oz/100 yds/57g each #138 cranberry and #171 gold
- Lion Brand Homespun bulky (chunky) weight yarn (6 oz/185 yds/170g per skein):
  2 skeins each #311 rococo and #309 deco
- Sizes G/6/4mm and H/8/5mm crochet hooks or sizes needed to obtain gauge
- Tapestry needle
- Sewing needle
- Heavy thread in matching colors

Rnd 5: Ch 1, sc in first sc, *ch 2, (sc, ch 2, sc) in center dc of next shell, ch 2, sc in next sc, rep from * around, working at each corner, ch 2, sk next 2 dc, (sc, ch 2, sc) in next dc, (sc, ch 3, sc) in next dc, (sc, ch 2, sc) in next dc, ch 2, sk next 2 dc, sc in next sc, join last ch 2 to beg sc, fasten off.
Rnd 6: Draw up a lp of chestnut heather in sc between 2 shells on side edge, ch 1, sc in same sc, *ch 2, sk next ch-2 sp and

next sc, (sc, ch 2, sc) in next ch-2 sp, ch 2, sk next sc and next ch-2 sp, sc in next sc, rep from * around, working at each corner, ch 2, sk next ch-2 sp and next sc, (sc, ch 2, sc) in next ch-2 sp, ch 1, (sc, ch 3, sc) in next ch-3 sp, ch 1, (sc, ch 2, sc) in next ch-2 sp, ch 2, sk next sc and next ch-2 sp, sc in next sc, join last ch 2 to beg sc, fasten off.

With care, block leaves with steam iron. ✂

Wild Lime Cloche
Continued from page 121

Continued from page 121

ch-1, ch 1, sk next ch-1 sp, [sc in next sc, ch 1, sk next ch-1 sp] around, join in beg sc.
Rnd 8: Rep rnd 7.
Rnd 9: Ch 1, sc in same sc as beg ch-1, *ch 1, sk next ch-1 sp, sc in next sc, ch 2, sk next ch-1 sp**, sc in next sc, rep from * around, ending last rep at **, join in beg sc.
Rnd 10: Ch 1, sc in same sc as beg ch-1, *ch 1, sk next ch-1 sp, sc in next sc, ch 2, sk next ch-2 sp**, sc in next sc, rep from * around, ending last rep at **, join in beg sc.
Rnd 11: Ch 1, sc in same sc as beg ch-1, *ch 2, sk next ch-1 sp, sc in next sc, ch 2, sk next ch-2 sp**, sc in next sc, rep from * around, ending last rep at **, join in beg sc.
Rnds 12–21: Ch 1, sc in first sc, ch 2, sk next ch-2 sp, [sc in next sc, ch 2, sk next ch-2 sp] around, join in beg sc. At the end of rnd 21, fasten off.
Rnd 22: With 1 strand of yarn, draw up a lp of C in first sc of previous rnd, ch 1, sc in same sc as beg ch-1, *sk next ch-2 sp, **shell** (see Special Stitch) in next sc, sk next ch-2 sp**, sc in next sc, rep from * around, ending last rep at **, join in beg sc, fasten off.
Rnd 23: Draw up a lp of each A and B in first sc of previous rnd, *ch 2, (sl st, ch 2, sl st) in 3rd dc of next shell, ch 2, sl st in next sc, rep from * around, fasten off.

Tie
With 2 strands of C held tog, leaving 4-inch lengths at beg, ch 120, leaving 4-inch lengths, fasten off.
Weave Tie under and over sc sts of rnd 21 from joining seam around. Tie ends in a bow. Place a wooden bead onto each end of Tie, then draw 3 strands of C each 8 inches in length through end of each Tie. Tie in an overhand knot under bead and trim ends as desired.

Flower
Rnd 1 (RS): With 1 strand of C, ch 6, join in first ch to form a ring, ch 1, 18 sc in ring, join in beg sc. *(18 sc)*
Rnd 2: Ch 6 *(counts as first hdc and ch-4)*, sk 2 sc, [hdc in next sc, ch 4, sk next 2 sc] 5 times, join in 2nd ch of beg ch-6. *(6 ch-4 sps)*
Rnd 3: Ch 1, (sc, hdc, 3 dc, hdc, sc) in each ch-4 sp around, join in beg sc. *(6 petals)*
Rnd 4: Working behind petals, sl st around hdc post of rnd 2, [ch 5, sl st around next hdc post of rnd 2] 6 times. *(6 ch-5 sps)*
Rnd 5: Ch 1, (sc, hdc, 5 dc, hdc, sc) in each ch-5 sp, join in beg sc, fasten off. *(6 petals)*
Position flower slightly above bow, leaving petals free, sew hdc sts of rnd 2 to Cloche. ✂

Neon Bright Winter Warmers

Continued from page 134

Thumb

Row 1: Attach A in first sk dc of rnd 6, ch 1, sc in same dc as beg ch-1, sc in each of next 7 dc, turn. *(8 dc)*

Row 2: Ch 3, dc in each of next 7 sc, turn.

Row 3: Ch 1, sc in each dc across, turn.

Size small only: leaving a length of yarn, fasten off.

Row 4 [sizes medium & large only]: Rep row 2.

Size medium only: leaving a length of yarn, fasten off.

Row 5 [size large only]: Rep row 3, leaving a length of yarn, fasten off.

Weave rem length of yarn through row 3 [4, 5] of Thumb sts, knot to secure, sew Thumb side seam.

Tassel

Make 2.

Cut 2 lengths of each of the 4 colors each 6 inches long. Tie another 6-inch length of A around the center of bundle; tie another length of A ½ inch down from top of Tassel. Trim ends of Tassel to 2½ inches. Tie Tassel to center top of Mitten centered over rnd 5. ✂

Royal Print Tote

Continued from page 137

print in sc at side of Bottom, ch 1, sc in each sc around, do not join rnds, use a st marker to mark rnds. *(60 sc)*

Rnd 2: Sc in each sc around.

Rnd 3: Rep rnd 2.

Rnd 4: Sc around, inc 1 sc at each end of oval curve. *(62 sc)*

Rnds 5–7: Rep rnd 2.

Rnds 8–27: Rep rnds 4–7. *(72 sc)*

Rnd 28: Rep rnd 4, sl st to join in beg sc, fasten off. *(74 sc)*

Border

Note: Mark Sides of tote 37 sts each side to line up with ends of Bottom piece.

Rnd 1 (RS): With size G hook, attach 2 strands of royal in marked sc, ch 1, sc in same sc as beg ch-1, *sk next 2 sc, **shell** (see Special Stitch) in next sc, sk 1 sc**, sc in next sc, rep from * around, ending last rep at **, join in beg sc, fasten off. *(15 shells)*

Note: On each long side edge of Tote, place a marker at center shell each side.

Rnd 2 (RS): Draw up 1 strand each royal and artist print in sc at either side, *ch 3, (sl st, ch 3, sl st) in center dc of next shell, ch 3, sl st in next sc, rep from * around, working at back center shell for button lp, ch 3, (sl st, ch 11, sl st in 2nd ch of ch-11, ch 1, sl st) in center dc of shell, ch 3, sl st in next sc, ending with sl st in same sc as beg ch-3, fasten off.

Sew button opposite button lp on opposite side of Tote.

Insert felt oval into Tote.

Handle

Make 2.

With size H hook, leaving 5-inch lengths at beg, holding 5 strands of royal tog, ch 32, leaving 5-inch ends, fasten off. Position and sew in place with beg and ending strands of yarn on inside of Tote at 2nd shell points from center sc at front and at each 2nd sc from center back. ✂

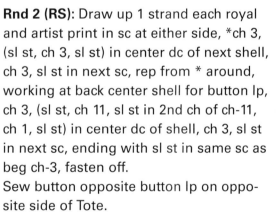

Diagonal Stripes Hat
Continued from page 135

[(sc, ch 3, tr) in next sc] twice, ending with sc in same sc as beg ch-3, change color to C. *(18 tr)*

Rnd 8: (Ch 3, tr) in same st as sc, *(sc, ch 3, tr) in next sc, rep from * 17 times, ending with sc in same st as beg ch-3, change color to D. *(18 tr)*

Rnds 9–19: Rep rnd 8, change color at the end of each rnd in the following sequence, E, [A, B, C, D, E] twice

Rnd 20: Rep rnd 8, fasten off.

Row 21: Now working in rows, fold rnd 20 of Hat flat with 9 tr each side edge, attach A with sl st through first ch-3 sp, working through both thicknesses, ch 1, 2 sc in same ch sp as beg ch-1, 3 sc through each of next 7 ch-3 sps, 2 sc in last ch-3 sp, sl st in same ch sp, fasten off.

Tassel
Make 2.
Wrap each of the 5 yarn colors around 10-inch edge of cardboard 5 times. Insert at separate length of A through top under the strands at top of cardboard and knot tightly. Cut yarn ends at opposite end. Tie a length of D tightly ¾ inch from top tightly around. Trim ends even. Sew Tassel to corner point of Hat.

Hair
Make 13.
With size H hook and 1 strand F, ch 30, 2 sc in 2nd ch from hook, 3 sc in each rem ch across, leaving a length of yarn, fasten off. Sew strands of Hair inside edge of Hat 1 inch apart centering at back. ✄

Black Magic Cardigan
Continued from page 125

off hook, fasten off.

Edging
With size J hook and A, sc around entire Sleeve, leaving a length of yarn, fasten off.

Assembly
Sew shoulder seams. Sew Sleeves into armhole openings, sew sleeve seam.

Sleeve Ribbing
Make 2.
Rnd 1: With size J hook, attach A at sleeve seam, ch 1, work 32 [35, 38, 41, 44] sc evenly sp around, join in beg sc. *(32 [35, 38, 41, 44] sc)*
Rnd 2: Ch 2, [**fpdc** *(see Stitch Guide)* around post of next st, **bpdc** *(see Stitch Guide)* around post of next st] around, join in 2nd ch of beg ch-2.

Rnds 3 & 4: Ch 2, [fpdc around fpdc, bpdc around bpdc] around, join in 2nd ch of beg ch-2. At the end of rnd 4, fasten off.

Finishing
Rnd 1: With size J hook, attach A at center back neck, ch 1, sc in same st as beg ch-1, sc around neck, down front, across bottom, up opposite front and around neck working 3 sc at bottom corners to keep work flat, join in beg sc.
Rnd 2: Ch 1, sc around neck, down front and across bottom working 3 sc in center sc of 3-sc group of previous rnd, sc in next 2 sc {ch 2, sk next 2 sc, sc in next 6 [7, 7, 8, 8] sc} 6 times *(buttonholes)*, sc in each rem sc, join in beg sc, fasten off.

Denim Fur Hat & Scarf

Continued from page 131

Rnds 10–16: Rep rnd 7. At the end of rnd 16, draw up a lp of beige blue print, fasten off dark blue.

Rnds 17–21: Ch 1, sc in each st around. At the end of rnd 21, sl st in next sc, fasten off.

Scarf

Row 1: With dark blue, ch 13, sc in 2nd ch from hook, sc in each rem ch across, turn. *(12 sc)*

Row 2: Ch 1, [sc in next sc, dc in next sc] across, turn.

Rows 3–43: Ch 1, [sc in dc, dc in sc] across, turn.

Row 44: Ch 1, sc in each st across, fasten off. *(12 sc)*

Trim

Row 1: Attach beige blue print in last st of previous row, ch 1, sc in each st across, turn.

Rows 2–25: Ch 1, sc in each sc across, turn. At the end of row 25, fasten off. Working on opposite side of foundation ch of Scarf, rep rows 1–25 of Trim.

Tie

Make 2.

Attach dark blue in first sc of row 44 of Scarf, ch 6, sl st in last sc of row 44, fasten off. Attach dark blue in first ch of row 1, ch 6, sl st in last ch of row 1, fasten off. Pass Trim end of Scarf through either Tie. ✁

Americana Cardigan

Continued from page 130

Row 2: Ch 3, dc in same dc as beg ch-3, dc in each dc across to last dc, 2 dc in last dc, turn. *(50 dc)*

Row 3: Rep row 1.

Row 4: Rep row 2. *(52 dc)*

Row 5: Rep row 1.

Row 6: Rep row 2. *(54 dc)*

Rows 7 & 8: Rep row 1.

[Rep Rows 2–8] 5 times. *(84 dc)*

Rep row 1, fasten off.

Assembly

With tapestry needle, sew shoulder seams, fold Sleeve in half lengthwise and pin center of Sleeve to sewn shoulder seam. Sew Sleeve to body of sweater. Sew Sleeve and side seams.

Border

Rnd 1 (RS): Attach MC in right side sewn seam, ch 1, sc in each st across bottom edge of right front, 3 sc in corner st, 84 sc evenly sp up right front to beg of neck shaping, 62 sc evenly around neck to beg of neck shaping on left front, 84 sc down left front to bottom corner, 3 sc in corner, sc in each st across bottom edge of left front, sc in each st across back, join in beg sc.

Rnd 2 (RS): Ch 1, sc in each sc across bottom edge, 3 sc in center corner st, sc in each of next 3 sc, [ch 2, sk each of next 2 sc, sc in each of next 11 sc] 6 times, ch 2, sk each of next 2 sc, sc in each rem sc to center corner *(7 buttonholes)*, 3 sc in center corner sc, sc in each rem sc around, working 3 sc in each rem center corner sc, join in beg sc.

Rnd 3: Ch 1, sc in each sc around, working 2 sc in each ch-2 sp of each buttonhole, join in beg sc, fasten off. With tapestry needle, sew buttons opposite buttonholes. ✁

Patchwork Blanket & Pillows

Continued from page 139

At the end of last rep, change color to B.
Row 65: With B, rep row 2 of Strip 1.
Rows 66–80: Rep rows 2–16.
Rows 81–96: With MC, rep row 2 of Strip 1. At the end of last rep, fasten off.

Strip 5
Row 1 (RS): With MC, ch 17, sc in 2nd ch from hook, sc in each rem ch across, turn. *(16 sc)*
Rows 2–16: Rep row 2 of Strip 1. At the end of last rep, change color to B.
Row 17: With B, rep row 2 of Strip 1.
Rows 18–32: Ch 1, sc in each sc across, changing color as indicated in Chart 3. At the end of last rep, change to B.
Rows 33–48: With B, rep row 2 of Strip 1. At the end of last rep, change color to C.
Row 49: With C, rep row 2 of Strip 1.
Rows 50–64: Ch 1, sc in each sc

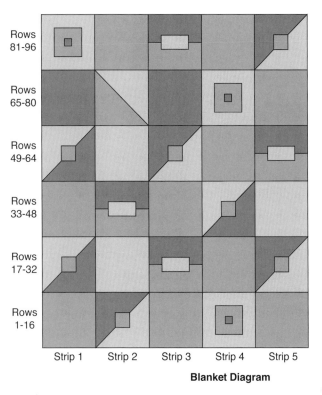

Reverse Single Crochet

across, changing color as indicated in Chart 4. At the end of last rep, change color to MC.
Row 65–80: With MC, rep row 2 of Strip 1. At the end of last rep, change color to B.
Row 81: With B, rep row 2 of Strip 1.
Row 82–96: With B, rep rows 18–32. At the end of last rep, fasten off.
Using diagram as a guide, sew strips tog.

Edging
Rnd 1: Attach MC with a sl st in top right corner, ch 1, sc evenly sp around, working 3 sc in each corner, join in beg sc.
Rnd 2: Ch 1, **reverse sc** *(see illustration at left)* in each sc around, join in beg sc, fasten off.

Pillow A
Front
Row 1 (RS): With B, ch 28, sc in 2nd ch from hook, sc in each rem ch across, turn. *(27 sc)*
Rows 2–30: Ch 1, sc in each sc across changing color as indicated by Chart 6, turn each row. At the end of row 30, fasten off.

Back
Row 1 (RS): With B, ch 28, sc in 2nd ch from hook, sc in each rem ch across, turn. *(27 sc)*
Rows 2–30: Ch 1, sc in each sc across, turn. At the end of row 30, fasten off.

Joining
Holding WS tog, with Front facing and working through both thicknesses, attach C, ch 1, sc in each st around, working 3 sc in each

Chart Numbers	
1	
2	
3	
4	
5	

Blanket Diagram

Rows 81-96 / Rows 65-80 / Rows 49-64 / Rows 33-48 / Rows 17-32 / Rows 1-16

Strip 1 / Strip 2 / Strip 3 / Strip 4 / Strip 5

corner on 3 sides, insert pillow form, continue to sc across 4th side, join in beg sc, fasten off.

Pillow B
Front
Row 1 (RS): With C, ch 31, sc in 2nd ch from hook, sc in each rem ch across, turn. *(30 sc)*

Rows 2–27: Ch 1, sc in each sc across changing color as indicated by Chart 7, turn each row. At the end of row 27, fasten off.

Back
Row 1 (RS): With C, ch 31, sc in 2nd ch from hook, sc in each rem ch across, turn. *(30 sc)*

Rows 2–27: Ch 1, sc in each sc across, turn. At the end of row 27, fasten off.

Joining
Holding WS tog, with Front facing and working through both thicknesses, attach B, ch 1, sc in each st around, working 3 sc in each corner on 3 sides, insert pillow form, continue to sc across 4th side, join in beg sc, fasten off. ✄

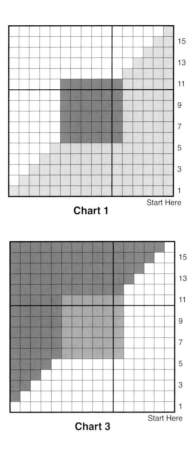

Chart 1

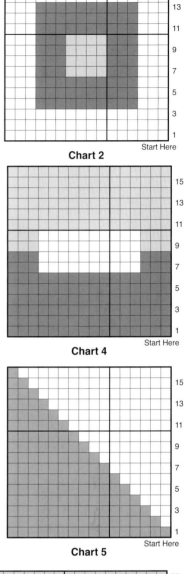

Chart 2

Chart 4

Chart 3

COLOR KEY
- ▨ MC
- ▢ Contrast A
- ☐ Contrast B
- ▦ Contrast C

Chart 5

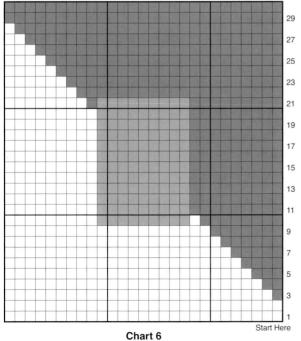

Chart 6

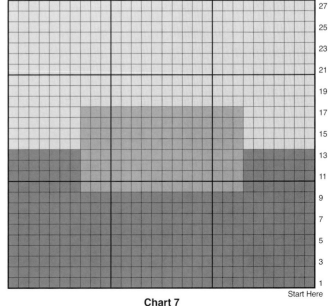

Chart 7

Every Day's a Holiday

Create some crochet magic with all those odds and ends of leftover yarn and thread to add an extra-special touch to festive occasions throughout the year. From Valentine's Day through Christmas, these fun, easy projects make great gifts and decorations for a variety of holidays and seasons and are sure to be enjoyed for years to come!

Design by Ellen Anderson Eaves

Spring Blossoms Afghan

Celebrate spring and the Easter season with this gorgeous afghan blooming with colorful flowers perfect for using virtually any shade of scrap yarn!

Gauge
Rnds 1 and 2 = 2¼ inches; Motif = 5½ inches square

Pattern Notes
Weave in loose ends as work progresses. Join rounds with a slip stitch unless otherwise stated.

Special Stitch
Picot: Ch 3, sl st in top of last st made.

Motif
Make 80.
Rnd 1: With light color, ch 6, dc in 6th ch from hook, (dc, ch 2) 5 times in same ch, join in 4th ch of beg ch-6, fasten off. *(6 dc; 6 ch-2 sps)*

Rnd 2: Attach dark color with sc in any st, 3 sc in next ch sp, [sc in next st, 3 sc in next ch sp] around, sl st to join in **back lp** *(see Stitch Guide)* of beg sc. *(24 sc)*

Rnd 3: Working this rnd in back lps only, ch 3 *(counts as first dc)*, dc in each st around, join in 3rd ch of beg ch-3.

Rnd 4: Attach shade of green with sl st in any dc of rnd 3, ch 8 *(counts as first dtr and ch-3)*, dtr in same st, *ch 1, tr in next st, ch 1, [dc in next st, ch 1] 3 times, tr in next st, ch 1** (dtr, ch 3, dtr) in next st, rep from * around, ending last rep at **, join in 5th ch of beg ch-8, fasten off. *(28 ch sps; 28 sts)*

Rnd 5: Attach white with sl st in any corner ch-3 sp, ch 3, (dc, ch 2, 2 dc) in same sp, dc in each st and in each ch-1 sp around with (2 dc, ch 2, 2 dc) in each corner ch-3 sp, join in 3rd ch of beg ch-3. *(17 dc on each side between corner ch sps)*

Rnd 6: Working this rnd in **front lps** *(see Stitch Guide)* only of rnd 2, attach flower color with sl st in any st, ch 3, (dc, **picot–** *see Special Stitch*, dc) in same st, sk next st, *(2 dc, picot, dc) in next st, sk next st, rep from * around, join in 3rd ch of beg ch-3, fasten off.

Assembly
Holding Motifs RS tog, matching sts, working through both thicknesses in front lps only, sc motifs tog in 8 rows of 10 Motifs each.

Border
Rnd 1: Working around outer edge in back lps only, attach white with sl st in first ch of

Continued on page 166

INTERMEDIATE

Finished Size
48½ x 59½ inches

Materials
- Red Heart Super
  Saver medium
  (worsted)
  weight yarn:
  28 oz/1400 yds/794g
    #311 white
  11 oz/550 yds/312g
    of assorted
    shades of green
  10 oz/500 yds/283.5g
    of assorted flower
    colors and dark
    colors
  3 oz/150 yds/85g
    of assorted
    light colors
- Size H/8/5mm
  crochet hook or
  size needed to
  obtain gauge
- Tapestry needle

Design by Michele Wilcox

Bee My Valentine

Pretty valentine cards are always appreciated, but how about giving a personal, handwritten note attached to this cute little guy to make a really memorable impression?

◼◻◻◻
BEGINNER

Finished Size
6 inches long

Materials
- Medium (worsted) weight yarn: 1 oz/50 yds/28.35g each yellow and black 18 yds off-white
- Size F/5/3.75mm crochet hook or size needed to obtain gauge
- Tapestry needle
- Stitch marker
- 18mm red heart-shaped button
- Fiberfill

Gauge
4 sc = 1 inch; 4 sc rnds = 1 inch

Pattern Notes
Weave in loose ends as work progresses.
Do not join rounds unless otherwise stated, use stitch marker to mark rounds.

Head
Rnd 1 (RS): With yellow, ch 2, 6 sc in 2nd ch from hook, place st marker at end of rnd, move marker as work progresses. *(6 sc)*
Rnd 2: 2 sc in each sc around. *(12 sc)*
Rnd 3: Sc in each sc around.

Continued on page 168

Bonny Belle Bunny

Design by Sue Childress

Pretty as a picture and dressed up in her spring finery, this little bunny is sure to be the cutest accessory to decorate a special little girl's Easter basket.

Gauge
6 dc sts = 1 inch
Check gauge to save time.

Pattern Notes
Weave in loose ends as work progresses. Join rounds with a slip stitch unless otherwise stated.

Work in **back loop** (see Stitch Guide) of stitches on each row or round unless otherwise stated.

Dress
Row 1 (RS): Beg at neck edge, with pink, ch 20, sc in 2nd ch from hook, [2 sc in next ch, sc in next ch] across, turn. (28 sc)

Row 2: Ch 2 (counts as first hdc throughout), hdc in each of next 4 sts, ch 4, sk next 4 sts (armhole opening), hdc in each of next 10 sts, ch 4, sk next 4 sts (armhole opening), hdc in each of next 5 sts, turn.

Row 3: Ch 2, hdc in each st and each ch across, turn. (28 hdc)

Row 4: Ch 2, [hdc in next st, 2 hdc in next st] 12 times, hdc in each of next 2 sts, turn. (40 hdc)

Continued on page 167

Pastel Beaded Jar Covers

Designs by **Dot Drake**

These pretty, fresh-as-spring covers stitched in size 10 crochet cotton and embellished with colorful beads make a great presentation for jars filled with homemade goodies.

Lavender Cover

Pattern Notes
Weave in loose ends as work progresses. Join rounds with a slip stitch unless otherwise stated.

Special Stitch
Picot: Ch 3, sl st in 3rd ch from hook.

Cover
Rnd 1 (WS): String beads onto lavender thread, push beads back along thread until needed, ch 5 *(counts as first tr, ch 1)*, tr in 5th ch from hook, ch 1, (tr, ch 1)10 times in same ch as last tr, join in 4th ch of beg ch-5. *(12 ch-1 sps)*

Rnd 2: Ch 1, sc in first ch sp, [ch 4, sc in next ch sp] around, ch 1, dc in beg sc to form last ch-4 sp.

Rnd 3: Ch 1, sc in joining ch sp, **picot** *(see Special Stitch)*, [ch 5, sc in next ch sp, picot] around, ending with ch 2, dc in beg sc.

Rnd 4: Ch 1, sc in joining ch sp, [ch 5, sc in next ch sp] around, ch 5, join in beg sc.

Rnd 5: Sl st into next ch sp, ch 5 *(counts as*

first dc and ch-2), (dc, ch 2) twice in same ch sp as beg ch-5, (dc, ch 2) 3 times in each ch sp around, join in 3rd ch of beg ch-5. *(36 ch sps)*

Rnd 6: Ch 1, sc in first ch sp, [ch 5, sc in next ch sp] around, ch 2, dc in beg sc.

Rnd 7: Ch 1, sc in joining ch sp, picot, [ch 5, sc in next ch sp, picot] around, ch 2, dc in beg sc.

Rnd 8: Ch 1, sc in joining ch sp, ch 5, [sc in next ch sp, ch 5] around, join in beg sc.

Rnd 9: Ch 1, 5 sc in each ch sp around, join in beg sc. *(180 sc)*

Rnd 10: Sl st in next st, ch 1, sc in next st, picot, [ch 5, sc in center st of next 5-sc group, picot] around, ch 2, dc in beg sc.

Rnd 11: Ch 1, sc in joining ch sp, picot, [ch 5, sc in next ch sp, picot] around, ch 2, tr in beg sc.

Rnd 12: Ch 1, sc in joining ch sp, picot, [ch 6, sc in next ch sp, picot] around, ch 3, tr in beg sc.

Rnd 13: Ch 1, sc in joining ch sp, picot, ch 4, draw up 1 bead, ch 4, [sc in next ch sp, picot, ch 4, draw up 1 bead, ch 4] around, join in beg sc, fasten off.

Leaf
Make 2.

With light green, ch 15, hdc in 5th ch from hook, ch 2, sk next ch, dc in next ch, ch 2, sk next ch, tr in next ch, ch 2, sk next ch, dc in next ch, ch 2, sk next ch, hdc in next ch, ch 2, sk next ch, sl st in last ch, working on opposite side of foundation ch, ch 1, 2 sc in next ch sp, [sc in next ch, 2 sc in next ch sp] 4 times, sc in next ch, 5 sc in ch sp at end for tip, [sc in next st, 2 sc in next ch sp] 5 times, join in beg sc, fasten off.

Rose
Rnd 1: With light pink, ch 6, dc in 6th ch from hook, ch 2, (dc, ch 2) 3 times in same ch as last st, sl st to join in 4th ch of beg ch-6. *(5 ch sps)*

Rnd 2: Ch 1, (sc, hdc, 2 dc, hdc, sc) in each ch sp around, join in beg sc. *(5 petals)*

Rnd 3: Working behind petals, ch 3, [sc in next st on rnd 1, ch 3] around, join in first ch of beg ch-3.

Rnd 4: Ch 1, (sc, hdc, 4 dc, hdc, sc) in each ch sp around, join in beg sc. *(5 petals)*

Rnd 5: Working behind petals, ch 4, [sc in next st on rnd 3, ch 4] around, join in first ch of beg ch-4.

Rnd 6: Ch 1, (sc, hdc, 6 dc, hdc, sc) in each ch sp around, join in beg sc, fasten off.

Center and sew Leaves and Rose to rnd 1 of Cover.

Cord

With light green, ch 2, sc in 2nd ch from hook, turn last st made to left so that back of the sc is facing, sc in strand on left side of st, *turn last st made to left, sc in parallel strands on left side of st, rep from * until cord is 21 inches long, fasten off.

Weave Cord in and out of sps on rnd 10 or any rnd to fit top of jar.

EASY

Finished Size

Cover is 7½ inches across

Materials

- Size 10 crochet cotton:
  50 yds lavender
  25 yds each
    light pink and
    light green
- Size 8/1.50mm steel crochet hook or size needed to obtain gauge
- 9mm pink beads: 36

Finished Size

Cover is 7½ inches
across

Materials

- Size 10 crochet
  cotton:
  50 yds yellow
  25 yds each pink
    and green
  15 yds each five
    desired flower
    colors
- Size 8/1.50mm
  steel crochet hook
  or size needed to
  obtain gauge
- Embroidery needle
- 9mm clear beads: 65

Yellow Cover

Pattern Notes

Weave in loose ends as work progresses.
Join rounds with a slip stitch unless otherwise stated.

Cover

Rnd 1: String 60 beads onto yellow thread, push beads back along thread until needed, ch 6, join in first ch to form a ring, ch 1, 15 sc in ring, join in beg sc. *(15 sc)*

Rnd 2: Ch 4 *(counts as first dc, ch 1)*, [dc in next st, ch 1] around, join in 3rd ch of beg ch-4.

Rnds 3 & 4: Ch 6 *(counts as first dc, ch 3 throughout)*, dc same st as ch-6 and next st tog, [ch 3, **dc dec** *(see Stitch Guide)* in same st as last st made and next st] 13 times, ch 3, dc in same st as last st made, join in 3rd ch of beg ch-6.

Rnd 5: Ch 1, sc in first st, (2 sc, ch 2, 2 sc) in next ch-3 sp, sc in each st around with (2 sc, ch 2, 2 sc) in each ch-3 sp, join with sl st in first sc.

Rnd 6: (Ch 6, dc) in first st, ch 2, sk next 4 sts and ch sp, *(dc, ch 3, dc) in next st, ch 2, sk next 4 sts and ch sp, rep from * around, join in 3rd ch of beg ch-6.

Rnds 7 & 8: (Ch 6, dc) in first st, sk ch sps, (dc, ch 3, dc) in each st around, join in 3rd ch of beg ch-6.

Rnd 9: Ch 1, sc in first st, 4 sc in next ch sp, sk next st, [sc in next st, 4 sc in next ch sp, sk next st] around, join in beg sc.

Rnd 10: (Ch 6, dc) in first st, ch 2, sk next 4 sts, *(dc, ch 3, dc) in next st, ch 2, sk next 4 sts, rep from * around, join in 3rd ch of beg ch-6.

Rnd 11: (Ch 6, dc) in first st, sk ch sps, (dc, ch 3, dc) in each st around, join in 3rd ch of beg ch-6.

Rnd 12: Ch 1, sc in first ch sp, [ch 5, sc in next ch sp] around, ch 2, dc in beg sc.

Rnd 13: Ch 1, sc in joining ch sp, ch 4, push up 1 bead, ch 4, [sc in next ch sp, ch 4, push up 1 bead, ch 4] around, join in beg sc, fasten off.

Leaf
Make 3.

With green, ch 13, sc in 2nd ch from hook, hdc in next ch, dc in each of next 2 chs, tr in each of next 6 chs, dc in next ch (hdc, 3 sc, hdc) in last ch, working on opposite side of foundation ch, hdc in next ch, dc in next ch, tr in each of next 6 chs, dc in each of next 2 chs, hdc in last ch, join in beg sc, fasten off.

Flower
Make 5.

With flower color, [ch 4, 2 dc in 4th ch from hook, ch 3, sl st in same ch as last st] 5 times, fasten off.
Sew 1 bead to the center of each Flower. Center and sew Leaves and 3 Flowers to rnds 1–3 of Cover.

Cord

With pink, rep Lavender Cord until piece is 22 inches long.
Weave Cord in and out of sps on rnd 9 or any rnd to fit over top of jar. Sew 1 Flower to each end of cord.

White Cover

Pattern Notes
Weave in loose ends as work progresses.
Join rounds with a slip stitch unless otherwise stated.

Special Stitch

Picot: Ch 3, sl st in top of last st made.

Cover

Rnd 1: With white, ch 7, join in first ch to form a ring, ch 1, 18 sc in ring, join in beg sc. *(18 sc)*

Rnd 2: Working this rnd in **front lps** *(see Stitch Guide)*, ch 1, sc in first st, **picot** *(see Special Stitch)*, sc in next st, [sc in next st, picot, sc in next st] around, join with sl st in **back lp** *(see Stitch Guide)* of first st of rnd 1.

Rnd 3: Working this rnd in back lps of rnd 1, ch 1, (sc, ch 12, sc) in first st, sc in each of next 2 sts, *(sc, ch 12, sc) in next st, sc in each of next 2 sts, rep from * around, join in beg sc. *(6 ch sps)*

Rnd 4: Ch 1, (6 sc, 2 hdc, 7 dc, 2 hdc, 6 sc) in first ch sp, sk next st, sc in each of next 2 sts, *sk next st, (6 sc, 2 hdc, 7 dc, 2 hdc, 6 sc) in next ch sp, sk next st, sc in each of next 2 sts, rep from * around, join in beg sc, fasten off.

Rnd 5: Sk first 6 sts, attach pink with sc in next st, sc in each of next 5 sts, picot, sc in each of next 5 sts, [ch 2, sk next 14 sts, sc in each of next 6 sts, picot, sc in each of next 5 sts] around to last 8 sts, sk last 8 sts, join in beg sc, fasten off.

Rnd 6: Attach white with sc in any ch-2 sp, 2 sc in same ch sp as joining sc, ch 4, sk next 3 sts, sc in next st, ch 7, sk next 4 sts and picot, sc in next st, ch 4, sk next 2 sts, [3 sc in next ch sp, ch 4, sk next 3 sts, sc in next st, ch 7, sk next 4 sts and picot, sc in next st, ch 4, sk next 2 sts] around, ch 1, dc in beg sc to form last ch sp.

Rnd 7: Ch 1, sc in joining ch sp, ch 5, sc in next ch sp, ch 5, (sc, ch 5, sc) in next ch sp, *ch 5, [sc in next ch sp, ch 5] twice, (sc, ch 5, sc) in next ch sp, rep from * around, ch 12, dc in beg sc.

Rnd 8: Ch 1, sc in joining ch sp, picot, [ch 5, sc in next ch sp, picot] around, ch 2, dc in beg sc.

Rnd 9: Ch 1, sc in joining ch sp, ch 6, [sc in next ch sp, ch 6] around, join in beg sc, fasten off.

Rnd 10: Attach pink with sc in any ch sp, 6 sc in same ch sp as joining sc, 7 sc in each ch sp around, join in beg sc, fasten off.

Rnd 11: String 42 beads onto white thread, push beads back along thread until needed, attach white with sl st in first st, ch 4, sk next st, dc in next st, ch 1, sk next st, [dc in next st, ch 1, sk next st] around, join with sl st in 3rd ch of beg ch-4.

Rnd 12: Ch 1, sc in first ch sp, [ch 5, sk next ch sp, sc in next ch sp] around to last ch sp, ch 2, sk last ch sp, dc in beg sc to form last ch sp.

Rnd 13: Ch 1, sc in joining ch sp, picot, [ch 5, sc in next ch sp, picot] around, ch 2, dc in beg sc.

Rnd 14: Ch 1, sc in joining ch sp, ch 4, push up 1 bead, ch 4, [sc in next ch sp, ch 4, push up 1 bead, ch 4] around, join in beg sc, fasten off.

Cord

String 2 beads onto green thread, push beads along thread until needed, ch 2, push up 1 bead, sc in 2nd ch from hook, turn last st made to left so that back of the sc is facing, sc in strand on left side of st, *turn last st made to left, sc in parallel strands on left side of st, rep from * for 22 inches, push up 1 bead, ch 1, fasten off. Weave Cord in and out of sps on rnd 10 or any rnd to fit top of jar. ✂

Finished Size

Cover is 7½ inches across

Materials

- Size 10 crochet cotton:
  50 yds white
  25 yds each pink and green
- Size 8/1.50mm steel crochet hook or size needed to obtain gauge
- 9mm clear pony beads: 44

Design by Katherine Eng

Fireworks Tote

Triple strands of navy, burgundy and royal blue worked together as one create both a rich tweed effect and extra durability in this classy tote stitched in Americana shades.

BEGINNER

Finished Size
12 x 14 inches

Materials
- Red Heart Fiesta medium (worsted) weight yarn (6 oz/316 yds/170g per skein):
  1 skein #6915 burgundy (A)
- Red Heart Super Saver medium (worsted) weight yarn (8 oz/425 yds/226g per skein):
  1 skein each #387 soft navy (B), #385 royal (C) and #376 burgundy (D)
- Size H/8/5mm crochet hook or size needed to obtain gauge
- Tapestry needle
- 1⅛-inch burgundy button

Gauge
Rows 1–3 = 1¾ inches; 4 sc = 1½ inches

Pattern Notes
Weave in loose ends as work progresses. Join rounds with a slip stitch unless otherwise stated.

Continued on page 169

Halloween Garland

This versatile little garland will add a fun, festive touch to your Halloween party or dress up your door in whimsical style to delight trick-or-treaters of all ages!

Gauge
7 sc = 2 inches; 7 sc rows = 2 inches

Pattern Notes
Weave in loose ends as work progresses. Join rounds with a slip stitch unless otherwise stated.

Garland
Row 1: With black, ch 220, sc in 11th ch from hook, sc in each rem ch across, ch 10, sl st in last sc, fasten off. *(210 sc; 2 ch-10 lps)*
Row 2: Working in opposite side of foundation ch of row 1, sk first ch-10 lp, attach orange with sc in next ch, sc in each ch across, leaving last ch-10 lp unworked, fasten off.

Pumpkin
Make 4.
Rnd 1: With orange, ch 2, 6 sc in 2nd ch from hook, join in beg sc. *(6 sc)*
Rnd 2: Ch 1, 2 sc in each sc around, join in beg sc. *(12 sc)*
Rnd 3: Ch 1, sc in first sc, 2 sc in next sc, [sc in next sc, 2 sc in next sc] around, join in beg sc. *(18 sc)*

Continued on page 173

Wine Bottle Cover

Design by Katherine Eng

For a great holiday gift, wrap a special bottle of wine in this festive cover worked in vintage shades of cranberry and mistletoe accented with sparkling gold highlights.

BEGINNER

Finished Size

Fits 12-inch wine bottle

Materials

- Caron Victorian medium (worsted) weight yarn:
  2½ oz/125 yds/71g #1950 cranberry
  5 yds #1953 mistletoe ombre
- Size H/8/5mm crochet hook or size needed to obtain gauge
- Tapestry needle
- 2 red pony beads

Gauge

Rnds 1–4 = 3¼ inches
Check gauge to save time.

Pattern Notes

Weave in loose ends as work progresses.
Join rounds with a slip stitch unless otherwise stated.

Special Stitch

Shell: 3 dc in indicated st.

Cover

Rnd 1 (RS): With cranberry, ch 4, join in first ch to form a ring, ch 1, 8 sc in ring, join in beg sc. *(8 sc)*

Rnd 2: Ch 1, 2 sc in each sc around, join in beg sc. *(16 sc)*

Rnd 3: Ch 1, [sc in next sc, 2 sc in next sc] around, join in beg sc. *(24 sc)*

Rnd 4: Ch 1, [sc in each of next 2 sc, 2 sc in next sc] around, join in beg sc. *(32 sc)*

Rnd 5: Ch 1, sc in each sc around, join in beg sc.

Rnd 6: Ch 1, [sc in each of next 7 sc, 2 sc in next sc] 4 times, join in beg sc. *(36 sc)*

Continued on page 170

Yuletide Trivets

Design by Katherine Eng

Dress up your holiday table with decorative mats stitched in gold-accented Victorian Christmas colors. Combine them with our Wine Bottle Cover on page 160 for an extra-special gift set!

■□□□
BEGINNER

Finished Size
Bell: 10 x 10½ inches
Star: 7½ inches

Materials
- Caron Victorian medium (worsted) weight yarn (1¾ oz/103 yds/50g per skein):
  1 skein each #1950 cranberry and #1953 mistletoe ombre
- Size H/8/5mm crochet hook or size needed to obtain gauge
- Tapestry needle

Gauge
Rows 1–3 = 1½ inches; 3 sc = 1 inch

Pattern Notes
Weave in loose ends as work progresses. Join rounds with a slip stitch unless otherwise stated.

Special Stitch
Shell: 5 dc in indicated st.

Bell
Row 1: With 1 strand each cranberry and mistletoe ombre held tog, ch 19, working in **back lp** (hump) of ch, sc in 2nd ch from hook, sc in each rem ch across, turn. (18 sc)
Row 2: Ch 1, sc in each sc across, turn.
Row 3: Ch 1, **sc dec** (see Stitch Guide) in next 2 sc, sc in each sc across to last 2 sc,

Continued on page 170

Evergreen Stocking

Stitched in a beautiful blend of pine forest hues, this unusual and eye-catching Christmas stocking will add a festive touch of greenery to your holiday decor.

Gauge

Size G hook: 14 sc = 4 inches; 15 sc rows worked in Body pattern = 4 inches
Size 2 steel hook: Bell is 1½ inches long; 3 sc rnds = ½ inch

Pattern Notes

Weave in loose ends as work progresses. Join rounds with a slip stitch unless otherwise stated.

Stocking

Cuff

Row 1: With size G hook and olive, ch 44, sc in 2nd ch from hook, sc in each rem ch across, turn. *(43 sc)*
Row 2: Ch 3 *(counts as first dc throughout)*, dc in each st across, turn.
Row 3: Ch 1, sc in each st across, turn.
Rows 4–11: Rep rows 2 and 3.
Row 12: Sl st in first st, [ch 1, sl st in next st] across, fasten off.

Body

Row 1: With size G hook and with front of row 1 on Cuff facing, working on opposite side of foundation ch, attach olive with sc in first ch, sc in each ch across, **change color** *(see Stitch Guide)* to rich sage green in last st, turn. *(43 sc)*
Row 2: Ch 1, sc in each st across, turn.
Row 3: Rep row 2, at end of row change color to olive.
Row 4: Ch 1, sc in first st **bphdc** *(see Stitch Guide)* around next st on row below last, [sc in each of next 3 sts on last row, bphdc around next st on row before last] across to last st on last row, sc in last st, turn.
Row 5: Ch 1, sc in each st across, change color to rich sage green, turn.
Rows 6 & 7: Rep rows 2 and 3.
Row 8: Ch 1, sc in next 3 sts, [bphdc around next st on row before last, sc in each of next 3 sts] across, turn.
Row 9: Rep row 5.
Rows 10–37: Rep rows 2–9 consecutively, ending with row 5. At the end of row 37, fasten off both colors.
For center back seam, sew ends of rows on Cuff and Body tog. Fold Cuff down over Body.

Heel

Row 1: Sk first 33 sts of last row on Body, attach rich sage green with sc in next st, sc in each of next 19 sts, sk center back seam

and next st of Body tog, sc in each of next 21 sts, sc next st of Body and first st on Heel tog, sc in each of last 9 sts of Heel, turn. *(41 sc)*

Row 2: Ch 1, sc in each st across, change color to olive in last st, turn.

Row 3: Ch 1, sc in each of first 22 sc, **fphdc** *(see Stitch Guide)* around next st on row before last, [sc in each of next 3 sts on last row, fphdc around next st on row before last] across to last 2 sts on last row, sc in each of last 2 sts, turn.

Row 4: Ch 1, sc in each st across, change color to rich sage green in last st, turn.

Rows 5 & 6: Ch 1, sc in each st across, turn. At the end of last row, change color to olive, turn.

Row 7: Ch 1, sc in each of first 4 sts, [fphdc around next st on row before last, sc in each of next 3 sts on last row] across to last st, sc in last st, turn.

Row 8: Ch 1, sc in each st across, change color to rich sage green in last st, turn.

Rows 9 & 10: Ch 1, sc in each st across, turn. At the end of last row, change color to olive in last st, turn.

Rows 11–20: Rep rows 3–10 consecutively, ending with row 4. At the end of last row, fasten off both colors.

Sew ends of rows tog.

Toe

Rnd 1 (RS): Now working in rnds, attach rich sage green with sc in first st, sc in each st around to last 2 sts, **sc dec** *(see Stitch Guide)* in next 2 sts, join in beg sc, turn. *(40 sc)*

Continued on page 172

Finished Size

20 inches long

Materials

- Patons Décor medium (worsted) weight yarn (3½ oz/210 yds/100g per ball): 1 ball each #01608 olive and #01637 rich sage green
- Size 3 pearl cotton: 32 yds green 16 yds each silver and red
- Size 2/2.20mm steel crochet hook or size needed to obtain gauge
- Size G/6/4mm crochet hook or size needed to obtain gauge
- Tapestry needle
- Stitch marker

and leaving rem sts unworked, turn. *(20 sc)*

Row 2: Ch 1, sc in each of first 13 sts leaving rem sts unworked, turn.

Row 3: Ch 1, sc in each first 6 sts leaving rem sts unworked, turn. *(6 sc)*

Rows 4–17: Ch 1, sc in each st across, sc in next unworked st, turn. At the end of last row, fasten off. *(20 sc at end of row 17)*

Sole

Row 1: With RS facing, attach rich sage green with sc in 11th st of last row of Heel, sc in each of next 8 sts, sc last st of Heel

Design by Patricia Hall

Christmas Rose Ornament

With small amounts of medium weight yarn, sparkling glitter, a plastic foam ball and a little bit of glue, you can create this glittering wild rose ornament in less than an hour!

●□□□
BEGINNER

Finished Size
3¼ inches in diameter, plus Flower and Leaves

Materials
- Plastic canvas medium (worsted) weight yarn (10 yds per skein):
  3 skeins blue or desired color
  2 skeins pink
  1 skein white
- Sizes D/3/3.25mm and G/6/4mm crochet hooks or sizes needed to obtain gauge
- Tapestry needle
- 2½-inch plastic foam ball
- Gold glitter
- Crystal glitter
- Fabric glue
- Hot-glue gun
- Stitch marker

Gauge
Size G hook: 4 sc = 1 inch
Size D hook: Flower = 2¾ inches in diameter

Pattern Notes
Weave in loose ends as work progresses.
Join rounds with a slip stitch unless otherwise stated.

Ball
Rnd 1 (RS): With size G hook and blue or desired color, ch 2, 5 sc in 2nd ch from hook, do not join rnds, use st marker to mark rnds. *(5 sc)*

Rnd 2: [2 sc in next sc] 5 times. *(10 sc)*

Rnd 3: [Sc in next sc, 2 sc in next sc] 5 times. *(15 sc)*

Rnd 4: [Sc in each of next 2 sc, 2 sc in next sc] 5 times. *(20 sc)*

Rnd 5: [Sc in each of next 3 sc, 2 sc in next sc] 5 times. *(25 sc)*

Rnd 6: [Sc in each of next 4 sc, 2 sc in next sc] 5 times. *(30 sc)*

Rnds 7–12: Sc in each st around. At the end of rnd 12, insert plastic foam ball.

Rnd 13: [**Sc dec** *(see Stitch Guide)* in next 2 sc, sc in each of next 4 sc] 5 times. *(25 sc)*

Rnd 14: [Sc dec in next 2 sc, sc in each of next 3 sc] 5 times. *(20 sc)*

Rnd 15: [Sc dec in next 2 sc, sc in each of next 2 sc] 5 times. *(15 sc)*

Continued on page 171

Santa Purse

Design by Michele Wilcox

Your favorite little girl will love this whimsical holiday purse stitched in medium weight yarn and sized just right to carry her gift list for a visit with Santa!

Gauge

4 sc = 1 inch; 4 sc rows = 1 inch

Pattern Notes

Weave in loose ends as work progresses. Join rounds with a slip stitch unless otherwise stated.

Purse Front

Row 1 (WS): With cream, ch 26, sc in 2nd ch from hook, sc in each rem ch across, turn. *(25 sc)*

Row 2: Ch 1, sc in each sc across, turn.

Rows 3–14: Rep row 2. At the end of row 14, fasten off.

Row 15: Draw up a lp of white, ch 1, sc in same st as beg ch-1, [dc in next sc, sc in next sc] across, turn.

Row 16: Ch 1, dc in first sc, [sc in next dc, dc in next sc] across, turn.

Row 17: Ch 1, sc in first dc, [dc in next sc, sc in next dc] across, turn.

Row 18: Rep row 16, fasten off.

Row 19: Draw up a lp of red, ch 1, sc in each st across, turn.

Rows 20–32: Rep row 2. At the end of row 32, fasten off.

Facial Features

Sew blue buttons between rows 9 and 10 for **eyes**, leaving 5 sc sts between buttons at center. With a length of red, embroider mouth centered below eyes over rows 5 and 6.

■□□□
BEGINNER

Finished Size

6½ x 7½, excluding beard and Shoulder Strap

Materials

- TLC Cotton Plus medium (worsted) weight yarn (3.5 oz/186 yds/100g per skein): 1 skein each #3907 red, #3100 cream and #3001 white
- Size G/6/4mm crochet hook or size needed to obtain gauge
- Tapestry needle
- 12mm blue buttons: 2
- Red crayon
- 3-inch piece of cardboard

With red crayon, color cheeks.

Purse Back

Row 1 (WS): With red, ch 26, sc in 2nd ch from hook, sc in each rem ch across, turn. *(25 sc)*

Row 2: Ch 1, sc in each sc across, turn.

Rows 3–32: Rep row 2.

Row 33: Ch 1, **sc dec** *(see Stitch Guide)* in next 2 sc, sc in each sc across to last 2 sc, sc dec in next 22 sc, turn. *(23 sc)*

Row 34: Ch 1, working in **back lps** *(see Stitch Guide)* for this row only, sc in each of next 21 sts, sc dec in next 2 sts, turn. *(22 sc)*

Row 35: Ch 1, sc dec in next 2 sc, sc in each rem sc across, turn. *(21 sc)*

Row 36: Ch 1, sc in each sc across to last 2 sc, sc dec in next 2 sc, turn. *(20 sc)*

Rows 37–54: Rep rows 35 and 36. At the end of row 54, fasten off. *(2 sc)*

Joining

Rnd 1: Holding Front and Back Purse pieces WS tog and with Front facing, attach red in side edge of row 33 of Back *(dec edge)*, ch 1, sc in same row as beg ch-1, sc in each row across dec edge to point of hat, work 3 sc in row 54, sc in each row of Back through row 33, working through both thicknesses, sc in each row **change color** *(see Stitch Guide)* to white after last red row, work 6 sc across white section, continue with white, start **beard**, [sc in next row, ch 5, 3 sc in 2nd ch from hook, 3 sc in each of next 3 chs, sc in each of next 2 rows] 18 times, working 3 sc in each bottom corner of Purse, sc across white section of hat, change to red, sc in each rem row, join in beg sc, fasten off.

Pompom

Wrap white yarn 80 times around cardboard. Pass a length of white under the strands and knot around bundle of strands, cut opposite ends, fluff, trim ends to shape Pompom. Sew Pompom to point of hat.

Shoulder Strap

Row 1: With red, ch 131, dc in 4th ch from hook, dc in each rem ch across.

Row 2: Fold row 1 in half, insert hook in first dc and opposite side of foundation ch and complete a sl st, [insert hook in next dc and next ch of foundation ch and complete a sl st] across, fasten off.
Sew handle to each side of Purse. ✂

Spring Blossoms Afghan

Continued from page 150

corner ch sp before one short end, ch 3, dc in same ch, ch 2, 2 dc in next ch, [dc in each st, in each of 2 chs on each side of seams and in each seam across to next corner ch-2 sp, 2 dc in next ch, ch 2, 2 dc in next ch] 3 times, dc in each st, in each of 2 chs on each side of seams and in each seam across, join in 3rd ch of beg ch-3. *(175 dc each short edge between corner ch sps; 219 dc each long edge between corner ch sps)*

Rnd 2: Sl st in next st, sl st in next ch sp, ch 4 *(counts as first dc and ch-1)*, (dc, ch 1, dc) in same sp, *[ch 1, sk next st, {dc in next st, ch 1, sk next st} across] to next corner ch sp, ({dc, ch 1} twice, dc) in next corner ch sp, rep from * twice, rep between [ ], join in 3rd ch of beg ch-4.

Rnd 3: Ch 3, (dc, picot, dc) in same st, (2 dc, picot, dc) in each st around, join in 3rd ch of beg ch-3, fasten off. ✂

Bonny Belle Bunny
Continued from page 153

Rnd 5 (RS): Now working in rnds, ch 3 *(counts as first dc throughout)*, dc in each st across, join in 3rd ch of beg ch-3. *(40 dc)*

Rnd 6: Ch 3, dc in same st as beg ch-3, 2 dc in each dc around, join in 3rd ch of beg ch-3. *(80 dc)*

Rnd 7: Working in both lps of sts, [ch 2, sk 1 dc, sc in next dc] around, sl st in same st as beg ch-2. *(20 ch-2 sps)*

Rnd 8: Ch 1, 3 sc in each ch-2 sp around, join in beg sc. *(60 sc)*

Rnd 9: Working in both lps of sts, ch 1, sc in same sc as beg ch-1, ch 2, sk 1 sc, [sc in next sc, ch 2, sk 1 sc] around, join in beg sc. *(30 ch-2 sps)*

Rnd 10: Sl st into ch-2 sp, ch 2, dc in same ch-2 sp, 2 dc in each ch-2 sp around, join in 3rd ch of beg ch-3. *(60 dc)*

Rnd 11: Working in back lps, ch 3, dc in each st around, join in 3rd ch of beg ch-3.

Rnd 12: Rep rnd 11.

Rnds 13–24: Rep rnds 7–12. At the end of rnd 24, fasten off.

Rnd 25: Attach white in joining st, rep rnd 7.

Rnd 26: Ch 1, [sc in next ch-2 sp, 5 dc in next ch-2 sp] around, join in beg sc.

Rnd 27: Ch 1, sc in same st as beg ch-1, ch 2, [sc in next st, ch 2] around, join in beg sc, fasten off.

Sleeve
Make 2.

Rnd 1: Attach pink at center under-arm, [ch 2, sc in next st] 12 times evenly around armhole opening, join in base of beg ch-2. *(12 ch-2 sps)*

Rnd 2: Sl st into ch-2 sp, ch 3, dc in same ch-2 sp, 2 dc in each ch-2 sp around, join in 3rd ch of beg ch-3. *(24 dc)*

Rnd 3: [Ch 2, sc in next dc] around, join in same st as beg ch-2, fasten off. *(24 ch-2 sps)*

Rnd 4: Attach white in any ch-2 sp, [ch 2, sc in next ch-2 sp] around, join in same st as beg ch-2, fasten off.

Neckline Edging

Row 1 (RS): Attach pink at base of left back opening, ch 1, 10 sc evenly sp up back opening, [ch 1, sc in next ch] across opposite side of foundation ch of neck, work 10 sc evenly down right back opening, turn.

Row 2: Ch 2, sc in 3rd and 4th sc, [ch 2, sk 1 sc, sc in each of next 2 sc] twice, fasten off. *(3 buttonholes)*

Sew buttons opposite buttonholes. Place Dress on bunny. Place necklace on bunny. Decorate ears with ribbon appliqués. ✂

BEGINNER

Finished Size
Fits 8-inch soft
  sculpture bunny

Materials
- Size 5 crochet cotton
  (50g per ball):
  1 ball each white
    and pink
- Size B/1/2.25mm
  crochet hook or
  size needed to
  obtain gauge
- Tapestry needle
- 10mm clear buttons: 3
- Pink ribbon-and-pearl
  appliqués: 2
- Small necklace
  (optional)
- 8-inch soft sculpture
  bunny

Bee My Valentine
Continued from page 152

Rnd 4: [Sc in next sc, 2 sc in next sc] around. *(18 sc)*

Rnd 5: [Sc in each of next 2 sc, 2 sc in next sc] around. *(24 sc)*

Rnds 6–10: Rep rnd 3.

Rnd 11: [**Sc dec** *(see Stitch Guide)* in next 2 sc] around, fasten off. *(12 sc)*

Facial Features

Using photo as a guide, with length of black yarn, embroider **satin st** *(see illustration)* **nose** over rnd 1, with **straight st** *(see illustration)* **mouth.** Embroider **eyes** in satin st 1 rnd above nose leaving ¼-inch sp between eyes.

Satin Stitch   Straight Stitch

Feeler
Make 2.

With black, ch 7, sl st in 2nd ch from hook, sl st in each rem ch across, fasten off. Sew 2 rnds above eyes, leaving 1 sc between Feelers.

Middle Body

Rnds 1 & 2: With black, rep rnds 1 and 2 of Head. *(12 sc)*

Rnd 3: Rep rnd 4 of Head. *(18 sc)*

Rnd 4: Rep rnd 5 of Head. *(24 sc)*

Rnds 5–9: Sc in each sc around.

Rnd 10: Rep rnd 11 of Head. *(12 sc)*

Stuff Middle Body and sew to Head.

Bottom Body

Rnd 1: Rep rnd 1 of Head. *(6 sc)*

Rnd 2: Sc in each sc around.

Rnd 3: 2 sc in next sc around. *(12 sc)*

Rnd 4: Rep rnd 2.

Rnd 5: [Sc in next sc, 2 sc in next sc] around. *(18 sc)*

Rnd 6: [Sc in each of next 2 sc, 2 sc in next sc] around. *(24 sc)*

Rnds 7–12: Rep rnd 2.

Rnd 13: [Sc dec in next 2 sc] around, sl st in next sc, fasten off. *(12 sc)*

Stuff and sew to Middle Body.

Leg
Make 6.

Row 1: With black, ch 4, sc in 2nd ch from hook, sc in each rem ch across, turn. *(3 sc)*

Rows 2–5: Ch 1, sc in each sc across, turn. At the end of row 5, leaving a length of yarn, fasten off. Fold Leg in half lengthwise, sew side seam from row 5 on down to row 1, and sew Leg to Middle Body. Sew 3 Legs to each side of Middle Body.

Wing
Make 2.

Rnd 1: With off-white, ch 2, 6 sc in 2nd ch from hook, place st marker at end of rnd, move marker as work progresses. *(6 sc)*

Rnd 2: 2 sc in each sc around. *(12 sc)*

Rnds 3–5: Sc in each sc around.

Rnd 6: [Sc dec in next 2 sc] 6 times, sl st in next sc, leaving a length of yarn on first Wing only, fasten off. *(6 sc)*

Sew Wings to Middle Body, on upper end near Head so that rnd 6 of each Wing is touching.

Sew heart-shaped red button to side edge of rnd 5 of Bottom Body. ✂

Fireworks Tote

Continued from page 158

Special Stitch

Shell: 3 dc in indicated st.

Front

Row 1 (RS): Beg at top of bag and working down, with 1 strand each A, B and C held tog, ch 30, sc in 2nd ch from hook, sc in each rem ch across, turn. *(29 sc)*

Row 2: Ch 1, sc in first sc, [ch 1, sk 1 sc, sc in next sc] across, turn.

Row 3: Ch 1, sc in first sc, [**shell** *(see Special Stitch)* in next sc, sc in next sc] across, turn. *(14 shells; 15 sc)*

Row 4: Ch 3 *(counts as first dc throughout)*, dc in first sc, [sc in center dc of next shell, shell in next sc] across, turn. *(15 shells; 14 sc)*

Row 5: Ch 1, sc in first dc, [shell in next sc, sc in center dc of next shell] across, ending with sc in last dc, turn. *(14 shells, 15 sc)*

Rows 6–15: Rep rows 4 and 5.

Rnd 16: Rep row 4.

Row 17: Ch 1, sc in first dc, [hdc in next dc, dc in next sc, hdc in next dc, sc in next dc] across, turn.

Row 18: Ch 1, sc in first sc, [ch 1, sk 1 st, sc in next st] across, turn.

Row 19: Ch 1, sc in each sc and each ch-1 sp across, fasten off.

Back

Rows 1–19: Rep rows 1–19 of Front.

Border

Note: *Border is worked on each Front and Back, adjusting on Back as specified for button lp.*

Rnd 1 (RS): With 1 strand each A and D, draw up a lp in any sc near center bottom *(row 19)*, ch 1, sc in each sc across working 3 sc in corner sc, working up side, sc in each of each sc row, sc in top of and over post at end of each dc row, 3 sc in corner ch, sc in each ch across to last ch, 3 sc in last ch, working across 2nd side, sc in each of each sc row, sc in top of and over post at end of each dc row, 3 sc in corner st, sc in each rem st across bottom, join in beg sc, fasten off.

Note: *Working across Back across foundation ch to work button lp, sc in center ch, ch 14, sl st in 3rd ch of ch-14, ch 3, sc in same center ch.*

Strap

Row 1 (RS): With 1 strand each A, B and C held tog, ch 4, sc in 2nd ch from hook, sc in each of next 2 chs, turn. *(3 sc)*

Rows 2–83: Ch 1, sc in each of next 3 sc, turn. At the end of row 83, leaving a length of yarn, fasten off.

With RS tog of row 83 and opposite side of foundation ch of row 1, whipstitch ends tog.

Border

Rnd 1: With 1 strand each A and D held tog, attach in side edge of any row, ch 1, sc in side edge of each row around Strap, join in beg sc, fasten off.

Rep rnd 1 on opposite side edge of Strap. Thread tapestry needle with a length of D, working through both lps of sts of Strap, Front and Back pieces, sew Strap around sides and bottom.

With a strand of A, sew button to Front opposite button lp. ✄

Wine Bottle Cover

Continued from page 160

Rnd 7: Ch 1, sc in first sc, ch 1, sk next sc, [sc in next sc, ch 1, sk next sc] around, join in beg sc, turn. *(18 sc; 18 ch-1 sps)*

Rnd 8: Ch 1, sc in next ch-1 sp, ch 1, [sc in next ch-1 sp, ch 1] around, join in beg sc, turn.

Rnds 9–31: rep rnd 8.

Rnd 32: Ch 4 *(counts as first dc, ch 1 throughout)*, [dc in next ch-1 sp, ch 1] around, join in 3rd ch of beg ch-4, turn.

Rnd 33: Ch 1, [sc in next ch-1 sp, ch 1] around, join in beg sc, turn.

Rnd 34: Ch 1, sc in next ch-1 sp, **shell** *(see Special Stitch)* in next ch-1 sp, [sc in next ch-1 sp, shell in next ch-1 sp] around, join in beg sc. *(9 shells; 9 sc)*

Rnd 35: Ch 4, sc in center dc of next shell, ch 1, [dc in next sc, ch 1, sc in center dc of next shell, ch 1] around, join in 3rd ch of beg ch-4.

Rnd 36: Rep rnd 34.

Rnd 37: Ch 1, sc in first sc, *ch 1, (sc, ch 2, sc) in center dc of next shell ch 1**, sc in next sc, rep from * around, ending last rep at **, join in beg sc, fasten off.

Tie

Holding 1 strand each cranberry and mistletoe tog, leaving 4-inch lengths at beg, ch 73, leaving 4-inch lengths, fasten off.

With joining seam at center back, weave ch under and over dc sts of rnd 32, insert bottle into Cover. Cut 2 lengths of each color 8 inches long. [Place a pony bead on end of tie, add a strand of each color to end of ch, tie all rem lengths in an overhand knot, trim ends to desired length] twice, tie ch ends in a bow. ✄

Yuletide Trivets

Continued from page 161

sc dec in next 2 sc, turn. *(16 sc)*

Rows 4–17: Rep rows 2 and 3. *(2 sc)*

Row 18: Ch 1, sc in each of next 2 sc, turn.

Border

Rnd 1: Ch 1, 2 sc in first sc, ch 3, 2 sc in next sc, working down side edge of rows, **shell** *(see Special Stitch)* in side edge of row 16, sc in side edge of row 13, shell in side edge of row 10, sc in side edge of row 7, shell in side edge of row 4, sc in side edge of row 2, 7 dc in first ch of opposite side of foundation ch, sc in next ch, sk next ch, [shell in next ch, sk next ch, sc in next ch, sk next 2 chs] twice, shell in next ch, sk next ch, sc in next ch, 7 dc in last ch, working across opposite edge of rows, sc in side edge of row 2, shell in side edge of row 4, sc in side edge of row 7, shell in side edge of row 10, sc in side edge of row 13, shell in side edge of row 16, join in beg sc.

Rnd 2: Ch 2, sk next sc, (sl st, ch 4, sl st) in ch-3 sp, ch 2, sk next sc, sl st in next sc, [ch 3, (sl st, ch 2, sl st) in center dc of next shell, ch 3, sl st in next sc] 3 times, working at corner, ch 3, sk 2 dc, sl st in next dc, ch 3, (sl st, ch 4, sl st) in center dc, ch 3, sl st in next dc, ch 3, sk 2 dc, sl st in next sc, ch 3, (sl st, ch 2, sl st) in center dc of next shell, ch 3, sl st in next sc, ch 3, sk next 2 dc, (sl st, ch 3, sl st) in next dc, (sl st, ch 6, sl st) in center dc, (sl st, ch 3, sl st) in next dc, working at corner, ch 3, sk next 2 dc, sl st in next dc, ch 3, (sl st, ch 4, sl st) in center dc, ch 3, sl st in next dc, ch 3, sk next 2 dc, sl st in next sc, [ch 3, (sl st, ch 2, sl st) in center dc of next shell, ch 3, sl st in next sc] 3 times, sl st to join in same st as beg ch-2, fasten off.

Star

Rnd 1: With 1 strand each cranberry and mistletoe ombre held tog, ch 5, join in first ch to form a ring, ch 1, 10 sc in ring, join in beg sc. *(10 sc)*

Rnd 2: Ch 1, (sc, ch 3, sc) in first sc, *ch 1, sk 1 sc**, (sc, ch 3, sc) in next sc, rep from * around, ending last rep at **, join in beg sc, turn. *(5 ch-3 sps)*

Rnd 3: Ch 1, *(sc, ch 2, sc) in next ch-1 sp, ch 3, rep from * around, join in beg sc, turn. *(5 ch-3 sps)*

Rnd 4: Ch 1, *(sc, 2 dc, ch 2, 2 dc, sc) in next ch-3 sp, (sc, ch 2, sc) in next ch-2 sp, rep from * around, join in beg sc.

Rnd 5: Ch 1, *sc in next 2 sts, hdc in next st, (2 dc, ch 2, 2 dc) in next ch-2 sp, hdc in next st, sc in each of next 2 sts, sk next sc, sc in next ch-2 sp, sk next sc, rep from * around, join in beg sc.

Rnd 6: *[Ch 2, sk 1 st, sl st in next st] twice, ch 2, (sl st, ch 5, sl st) in next ch-2 sp, ch 2, sl st in next st, [ch 2, sk 1 st, sl st in next st] twice, ch 3, sc in first ch, sk next st, sl st in next st, rep from * around, ending on last rep with sl st in joining sl st of last rnd, fasten off. ✂

Christmas Rose Ornament

Continued from page 164

Rnd 16: [Sc dec in next 2 sc, sc in next sc] 5 times. *(10 sc)*

Rnd 17: [Sc dec in next 2 sc] 5 times. *(5 sc)*

Rnd 18: Ch 5 *(hanging lp)*, sk next 2 sts, sl st in next st, fasten off.

Flower

Rnd 1: With size D hook and pink, ch 6, join in first ch to form a ring, [3 sc in ring, ch 7] 6 times, join in beg sc. *(18 sc; 6 ch-7 lps)*

Rnd 2: Ch 1, sc in same sc as beg ch-1, *2 sc in next sc, sc in next sc, 15 hdc in next ch-7 sp**, sc in next sc, rep from * around, ending last rep at **, join in beg sc, fasten off. *(90 hdc; 24 sc)*

Bud

Row 1: With size D hook and pink, ch 9, 3 sc in 2nd ch from hook, 3 sc in each rem ch across, fasten off. *(24 sc)*

Leaf

Make 3.

Row 1: With size D hook and white, ch 6, sl st in 2nd ch from hook, sc in next ch, hdc in each of next 2 chs, (2 sc, ch 1, sl st in top of last sc, sc) in last ch, working on opposite side of foundation ch, hdc in each of next 2 chs, sc in next ch, sl st in last ch, fasten off.

Finishing

Using photo as a guide, place fabric glue on front of each Leaf and coat with crystal glitter. Let dry.

Draw hanging lp through center of any Flower petal *(will be off center)*, glue Flower to Ball. Roll Bud and glue to left of hanger. Glue Leaves evenly sp around Flower and glue in place. Place fabric glue in center of Flower and coat center of Flower with gold glitter. ✂

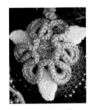

Evergreen Stocking
Continued from page 163

Rnd 2: Ch 1, sc in each st around, join in beg sc, turn.

Rnd 3: Ch 1, sc in first st, sc dec in next 2 sts, [sc in each of next 6 sts, sc dec in next 2 sts] 4 times, sc in each of last 5 sts, join in beg sc, turn. *(35 sc)*

Rnd 4: Rep rnd 2.

Rnd 5: Ch 1, sc in first st, sc dec in next 2 sts, [sc in each of next 5 sts, sc dec in next 2 sts] 4 times, sc in each of next 4 sts, join in beg sc, turn. *(30 sc)*

Rnd 6: Rep rnd 2.

Rnd 7: Ch 1, sc in first st, sc dec in next 2 sts, [sc in each of next 4 sts, sc dec in next 2 sts] 4 times, sc in each of last 3 sts, join in beg sc, turn. *(25 sc)*

Rnd 8: Rep rnd 2.

Rnd 9: Ch 1, sc in first st, sc dec in next 2 sts, [sc in each of next 3 sts, sc dec in next 2 sts] 4 times, sc in each of last 2 sts, join in beg sc, turn. *(20 sc)*

Rnd 10: Rep rnd 2.

Rnd 11: Ch 1, [sc dec in next 2 sts] 10 times, join in beg sc, turn. *(10 sc)*

Rnd 12: Ch 1, sc in each st around, join, leaving a long length, fasten off.

Weave rem length through sts of rnd 12, draw opening closed, secure end.

Bell
Note: Do not join rnds unless otherwise stated, use st marker to mark rnds.

Rnd 1: With size 2 steel hook and silver, ch 2, 6 sc in 2nd ch from hook. *(6 sc)*

Rnd 2: 2 sc in each sc around. *(12 sc)*

Rnd 3: [Sc in next st, 2 sc in next st] around. *(18 sc)*

Rnds 4–7: Sc in each st around.

Rnd 8: [Sl st in next st, ch 1] around.

Rnd 9: [Sl st in next ch sp, ch 2] around, to join sl st in first sl st, fasten off.

Holly Leaf
Make 2.

With size 2 steel hook and 2 strands of green held tog, ch 12, sc in 2nd ch from hook, [ch 3, sl st in next 2 chs] 4 times, ch 3, sl st in next ch, (sl st, sc, sl st) in last ch, [ch 3, sl st in next 2 chs] 4 times, ch 3, sl st in last ch, join with sl st in first sc, fasten off.

Bow
With size 2 steel hook and red, ch 100, sl st in 2nd ch from hook, sl st in each rem ch across, fasten off. Tie a knot in each end.

Finishing
Use photo as a guide. With tapestry needle and 2 strands of red held tog, wrapping thread around tapestry needle 3 times, embroider 7 French knots at random over front of Stocking.

Position Holly leaves on Cuff; embroider 4 French knots at center between leaves.

Cut 4 strands of red, each 6 inches long. Fold each strand in half, tie into a knot ½ inch below fold. Insert loose ends of each piece through rnd 1 of Bell working from inside to outside *(knots rem inside of Bell).* Placing Bell below Holly Leaves as shown, draw ends through sts on Cuff, tack in place and secure ends.

With size G hook, attach olive with a sl st in center back seam at top of Cuff, [ch 15, sl st in same sp] 3 times, fasten off.

Insert red ch Bow through any ch-15 hanging lp, tie ends in a bow. ✂

Halloween Garland

Continued from page 159

Rnd 4: Ch 1, [sc in each of next 2 sc, 2 sc in next sc] around, join in beg sc. *(24 sc)*
Rnd 5: Ch 1, [sc in each of next 3 sc, 2 sc in next sc] around, join in beg sc, fasten off. *(30 sc)*
Row 6: Now working in rows, for stem, attach green in first sc of previous rnd, ch 5, sc in 2nd ch from hook, sc in each of next 3 chs, sl st in same sc as joining, fasten off.

Finishing
Glue 2 oval wiggle eyes sp ⅜ inch apart over rnds 2 and 3.
From black felt for **nose**, cut ⅜ x ½-inch wide triangle. Glue to center of rnd 1.
Using photo as a guide, from black felt for **mouth**, cut ¼ x 1⅜-inch wide curved piece. Glue centered below nose.

Cat
Make 3.
Body
Rnds 1–4: With black, rep rnds 1–4 of Pumpkin. *(24 sc)*
Rnd 5: For **tail**, ch 10, sl st in 2nd ch from hook, sl st in each rem ch across, sl st in next sc of rnd 4, fasten off.

Head
Rnds 1–3: With black, rep rnds 1–3 of Pumpkin. *(18 sc)*
Rnd 4: Ch 1, sc in first st, ch 2, sl st in 2nd ch from hook *(first ear)*, sl st in each of next 4 sts, ch 2, sl st in 2nd ch from hook *(2nd ear)* sl st in next st, leaving rem sts unworked, fasten off.
Using photo as a guide, sew Head over top of rnd 4 on Body.

Finishing
Glue 2 round wiggle eyes over top of rnd 2 on Head sp ⅛ inch apart.

For **whiskers**, tie a 3-inch piece of white into knot around center of rnd 1 on Head. Separate plies of yarn, trim whiskers to ¾ inch.

Ghost
Make 3.
Head
Rnds 1–3: With white, rep rnds 1–3 of Pumpkin. *(18 sc)*

Body
Row 4: Now working in rows, ch 1, sc in each of next 6 sc, turn. *(6 sc)*
Rows 5 & 6: Ch 1, 2 sc in first sc, sc in each sc across to last sc, 2 sc in last sc, turn. *(10 sc)*
Rows 7–12: Ch 1, sc in each sc across, turn.
Row 13: Ch 1, sc in first sc, [ch 2, sc in next sc] across, fasten off.
Glue half round beads to top of rnds 1 and 2 on Head ⅛ inch apart.

Ties
For each Pumpkin, cut 1 strand of black each 6 inches long. For each Cat, cut 1 strand of green each 6 inches long. For each Ghost, cut 1 strand of orange each 6 inches long. Draw each Tie through center top of each piece.
Sk first 6 on row 2 of Garland, [attach a Pumpkin to next st of Garland, tie ends in a bow, sk next 21 sts, attach a ghost to next st of Garland, tie ends in a bow, sk next 21 sts, attach a Cat to next st of Garland, tie ends in a bow, sk next 21 sts] 3 times, attach a Pumpkin to next st of Garland, leaving last 5 sts unworked. ✂

▰▰▰▱
INTERMEDIATE

Finished Size
Garland 62½ inches
across

Materials
- Medium (worsted) weight yarn: 1 oz each black, orange, white and green
- Size H/8/5mm crochet hook or size needed to obtain gauge
- Tapestry needle
- Hot-glue gun
- 11mm round wiggle eyes: 3 pair
- 10 x 15mm oval wiggle eyes: 4 pairs
- 8mm half round black beads: 6
- 4-inch square black felt

General Instructions

Please review the following information before working the projects in this book. Important details about the abbreviations and symbols used are included.

Hooks

Crochet hooks are sized for different weights of yarn and thread. For thread crochet, you will usually use a steel crochet hook. Steel crochet-hook sizes range from size 00 to 14. The higher the number of the hook, the smaller your stitches will be. For example, a size 1 steel crochet hook will give you much larger stitches than a size 9 steel crochet hook. Keep in mind that the sizes given with the pattern instructions were obtained by working with the size thread or yarn and hook given in the materials list. If you work with a smaller hook, depending on your gauge, your project size will be smaller; if you work with a larger hook, your finished project's size will be larger.

Gauge

Gauge is determined by the tightness or looseness of your stitches, and affects the finished size of your project. If you are concerned about the finished size of the project matching the size given, take time to crochet a small section of the pattern and then check your gauge. For example, if the gauge called for is 10 dc = 1 inch, and your gauge is 12 dc to the inch, you should switch to a larger hook. On the other hand, if your gauge is only 8 dc to the inch, you should switch to a smaller hook.

If the gauge given in the pattern is for an entire motif, work one motif and then check your gauge.

Understanding Symbols

As you work through a pattern, you'll quickly notice several symbols in the instructions. These symbols are used to clarify the pattern for you: brackets [], curlicue braces {}, parentheses () and asterisks *.

Brackets [] are used to set off a group of instructions worked a specific number of times. For example, "[ch 3, sc in next ch-3 sp] 7 times" means to work the instructions inside the [] seven times.

Occasionally, a set of instructions inside a set of brackets needs to be repeated, too. In this case, the text within the brackets to be repeated will be set off with curlicue braces {}. For example, "[dc in each of next 3 sts, ch 1, {shell in next ch-1 sp} 3 times, ch 1] 4 times." In this case, in each of the four times you work the instructions included in the brackets, you will work the section included in the curlicue braces three times.

Parentheses () are used to set off a group of stitches to be worked all in one stitch, space or loop. For example, the parentheses () in this set of instructions, "Sk 3 sc, (3 dc, ch 1, 3 dc) in next st", indicate that after skipping 3 sc, you will work 3 dc, ch 1 and 3 more dc all in the next stitch.

Single asterisks * are also used when a group of instructions is repeated. For example, "*Sc in each of the next 5 sc, 2 sc in next sc, rep from * around, join with a sl st in beg sc" simply means you will work the instructions from the first * around the entire round.

Double asterisks ** are used to indicate when a *partial* set of repeat instructions are to be worked. For example, "*Ch 3, (sc, ch 3, sc) in next ch-2 sp, ch 3**, shell in next dc, rep from * 3 times, ending last rep at **" means that on the third repeat of the single asterisk instructions, you stop at the double asterisks.

Buyer's Guide

Bernat
P.O. Box 40
Listowel, ON N4W 3H3
CANADA
(800) 265-2684

Caron International Inc.
P.O. Box 222
Washington, NC 27889
(800) 868-9194

Coats & Clark Inc.
Consumer Services
P.O. Box 12229
Greenville, SC 29612-0229
(800) 648-1479

DMC Corp.
Hackensack Ave. Bldg. 10F
South Kearny, NJ 07032
(800) 275-4117

Elmore-Pisgah Inc.
P.O. Box 187
Spindale, NC 28160
(800) 633-7829

Lion Brand Yarn Co.
34 W. 15th St.
New York, NY 10011
(800) 795-5466

Patons Yarns
P.O. Box 40
Listowel, ON N4W 3H3
CANADA
(519) 291-3780

Stitch Guide

ABBREVIATIONS

beg	begin/beginning
bpdc	back post double crochet
bpsc	back post single crochet
bptr	back post treble crochet
CC	contrasting color
ch	chain stitch
ch-	refers to chain or space previously made (i.e. ch-1 space)
ch sp	chain space
cl	cluster
cm	centimeter(s)
dc	double crochet
dec	decrease/decreases/decreasing
dtr	double treble crochet
fpdc	front post double crochet
fpsc	front post single crochet
fptr	front post treble crochet
g	gram(s)
hdc	half double crochet
inc	increase/increases/increasing
lp(s)	loop(s)
MC	main color
mm	millimeter(s)
oz	ounce(s)
pc	popcorn
rem	remain/remaining
rep	repeat(s)
rnd(s)	round(s)
RS	right side
sc	single crochet
sk	skip(ped)
sl st	slip stitch
sp(s)	space(s)
st(s)	stitch(es)
tog	together
tr	treble crochet
trtr	triple treble
WS	wrong side
yd(s)	yard(s)
yo	yarn over

Chain—ch: Yo, pull through lp on hook.

Slip stitch—sl st: Insert hook in st, yo, pull through both lps on hook.

Single crochet—sc: Insert hook in st, yo, pull through st, yo, pull through both lps on hook.

**Front loop—front lp
Back loop—back lp**

Front Loop   Back Loop

Front post stitch—fp: Back post stitch—bp: When working post st, insert hook from right to left around post st on previous row.

Back   Front

Post of Stitch

Half double crochet—hdc: Yo, insert hook in st, yo, pull through st, yo, pull through all 3 lps on hook.

Double crochet—dc: Yo, insert hook in st, yo, pull through st, [yo, pull through 2 lps] twice.

Change colors: Drop first color; with second color, pull through last 2 lps of st.

Treble crochet—tr: Yo twice, insert hook in st, yo, pull through st, [yo, pull through 2 lps] 3 times.

Double treble crochet—dtr: Yo 3 times, insert hook in st, yo, pull through st, [yo, pull through 2 lps] 4 times.

Single crochet decrease (sc dec): (Insert hook, yo, draw up a lp) in each of the sts indicated, yo, draw through all lps on hook.

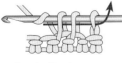

Example of 2-sc dec

Half double crochet decrease (hdc dec): (Yo, insert hook, yo, draw lp through) in each of the sts indicated, yo, draw through all lps on hook.

Example of 2-hdc dec

Double crochet decrease (dc dec): (Yo, insert hook, yo, draw lp through, yo, draw through 2 lps on hook) in each of the sts indicated, yo, draw through all lps on hook.

Example of 2-dc dec

US		UK
sl st (slip stitch)	=	sc (single crochet)
sc (single crochet)	=	dc (double crochet)
hdc (half double crochet)	=	htr (half treble crochet)
dc (double crochet)	=	tr (treble crochet)
tr (treble crochet)	=	dtr (double treble crochet)
dtr (double treble crochet)	=	ttr (triple treble crochet)
skip	=	miss

For more complete information, visit

StitchGuide.com

Special Thanks

Sandy Abbate
Free Spirit Poncho, Neon Bright Winter Warmers

Mindy Al-Aaraji
Double Triquetra Coaster

Svetlana Avrakh for Patons
Patchwork Blanket & Pillows

Vicki Blizzard
Princess Pooch Scarf & Booties

Vashti Braha
Far-Out Fur Accents, Groovy Beaded Curtain, Lunar Landscape Window Fringe, Mini Tech Totes

Gina Carlson-Brown
Funky Helmet

Cindy Carlson
Denim Fur Hat & Scarf

Belinda "Bendy" Carter
Jazzy Jewelry Head to Toe, Little Jeweled Bag, Rainbow Purse

Sue Childress
Dainty Handkerchiefs, Blue Post Stitch Booties, Bonny Belle Bunny, Green V-Stitch Booties

Dot Drake
Pastel Beaded Jar Covers

Ellen Anderson Eaves
Spring Blossoms Afghan

Katherine Eng
Citrus Party Mats, Colors of Fall Capelet, Fireworks Tote, Fluorescent Fun Shawl, Jingle Bells Necklace, Maple Leaves Afghan, Peace Garden Hat, Royal Print Tote, Sassy Stripes Tank Top, Sea Breeze Poncho, Wild Lime Cloche, Wine Bottle Cover, Yuletide Trivets

Paula Gron
Collared Drawstring Purse

Patricia Hall
Christmas Rose Ornament

Anne Halliday
Flower Power

Kim Harmon
The Blues Belt

Hazel Henry
Pineapples & Picots Pot Holder

Tammy Hildebrand
Dig-It Flowerpot Cover, Raspberry Fantasy Beaded Scarf

Mary Layfield
Bee-autiful Rose Slippers, Bold & Beautiful Necklaces, Patriotic Garden Pot Holder

Terrie Mays for Caron International
Diagonal Stripes Hat

Beverly Mewhorter
Halloween Garland

Shirley Patterson
Chain Waves Carryall, Little Miss Fingerless Mitts, Pick a Pretty Pair, Summer Garden Shadow Box

Darla Sims
Go-Go Granny

Ann Smith
Evergreen Stocking

Diane Stone
Winter Rose Pot Holder

Brenda Stratton
Sweet Scents Jar

Kathleen Stuart
Baby Wrist Rattles

Becky Symons for Mary Maxim
Americana Cardigan

Elizabeth Ann White
Dainty Flowers Headband, Pink Love Knot Booties

Michele Wilcox
Bee My Valentine, Cutie-Pie Sundress, Santa Purse

Lori Zeller
Black Magic Cardigan, Bodacious Beanbag Chair, My Friend Wendy, Pearls & Lace Wedding Cards